*Child Care and Culture* examines parenthood, infancy, and early childhood in an African community, raising provocative questions about "normal" child care. Comparing the Gusii people of Kenya with the American white middle class, the authors show how divergent cultural priorities create differing conditions for early childhood development.

Gusii mothers, who bear ten children on average, focus on goals of survival during infancy and compliance during early childhood, following a cultural model of maternal behavior for achieving these goals. Their practices are successful in a local context but diverge sharply from those considered normal or optimal in North America and Europe, especially in terms of cognitive stimulation, social engagement, emotional arousal, verbal responsiveness, and emotional support for exploration and conversation. Combining the perspectives of social anthropology, pediatrics, and developmental psychology, the authors demonstrate how child care customs can be responsive to varied socioeconomic, demographic, and cultural conditions without inflicting harm on children.

Child care and culture

# Child care and culture
## Lessons from Africa

**Robert A. LeVine**
*Harvard University*

**Suzanne Dixon**
*University of California*
*San Diego Medical School*

**Sarah LeVine**
*Harvard University*

**Amy Richman**
*Work-Family Directions, Inc.*

**P. Herbert Leiderman**
*Stanford University Medical Center*

**Constance H. Keefer**
*Harvard Medical School*

**T. Berry Brazelton**
*Harvard Medical School*

*with the collaboration of*
James Caron, Rebecca New, Patrice Miller,
Edward Z. Tronick, David Feigal, and Josephine Yaman

CAMBRIDGE
UNIVERSITY PRESS

Published by the Press Syndicate of the University of Cambridge
The Pitt Building, Trumpington Street, Cambridge CB2 1RP
40 West 20th Street, New York, NY 10011–4211, USA
10 Stamford Road, Oakleigh, Melbourne 3166, Australia

First published 1994

Printed in the United States of America

*Library of Congress Cataloging-in-Publication Data*
Child care and culture : lessons from Africa / Robert A. LeVine . . .
[et al.].
   p.  cm.
Includes bibliographical references and index.
ISBN 0-521-33171-4
1. Children, Gusii – Kenya – Kisii District.  2. Women, Gusii –
Kenya – Kisii District – Family relationships.  3. Child rearing –
Kenya – Kisii District – Cross-cultural studies.  4. Socialization –
Kenya – Kisii District – Cross-cultural studies.  5. Child rearing –
Massachusetts – Boston – Cross-cultural studies.  6. Socialization –
Massachusetts – Boston – Cross-cultural studies.  I. LeVine, Robert
Alan, 1932 –
DT433.545.G86C55    1994
305.23'1'096762–dc20                         93-33584
                                                    CIP

A catalog record for this book is available from the British Library.

ISBN 0-521-33171-4 hardback

# Contents

# Tables and figures

---

# Foreword

URIE BRONFENBRENNER

This book is about cultural lessons from Africa and from the United States, and what each culture can learn from the other about the forces that shape human character. It offers lessons not only for contemporary developmental science but also for today's societies on both continents. These scientific and social lessons are especially timely, for although some of them were learned – and taught – years ago, in recent decades they have gone out of fashion. Yet, as I shall suggest here, American society may need these lessons more today than ever before in its history.

What has gone out of fashion is summarized in a single word, a concept that from the 50s to the early 70s dominated the study of human development across disciplines in psychology, sociology, and anthropology. That key construct is *socialization,* defined as "the process through which individuals acquire the knowledge, skills, and dispositions that enable them to participate as more or less effective members of groups and the society."[1] In 1969, an entire handbook of more than 1,000 pages was published on theory and research pertaining to this subject.[2] But from today's perspective, socialization is no longer of commanding research interest. In the words of a leading contemporary scholar of human development: "After peaking during the 1960s and early 70s, socialization studies began to decline in all areas."[3]

Yet, *socialization* is exactly what this new book by Robert A. LeVine and his colleagues is all about. It exploits a dramatic experiment of nature by comparing conditions, processes, and outcomes of early child rearing among the Gusii people of northeastern Africa and their middle-class counterparts in the northeastern United States, specifically in Boston, Massachusetts. In a number of respects, the two cultures produce rather different kinds of human beings. For example, by contrast with the Americans, the Gusii are much less expressive of their feelings. "They rarely show approval, anger, or shock . . . they avoid disclosing information, particularly pleasurable facts about oneself, which Americans routinely share" (Chap. 1, p. 14). In addition, both children and adults are more compliant to authority, and ask fewer questions. These patterns begin early in life. For instance, the Gusii babies at 3 to 4 months cried less than half of the time that their American counterparts did.

What is most intriguing about the authors' findings, however, is not the systematic differences in personality that they found but the persuasive evidence and argument they present regarding the forces that give rise to the contrast. These forces operate at two levels – one more proximal and direct, the other more distal, inferential, yet ultimately more powerful. In the more immediate sphere, the differences in personality, which begin to emerge in the very first year of life, and are shown to be the product, in substantial degree, of the contrasting ways in which infants in the two cultures are treated by their mothers.

> The distribution . . . across categories is extremely different for the Gusii and Boston mothers: For the Gusii, holding and physical contact are most frequent at all age periods, whereas for the Bostonians, looking and talking are relatively frequent at first and become the most frequent behaviors by 9 months. (Chap. 8, p. 197)[4]

A further contrast is seen in the temporal distribution of maternal attention over the first 2 years.

> In the American model . . . it increases over time, as the toddler becomes more capable not only of conversations with the mother but also of attracting and keeping maternal attention through solicitations, demands, long dialogues, displays of accomplishment, tantrums, and other maneuvers of the 2-year old. Having fostered the infant's capacity for verbal communication and active engagement, the mother finds herself engaged in an expanding relationship with a toddler who sleeps less, talks more, and takes the initiative in interaction. . . .
> American mothers frequently use questions to promote the infant's excited participation in social exchange: They create a protoconversation with repeated questioning, lavishing praise on the infant for each vocal or motor response, which is taken as if

it were an answer to the question. . . . In terms of the American Pedagogical model, both questions and praise are essential to the encouragement of learning and social engagement in the pre-school child. (Chap. 10, pp. 252–253)

The contrast is highlighted in an analysis by LeVine and his colleagues of a more general aspect of parent–child relationships that has emerged in contemporary research as especially influential in shaping young children's development: the degree of *reciprocity* between the behavior of the infant and the mother. Here the results reveal that Gusii mothers are less likely than their American counterparts to respond with speech to their babies' vocalizations or to seek or return eye contact. More generally, the authors find "In comparison with American white middle-class mothers, then, Gusii mothers try to keep their babies calm, avoiding positive or negative arousal states by preventing or dampening excitement" (Chap. 8, p. 201).[5]

But how and why should such a pattern of maternal care arise? It is here that the authors' second level of analysis comes into play. In their view, the two societies have sharply different cultural goals, which in turn are dictated by historical experience in the environment in which each group has lived. For the Gusii, an especially critical experience over decades has been an extraordinarily high infant death rate, arising from life-threatening illnesses and physical hazards. It is the authors' first and foremost "distal" hypothesis that, in order to survive, the Gusii culture has placed an exceptionally high value both on having children and providing them with intensive care during the first 2 years of life, when infant survival is most seriously threatened. This value is principally reflected in two domains. The first is one of the highest fertility rates in the world; at the time the fieldwork was carried out, the average woman was bearing about ten children and losing about two. The second value is reflected in the intensive care given to infants during the first 2 years of life (to which the authors give plausible credit for minimizing the losses).

LeVine and his colleagues also have an additional cultural hypothesis. Up to the present time, the Gusii have been a "pastoral-agrarian" society, depending in substantial degree on women to work in the fields while the men attended to the cattle. Consistent with this division of roles, it is customary for mothers to return to work in the second year of a baby's life.

Both in preparation for and after this transition, responsibilities for the care of the young are shared in substantial degree by older siblings. The authors argue that, under these circumstances, it also becomes culturally adaptive to minimize the trauma of separation by discouraging the development of a strongly dependent relationship between the mother and the infant. Hence, the early minimalization of overt excitement, pleasurable or painful, in interpersonal contexts.

The authors point out further that the necessity of the mother's early return to work in the fields places a premium on having young children who, as they move beyond early infancy, are easily managed, will not interfere, and will do what they are told without complaint. Accordingly, in Gusii child rearing there is an early emphasis on compliance – at first in terms of refraining from misbehavior or making demands, later in assisting with household tasks and work responsibilities. "Conversations between mother and child are not encouraged or expected. . . . More frequent is the kind of interaction in which a toddler asks for something and the mother gives it, or the mother issues a command and the toddler obeys with action, not words" (Chap. 10, p. 254).

From the perspective of Gusii cultural values, this pattern of socialization has obvious advantages: "Gusii parents expect to benefit from having children who are easy to manage as infants, participate in domestic production during childhood, and continue to help their parents as adults" (Chap. 10, p. 264).

In sum, we have the authors' first general thesis: Gusii modes of early socialization are culturally adaptive. Or at least they *were* so. The qualification is the authors' own:

> But parental practices that are adaptive or effective under one set of historical conditions may not be so when conditions change. The Gusii goal of maximizing the number of surviving children made more adaptive sense at the onset of the 20th century, when mortality was high, landholdings were large, and children were available to work under parental control, than 75 years later, when most of the children survived, land was scarce, and children's futures depended on school attendance and employment rather than working for parents. In other words, Gusii reproductive and child care practices viewed as a parental investment strategy had lost much of their basis in economic utility by the 1970s. (Chap. 10, p. 269)

Viewing Gusii culture "from the American middle-class perspective," the authors point to other possible costs as well:

> failure to prepare the child for schooling through the early development of language skills, self-confidence, and assertiveness, and an excessive emphasis on compliance to authority instead of equality and independence – thus leaving the child without the skills and virtues thought to be needed in the modern world. (Chap. 10, pp. 264–265)

LeVine and his colleagues contend, however, that "at the level of practice . . . a different understanding emerges. . . . Despite the ideological emphasis on respect and obedience, then, the practical system of control over children has always been loose, and it was expected by parents that their children would misbehave in the pastures and other places outside the home" (Chap. 10, p. 266). In the authors' view, this freedom, both alone and in the peer group, combined with the self-discipline and skills gained through subsequent apprenticeship – first within, and then beyond the family, in the larger community – can counteract the influence of an earlier, more restrictive emotional and cognitive environment. In support of this conclusion, LeVine and his colleagues note that, in a follow-up conducted when the children were 13 to 14, "there were no glaring mental defects or psychiatric abnormalities" (Chap. 10, p. 273) and that the "sample as a whole seemed average in their academic performance, with almost two-thirds at or near their proper grade level. . . . There is evidence of resilience here that warns against exaggerating the influence of the early years and emphasizes the importance of greater exactitude in our assumptions concerning what that influence is – and what it is not" (Chap. 10, p. 268).

In the spirit of that same "greater exactitude," one can learn still more from LeVine's much-needed socialization perspective. First, along with change, there is evidence for continuity, for despite the liberating influence of experiences in later childhood and adolescence, as adults the Gusii still manifest the restraint of emotional expression rooted in modes of maternal care from their earliest infancy. And although the majority of the children in the sample were able to perform satisfactorily in the rural primary schools of 1980s Kenya, "this does not mean that . . . [they] were performing at the level of their urban middle-class counterparts in Nairobi, Europe, or North America" (Chap. 10, p. 268).

Nevertheless, there remains the powerful subtitle that the authors have selected for their book: "Lessons from Africa." The implication, of course, is that these lessons are primarily *for* the United States. LeVine and his co-authors never say explicitly what these lessons are, but I shall presume to do so for them. Here and there throughout this volume, and especially in the last chapter, one senses the implication that, with all the problems besetting the well-being and development of children in Gusii society, their culture contains a resource for psychological growth lacking in our own.

What might that resource be? Clearly, it does not lie in the domain of maternal fostering of the infant's "capacity for active engagement, promoting excited participation in social exchange, and lavishing praise for each vocal or motor response, which is taken as if it were an answer to the question." On the contrary, that is presumably our own culture's powerful discovery for developing psychological competence in the next generation. LeVine and his colleagues come close to saying so, but stop short – and for good reason.

As I have documented elsewhere,[6] there is evidence that such processes of progressively more complex reciprocal interaction between mother and infant – and, more generally, between adults and children – are breaking down in American society. They are becoming both less frequent, and less powerful in their impact. One major reason is that a key requirement for their operation is not being met; namely, to be effective, *they must take place on a fairly regular basis over extended periods of time.* Only then can patterns of reciprocal interaction exert a cumulative developmental effect, and become internalized as sources of motivation and direction for one's future life course. Today, the hectic pace and increasing chaos of contemporary American life undermine the evolving consistency and continuity that are essential for psychological growth. And it is precisely this necessary degree of stability that is still to be found in more traditional cultures, such as that of the Gusii people. Therein lies perhaps the most important cultural lesson from us to them, and from them to us. We are indebted to Robert LeVine and his colleagues for helping to bring that lesson home, where it most belongs.

NOTES

1.  Brim, O. G., Jr. (1966). Socialization through the Life Cycle. In O. G. Brim, Jr. & S. Wheeler. *Socialization after Childhood.* New York: Wiley.
2.  Goslin, D. A. (1969). *Handbook of Socialization Theory and Research.* Chicago: Rand McNally.
3.  Elder, G. H., Jr. (1993). Time, human agency, and social change: Perspectives on the life course. *Cooley-Mead Lecture,* American Sociological Association, August 1993.
4.  Indeed, in each of these contrasting categories the proportion of time spent by mothers in one culture is more than twice as great as that for mothers in the other (see Tables 8.1, 8.2, 8.3).
5.  As already noted, it would appear that the effort is successful. In this connection, the authors cite an incident in which Gusii mothers became upset while viewing a videotape of an American mother changing a diaper, with the infant screaming on the changing table. "They saw the American mother as incompetent" (Ch. 6, p. 149).
6.  Bronfenbrenner, U. (1989). *Who Cares for Children?.* Invited Address to UNESCO. Bilingual publication No. 188. Paris: Unit for Co-operation with UNICEF and WFP; Bronfenbrenner. U. (1992). Child care in the Anglo-Saxon Mode. In M. E. Lamb, K. Sternberg, C. P. Hwang, & A. G. Broberg (Eds.), *Child Care in Context: Cross-Cultural Perspectives* (pp. 281–291). Hillsdale, NJ: Erlbaum; Bronfenbrenner, U. (1993). The Ecology of Cognitive Development: Research Models and Fugitive Findings. In R. H. Wozniak & K. Fischer (Eds.), *Specific Environments: Thinking in Contexts* (pp. 3–44). Hillsdale, NJ: Erlbaum; Bronfenbrenner, U. & Ceci, S. J. (1993). Heredity, Environment and the Question "How?": A New Theoretical Perspective for the 1990's. In R. Plomin & G. E. McClearn (Eds.), *Nature, Nurture, and Psychology* (pp. 313–324). Washington, DC: APA Books.

# Acknowledgments

The Gusii Infant Study involved a group of research collaborators and received assistance from numerous agencies and individuals. Financial support for the fieldwork came from the National Science Foundation (SOC 74-12692), the National Institute of Mental Health (Research Career Scientist Award to Robert A. LeVine), and Children's Hospital Medical Center in Boston; support for analysis, writing, and comparative analyses came from the National Science Foundation (BNS 77-09007), the Spencer Foundation, and the Population Council (Subordinate Agreement CP 82.47A). In Kenya, we were helped by Dr. Albert Maleche, Director of the Bureau of Educational Research, then of the University of Nairobi, who provided the institutional affiliation through which the project received permission from the Government of Kenya to conduct research. In Kisii, the project received support from the District Commissioner, D. O. Mulama, and from many Gusii notables, including Simeon Nyachae, Lawrence Sagini, and Dr. Zakariah Onyonka (the first two of whom had worked with Robert LeVine in the 1950s). We are grateful to all of them.

The study in Kisii District involved a complex data collection program combined with the operation of a pediatric clinic for the research population. Pediatric service was provided by American physicians: T. Berry Brazelton, Suzanne Dixon, David Feigal, Constance Keefer, and P. Herbert Leiderman, all of whom doubled as developmental investigators. The project depended on a staff of Gusii field assistants. Some were local residents of the area we call Morongo in this book – Christopher Getoi, Joseph Obongo, Agnes Nyabeta, Clemencia Otara, Ruben Sosi Sabani, Anna Getoi, and Dinah Orora. Others were students at the University of Nairobi or other educational institutions who worked with us for varying lengths of time: Joel Momanyi, John Orora,

Teresa Monari, Drucilla Ombui, Agnes Nyandika, Truphena Onyango, Mary Kepha Ayonga. A non-Gusii student from Cambridge University, Edmund Law, worked as a volunteer field assistant during 1976. All contributed significantly to the research presented in this book.

In analyzing the data from the project, we were assisted by many students and colleagues, including James Caron, Rebecca New, Patrice Miller, Josephine Yaman, Susan Templeton, Hsaio-Ti Falcone, Roseanne Kermoian, Guy Reed, and Elizabeth Momanyi. Justus Ogembo provided ethnographic advice at a late stage in the manuscript preparation.

There are many others who helped make this book possible, including Michael Hennessy, M.D., an adventurous orthopedic surgeon who provided unique services at the Kisii General Hospital, conducted research on Gusii children's gait (Hennessy, Dixon, & Simon, 1984), and took some of the photographs appearing herein; Eliza Klein, who took some of the other photographs for the book; Edward Z. Tronick, Gloria Leiderman, Audrey Naylor, M.D., and Renate Lellep Fernandez, who gave helpful advice; Bambi Schieffelin and two anonymous reviewers for Cambridge University Press, who also did so; and the Swedish Collegium for Advanced Study in the Social Sciences, in Uppsala, who provided Robert A. LeVine with the time, space, and facilities to bring the manuscript to completion.

A prosperous Gusii father with his first wife and three of their nine children at her house in Morongo. His other wife lives and works at his shop in town 7 miles away. Photograph by Eliza Klein.

A Gusii homestead (*omochie*) with several houses and outbuildings. Each residential house (*enyomba*) has a thatched roof with a steeple (*egechuria*), the latter signifying that a man *owns* the house, though it is uniquely identified with one of his wives. The mud walls of the nearer houses have worn away, revealing their wattle frames. A woman stands in the yard; behind her is a granary (*ekiage*) with a metal roof. Photograph by Michael Hennessy.

A Gusii mother holds her infant child, as one of her children tries to play with the baby. Children are considered appropriate playmates for babies, but mothers are not. Photograph by Eliza Klein.

A group of siblings and half-siblings from one homestead. Gusii children spend their days with children older and younger than themselves. Photograph by Eliza Klein.

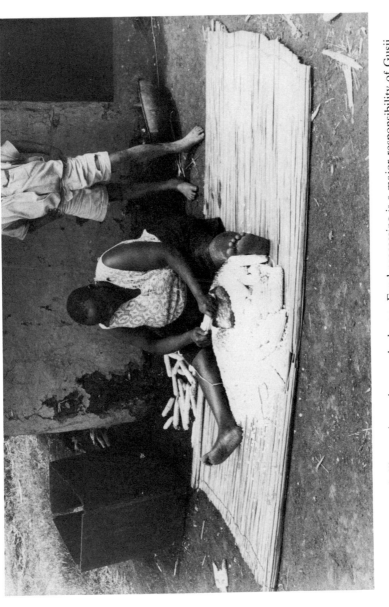

A woman shelling maize as her son looks on. Food-processing is a major responsibility of Gusii women. Photograph by Sarah LeVine.

A sample mother sitting with her baby gives a small bowl to her toddler, telling him to carry it elsewhere. This is deliberate training in obedience to maternal commands. Photograph by Eliza Klein.

Siblings in a maize field near their house. The two children at the ends are wearing school uniforms. Photograph by Sarah LeVine.

The yard of a house is the family center of daytime activity and social interaction. Maize kernels dry on wooden trays (*chingambo*) in front of the house, as chickens wander freely and children of all ages converse. Photograph by Sarah LeVine.

Day care: The *omoreri* (child nurse) carries her infant brother, keeping him out of harm's way and giving him constant access to a source of comfort. Photograph by Eliza Klein.

The elders (*abagaaka*) drink hot millet-beer (*amarwa*) from a common pot and discuss community affairs. Such gatherings of senior men represent moral and spiritual authority in the local patrilineage (*riiga*) and operate as the first level of governance beyond the homestead. Photograph by Sarah LeVine.

# Introduction

This book examines parenthood, infancy, and early childhood in an African community, revealing patterns and practices unanticipated by theories of child development and proposing a cultural approach to the understanding of early environments. In comparing the Gusii people of Kenya with the American white middle class, we show their differing patterns of reproductive behavior and child care to be goal-driven, not by goals fixed in the course of human evolution but by historically conditioned cultural models that set a parental agenda for optimizing certain potentials of human development over others. Gusii parents give priority to their own fertility, the survival of their infants, and the compliance of their children – goals they have been largely successful in attaining during the 20th century. (The Gusii have one of the highest fertility rates in the world.) In describing Gusii family life and infant care practices, we demonstrate how their organization as parental strategies was coherent and efficacious in the indigenous context while becoming increasingly problematic under new conditions.

This study of 28 Gusii children and their environments over 17 months provides a profile of care from birth to 30 months of age, includes comparisons of Gusii and American mother–infant interaction, and indicates many specific differences in caregiving environments. Gusii mothers breast-feed for 16 months, sleep with their infants, leave them during the daytime with child caregivers as young as 5 years old, and avoid praising or questioning toddlers or engaging them in extended conversations. Gusii infants grow up in bodily contact with their caregivers and are present at virtually all family activities, but are rarely the centers of verbal or visual attention. They have relatively little opportunity for motoric exploration during the first 18 months, and they have *less* access to maternal attention as they reach the transition from infancy to early childhood. These practices diverge sharply from those considered normal or optimal in North America and Europe, namely, infant care that is visually stimulating and socially engaging from the start (while affording long periods of sleep), with a verbally responsive and emotionally supportive mother who facilitates exploratory behavior and conversational interaction during the transition from infancy to early childhood. What are we to make of Gusii practices from this point of view? Do they constitute a form of neglect or deprivation? Or do our assumptions about the "average expectable environment" of the human infant have to be changed?

In this book we take up the challenge of answering these questions through an analysis of Gusii practices of reproduction and infant care in their own cultural context and in comparison with American practices. Gusii mothers are devoted to the welfare and development of their infants, and their sense of what is best for them is framed in terms of indigenous cultural models that assume high infant mortality, high fertility (but with protective birth-spacing), and a domestic age-hierarchy in which young children acquire useful skills and moral virtues through participation in household food production. The accuracy of these assumptions has been eroded by changing conditions, but the models based on them – putting more emphasis on survival, soothing, and compliance, less emphasis on talking and interactive excitement than American models – remained the dominant guides to parental behavior at the time of our field study.

The Gusii care raises questions for child development research: How do we conceptualize the needs of infants and young children in face of the diversity revealed in this study? To what extent to human populations with divergent conceptions of the life course facilitate different maturational processes in the early years, and what price do they pay for developing one potential of human development rather than another? Have theories of early development exaggerated the universality of infant social environments in the absence of convincing evidence about their diversity? Have theorists misinterpreted infant care practices that enhance school-related skills, and other behavioral tendencies valued in the West, as prerequisites for human development in general? Finding the answers must begin with a hard and detailed look at evidence from non-Western cultures. This book takes such a look at the Gusii, from the combined perspectives of social anthropology, pediatrics, and developmental psychology – examining the child and the environment over time, describing practices in context, analyzing their benefits and costs, and appraising some of their developmental and health consequences.

Chapter 1 offers a comparative framework for studying child care at the population level across diverse cultures. In Chapter 2 we review the evidence on infant care in the agricultural societies of sub-Saharan Africa from several disciplines. In Part II of the book (Chapters 3–5), we focus on the Gusii people of Kenya – their changing culture and family life as an environment for child rearing, and their practices during pregnancy and childbirth.

Part III presents the results of our longitudinal study, with an examination of the care and interpersonal environment of Gusii infants (Chapter 6), their health and nutrition (Chapter 7), their social interaction and communication (Chapter 8), and variations in their early caregiving relationships (Chapter 9). In Part IV (Chapter 10), we interpret the data in cultural and psychological terms, comparing Gusii infant care with that of the American white middle class and considering the lessons to be learned from this research.

*Part I*

# African infancy: Frameworks for understanding

# 1

## The comparative study of child care

Ever since Margaret Mead published *Growing Up in New Guinea* in 1930, it has been evident that knowledge of cultural variations in child rearing is essential to an understanding of human development. Mead introduced the idea that the diverse peoples of the world constitute a great laboratory of child development, with each culture representing a different set of experimental conditions for the rearing of children. The anthropological observer interested in questions of early education had only to "read the answers" from the experiment conducted for over a thousand years by a particular culture. Mead envisioned, for example, that her ethnographic report on the Manus people, whose children spent their days free of parental control, would help resolve the debate over "permissive" child rearing in America at that time.

The notion of cultural diversity as a laboratory offering "natural experiments" to the child development investigator has continued to excite interest in the cross-cultural study of child rearing, but reading the answers proved more complicated than Mead anticipated in 1930.[1] This is partly because the metaphor of a laboratory experiment makes the interpretation of results seem simpler than it is. In an experiment, the investigator controls the background conditions thought likely to affect the outcome in order to focus on one or two factors of interest, which are permitted to vary. But the conditions of childhood in Manus differ from those of American children in a great many ways other than the amount of parental supervision, and predicting the effects of "permissiveness" in the United States from observations made in New Guinea is highly conjectural. Anthropological students of child rearing resemble laboratory researchers in the experimental tradition less than they do naturalists in the Darwinian tradition of field observation.

In field research, the central question is what to observe, and the answers to that question concerning child development have changed over the years since Mead's pioneering study, with the emergence of new theories and evidence of what children learn at various ages and how they experience their environments. Field studies conducted at different times and from distinct theoretical perspectives have been focused on dissimilar aspects of childhood, resulting in something less than a cumulative record of empirical findings from which general conclusions can be drawn. Indeed, progress in this field has been marked primarily by studies calling attention to "new" aspects of childhood, those hitherto unexamined by anthropologists but which research in psychology, linguistics, or other disciplines has shown to be significant in the development of the child.

In the 1960s and early 1970s, for example, experimental studies showed human infants to be far more capable of perception, learning, communication, and the formation of social relationships during the first year of life than had previously been known. This stimulated more detailed field research on infant care in diverse human societies – including the study reported in this volume – that examined early environments in the light of the new developmental knowledge. Thus there have been many changes in, and continuing divergence concerning, what constitutes an adequate case study of child rearing in cultural context.

Ideology has also played a role in preventing a simple "reading of the answers" to questions of child development from world cultural diversity in child rearing. Much child development research in the 20th century has been driven by the fields of education and psychiatry in seeking to find the determinants of academic achievement and mental disorder within Western societies. This practical agenda has narrowed the range of problems selected for investigation and given a normative bias to interpretations of the evidence. Just as Mead framed her Manus material in terms of the permissiveness debate in the United States during the 1920s, subsequent analyses of cultural diversity in child rearing have often addressed questions arising from American middle-class concerns about school performance and mental health – usually recast as cognition, competence, or emotional development – and have reflected Western assumptions about child development, without taking account of the local contexts and conceptions of the people under discussion.

Furthermore, ideologies of child rearing in the Anglo-American West have changed over the last 60 years: The concern with hygiene, schedule, and discipline among child care "experts" of the 1930s was replaced after World War II by an emphasis on infants' need for love and emotional support. From the older perspective, for example, African customs of breast-feeding on demand for 18 to 36 months could be interpreted as "overindulgence" and classified in Freudian terms as excessive gratification at the oral stage of psychosexual development;[2] from the later perspective, the same practices, insofar as they were not accompanied by visual and verbal expressions of the mother's love that were familiar to Western observers, were occasionally interpreted as neglectful of the infant's emotional needs.[3] Do African mothers "indulge" their infants too much – or too little? Both the question and its answers reflect the biases of observers rather than the indigenous contexts that shape infant experience.

Thus Margaret Mead's dream of a world laboratory of variations in child care providing clear answers to the educational questions of middle-class America has not been realized, partly because the world is not a laboratory (even though it is varied), partly because our questions change as we know more, and also because many of our questions are rooted in local concerns and assumptions that have constrained the search for answers. Yet Mead's basic message to the child development field remains as valid today as in 1930: To understand how children grow up under varied environmental conditions, one must be willing to go to where those conditions already exist, to examine them with respect and in detail, and to change one's assumptions in the face of new observations.

Mead also recognized some fundamental issues to which anthropological evidence on childhood environments should be addressed: the issues of universality and variability, heredity and environment, normality and pathology. These issues are as important now – and as controversial – as they were in 1930, though they are debated in the context of more specialized bodies of knowledge.

For example, some investigators of infant development, following Hartmann's concept of an "average expectable environment" to which all human infants are genetically "preadapted,"[4] have proposed that there is a species-wide pattern of infant caregiving that promotes normal social and emotional development; that human parents as well as infants are preadapted to engage in this type of interaction; and that violating the infant's expectations for this pattern of interaction can lead to emotional disorder.[5] Other, more socially oriented students of child development, however, argue that the patterns of interaction proposed as universally necessary for normal development are actually derived from contemporary middle-class Anglo-American norms and that evidence from a broader range of populations would show a variety of infant caregiving patterns to be consistent with normal social and emotional development – thus casting doubt on both the genetic determination of early interactions and their contributions to emotional disorders. According to this perspective, early environments provide culture-specific patterns of interaction from which infants begin to acquire the codes of communication and interpersonal conduct prevailing in the community into which they were born.[6]

This difference of views about the interactive aspects of infant environments indicates a general problem of child development research: Investigators tend to make theoretical claims or assumptions about the human species as a whole but they tend to support them with locally collected data from their own, usually Euroamerican, populations. More evidence from diverse cultural settings is needed to help resolve, or reframe, long-standing issues in the field. We also need a broader and more inclusive conceptual framework than has been available to integrate evidence of human cultural diversity into child development research and to guide our search for further knowledge.

## A POPULATION PERSPECTIVE ON CHILD DEVELOPMENT

The child development field has been primarily concerned with *species-specific* and *person-specific* characteristics of humans. The general theories (e.g., of Freud, Piaget, Erikson, and Bowlby) have been offered as formulations applicable to all humans, positing stages and processes connected directly and indirectly with the

Table 1.1. *Framework for the comparative analysis of child care*

| Adaptive needs | Population-level patterns | Cultural goals of child care |
|---|---|---|
| *Subsistence:* Provision of food | Economic systems: foraging, agrarian, industrial | Economic competence |
| *Reproduction:* Somatic continuity | Marriage and kinship systems, demographic regimes, norms of infant care | Childbearing and survival, acquisition of gender roles |
| *Communication:* Sharing of information | Languages and other symbol systems | Communicative competence |
| *Social regulation:* Maintenance of order | Social hierarchies, conventions of face-to-face relations | Self-control, situationally appropriate behavior |

maturation of the central nervous system during childhood. Empirical research on child development, however, has focused largely on individual differences within relatively homogeneous populations, seeking to identify person-specific environmental or temperamental variables that predict person-specific behavioral outcomes. *Population-specific* characteristics have usually been regarded merely as an extension of individual differences, if they are taken into account at all. From a biological point of view, however, population-specific characteristics are of central significance in the analysis of human adaptation.

Population-level variation in social organization and social behavior is a characteristic of the human species.[7] Fundamental adaptive processes such as subsistence, reproduction, communication, and social regulation, far from being simply replicated across human populations, are highly variable in their pattern and organization, as indicated in Table 1.1. Patterns of social organization and behavior such as mating patterns (e.g., monogamy vs. polygamy) and emotional display rules, which vary across *species* in much of the animal kingdom, vary across *populations* in homo sapiens.

Populations can be defined as interactional networks within which mating and other communicative processes tend to be concentrated. Human populations vary greatly in size, complexity, and stability of boundaries, and form local associations, endogamous groupings, and speech communities, at national and subnational levels in the contemporary world. A population tends to share an environment, symbol systems for encoding it, and organizations and codes of conduct for adapting to it.[8] It is through the enactment of these population-specific codes of conduct in locally organized practices that human adaptation occurs.

Human adaptation, in other words, is largely attributable to the operation of specific social organizations (e.g., families, communities, empires) following culturally prescribed scripts (normative models) in subsistence, reproduction, and other domains of animal behavior.[9] The description and analysis of these organizations and scripts are the primary tasks of social anthropology. No account of ontogeny in human adaptation could be adequate without inclusion of the population-specific patterns that establish pathways for the behavioral development of children. All too often, however, child development theorists have leaped from species-wide determinants to person-specific behaviors without sufficient attention to the intervening contexts created by social and cultural systems, and investigators have studied individual differences without examining their ecological relationships. Seeking to identify the neuropsychological "hardware" or capacities for behavioral development, they have frequently overlooked the cultural "software" that gives it direction.

Table 1.1 outlines a framework for the comparative analysis of human child care, showing dimensions of population-level variation and the goals of child care corresponding to each of four adaptive needs or functions: subsistence, reproduction, communication, and social regulation. These functions are vital to survival and are socially organized, in homo sapiens as well as in other animal species.[10] In humans, the socially organized patterns vary at the population level, as indicated in the second column, and particular patterns influence the survival and behavioral development of offspring through the provision of goal-directed child care environments, as specified in the third column.

In biology, survival is the ultimate criterion of adaptation, achieved not only through spawning and protection of the newborn but also indirectly through the social processes involved in the provision of food, sharing of information, and maintenance of social order – in all animals. A description of child care in any human population must begin with how these adaptive functions are socially and culturally organized in the local environment of the child.

Consider the Gusii people of Kenya, who are described in this book, and the middle-class Americans with whom we are comparing them. The Gusii were until recently (the 1960s) "agro-pastoralists," that is, subsistence cultivators with herds of cattle, sheep, and goats. Each mother–child household grew its own food; now mothers grow some of their own food and buy some in the market with money earned through cash crops or provided by employed husbands. The mother depends on her children to help in cultivation, food-processing, and household tasks (including child care) that give her the time to work in the fields. Children participate in the domestic labor force from their early years, and their obedience and responsibility are important to the household economy. Gusii parents define economic competence in terms of their children's manifest obedience and responsibility, which they see as essential to their future economic careers as well as their present tasks.[11] The U.S. parents, by contrast, participate in a highly specialized industrial economy in which only 2% of working adults are involved in food production, and child rearing is geared to the schooling children will need to acquire specialized economic skills in adolescence and adulthood – a delayed goal permitting American children more time for play, which is also defined as educationally useful. The different patterns of subsistence translate into distinct goals for child rearing and dissimilar patterns of childhood experience.

The reproductive environments of Gusii and American parenthood are equally dissimilar. Gusii women marry in their teens, reside with their husbands' parents, become co-wives in polygynous unions (rare now, but frequent in earlier cohorts),[12] and are expected to bear a child every 2 years until menopause, when they have had about ten children on average. Their goals in child care are oriented to the child's survival and health in the first 2 years, participation in the sibling group thereafter, and resocialization for gender-specific reproductive roles, through the male and female initiation ceremonies, before puberty. These goals reflect the early stage of demographic transition in which the Gusii find themselves: Their child mortality rates are still high enough to make survival a concern during the early years; their high fertility, based on the traditional assumption that one can never have too many offspring (as labor, risk insurance, and social continuity), provides a large sibling group in which children socialize each other and also supports the initiation ceremonies as a valued transition to mature reproductive roles.

The middle-class Americans, on the other side of the demographic transition, marry relatively late, have only a few children and live with them in nuclear family households. Although American parents are protective of their children's health and tend to promote their acquisition of culturally constructed gender roles, they assume that child survival is assured by specialized medical care and that the child's mating and fertility represent future choices to be made by the child in adulthood. Reproductive issues in this sense are not as much in the forefront of parental attention for the Americans as they are for Gusii.

As for communication, the Gusii and American parents not only speak unrelated languages (the Gusii language has 94 tenses and no gender),[13] but also maintain different norms for expressing emotions and disclosing personal information. The Gusii are emotionally inexpressive by American standards; they rarely show approval, anger, or shock through facial expressions or in words, and they avoid disclosing information, particularly pleasurable facts about oneself, which Americans routinely share. This reflects a code of morally restrained conduct, described in Chapter 3, that parents want their children to acquire. Thus the standards of communicative competence shaping the speech environment of Gusii children diverge extremely from those of their American counterparts (Chapter 8).

Social regulation is another domain of contrast. Gusii children grow up in a hierarchical environment in which respect for those older or otherwise of higher status is the paramount virtue. This means not initiating conversation with those above you or calling attention to yourself in social gatherings. By Gusii standards, normal American children are excessively assertive and unruly. Gusii parents are convinced that proper respect will serve a child well during the rest of his or her life; American parents are equally convinced that self-confidence and initiative are useful virtues.

Thus when two human populations vary as drastically in the institutions through which they attain fundamental adaptive goals as the Gusii and middle-class Americans do, it will affect parents' conceptions of child care and their agenda for the development of children. The shape of childhood environments will be correspondingly differentiated, and childhood experience, though varying from one individual to another even in the same family, will reflect the dominant cultural scripts for social interaction, emotional expression, and other psychologically significant aspects of social behavior.

## DEVELOPMENTAL ISSUES: UNIVERSALS, PATHOLOGY, AND EARLY EXPERIENCE

Our case study of the Gusii is addressed to several long-standing issues of child development, reformulated from a population perspective and in terms of contemporary infancy research: What are the universals of child care and development in the human species? What are the contributions of social organization and culture to parent–child interaction? How do infants participate in and shape their own environments? Which forms of care are beneficial and which are harmful to children, that is, to what extent do they reduce or increase the environmental risks to survival or healthy development? To what extent do children's early experiences shape their later behavior? Although no study of a single society, even in comparison with populations previously studied in child development research, can answer such broad questions, it should be possible to learn lessons from the Gusii research that will shed new light on these issues, perhaps leading to their reformulation for future research.

More specifically, a case study of infant care in an environment that differs as much from Euroamerican populations as that of the Gusii does from middle-class Americans should reveal (1) whether presumed universals of infant care and development hold up in such a different setting; (2) how the conditions of infant experience in that setting affect the environmental risks to children; (3) which aspects of the setting influence parental behavior and permit or constrain the infant's contribution to the interaction; and (4) to what extent infant experience there represents early enculturation, that is, acquisition of the local culture. The case study should also seek to understand the context of family life and child care in the particular site and the social as well as psychological processes that influence parent and child behavior there.[14] Furthermore, it should examine infant care from three perspectives: that of the parent, that of the child, and that of cross-cultural comparison.[15]

Beyond this multiplicity of issues, questions, contexts, and perspectives, a case study must have a point of view that takes account of the biopsychological, socioeconomic, and cultural dimensions of human development and is formulated in relation to existing positions in the field. The ecological framework of Urie Bronfenbrenner,[16] in conceptualizing the levels of institutional environment that condition the child's interactions with others, is compatible with our perspective but was designed for the analysis of child development in large-scale modern societies with highly specialized institutions. There remains the need for a conceptualization that is both more general, in the sense of being potentially applicable to societies with less differentiated institutions, and more specific to cross-cultural variations in the parental predicament.

In Figure 1.1 we have depicted four points of view concerning human parental behavior. Each of the three boxes at the top of the figure summarizes not only a kind of condition but also a single explanatory model of parental behavior, as indicated by the black arrows, whereas the white arrows display the *Cultural Mediation model,* which combines the other three in a specific order, with headings derived from a computer analogy: "organic hardware," "ecological firmware," and "cultural software."[17]

The first box refers to those aspects of human parental care and ontogeny that reflect *species-wide* anatomy, reproductive physiology, neurophysiology, and growth patterns: for example, the capacities for maternal lactation and sensitivity to infant signals on the part of parents; the gradually maturing central nervous system of the child, which is remarkably capable even at birth but manifests new capabilities throughout childhood and adolescence. These are among the *hard-wired* aspects of reproduction and child development.[18] All of these features evolved through natural se-

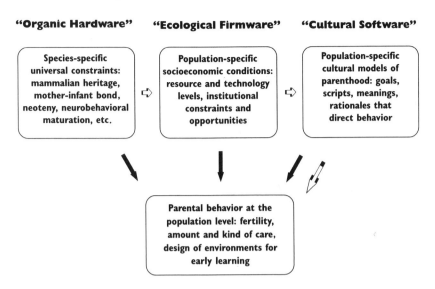

**"Organic Hardware"**     **"Ecological Firmware"**     **"Cultural Software"**

Species-specific universal constraints: mammalian heritage, mother-infant bond, neoteny, neurobehavioral maturation, etc.

Population-specific socioeconomic conditions: resource and technology levels, institutional constraints and opportunities

Population-specific cultural models of parenthood: goals, scripts, meanings, rationales that direct behavior

Parental behavior at the population level: fertility, amount and kind of care, design of environments for early learning

1.1 Analyzing human parental behavior at the population level.

lection and are still evolving, but in the perspective of historical (as opposed to evolutionary) time are treated as if they were unchangeable.[19]

The second box, ecological firmware, refers to population-level characteristics of human environments that affect the resources available to children in the form of food, protection from health risks, other material goods, and social attention. These are termed *firmware* in the computer analogy because although they can remain fixed like hardware, they are also (unlike hardware) capable of being altered in historical time, and include features such as fertility and mortality rates and levels of material welfare.[20] Historical changes in these settings have created wide variations among populations, such as the current gap between the affluent countries of the north and the poor countries of the south on birth and child death rates and per capita incomes.

The ecological parameters affecting parents in a given population can be seen as constituting the constraints and incentives for an *optimal parental investment strategy*. For Gusii parents of the past, with labor-intensive domestic food production and high levels of mortality, the optimal strategy for parents was to bear many children and attend to their early protection, thus minimizing risks to survival (as much as possible without modern disease control) and maximizing the number of participants in domestic production. Put another way, the economic and demographic situation of Gusii parents encouraged high fertility and physically protective infant care. For contemporary American middle-class parents, with low mortality, a household economy in which children figure as costs rather than assets, and with a competitive adult environment in the future of each child, the balance of incentives favors bearing few children and attending to the prolonged training of each one. An optimal parental investment strategy can be seen as resolving not only the trade-off between the number of children and the amount of resources invested per child but also the distribution of maternal energy across child care and other tasks. If mothers are called upon to do productive work during their childbearing years, then their time and energy become a scarce resource that can, theoretically, be allocated in an optimal way. In a situation like that of the Gusii, where women are manifestly overburdened by the demands of food production, reproduction, and child care, they need an optimal formula to perform effectively the multiple tasks demanded by their domestic roles.

The third box contains the software, that is, the ideas that influence parents in a particular population, and give them a common sense of what is natural, normal, and necessary in reproductive behavior and child care. Gusii conceptions of high fertility and protective infant care as aims for parents, and respect and restrained conduct as goals for child development, plus their prescribed means of attaining these goals, are examples of cultural models and scripts that have acquired directive force as personal codes of conduct. The codes, models, and scripts are based on historical traditions but change as they are communicated from one generation to another.

Each of these boxes refers to factors that have been given the status of "simple and sovereign" determinants by theorists of the biological and social sciences.

### Biopsychological models

The black arrow on the left of Figure 1.1 represents the explanatory model in which the organic equipment of the human animal provides the primary structure and meaning to parenthood everywhere regardless of history and culture. Population-level variations in infant environments tend to be ignored or minimized as influences on development; the child's maturational schedule is held to be robust enough to guarantee basic competence in social interaction and language and cognitive development, even under conditions of apparent deprivation.

### Economic Utility models

The middle black arrow represents the position that reproductive and parental behavior reflects primarily the socioeconomic conditions of childbearing and family life, with populations at a particular technological and demographic state, and in a particular social location, rationally regulating their fertility and resource allocations to children in response to economic incentives. Utilitarian models vary in their specific concepts of the parental predicament, but they all assume that economic rationality will overwhelm preferences to the contrary and that parental striving, whatever its cultural appearance, can be reduced to economic motives.

### Semiotic models

The black arrow on the right signifies the view that cultural scripts and their embedded meanings, derived from the traditions and popular ideologies of a particular culture, guide parental behavior. The assumption is that parents are influenced primarily by conventionalized images of what is and what ought to be in the domains of reproduction and child care, applying ideal standards in their daily lives, and seeking to implement an agenda derived from culture-specific concepts of virtue rather than making decisions based on economic calculation or developmental realities. Parental behavior is symbolic action, organized and driven by the shared meanings with which every aspect of reproduction and caregiving is endowed in the context of a local culture. Thus the Semiotic approach, like the Biopsychological and Economic Utility approaches, can be used as an explanatory model that takes little or no account of alternative points of view.

### Cultural mediation model

The working model we have adopted in this study is indicated by the white arrows and is based on the concept of cultural mediation and the hardware–software analogy. The white arrows represent *underdetermining* influences that provide capacities, constraints, or directions without *compelling* a specific outcome in parental behavior. Thus the organic hardware of parenthood and child development provides a basic set of parameters that limit the number of children women can bear at one time, the ages at which children can acquire speech and participate in the household economy, and the levels of performance that children can reach at given ages. These constraints, however, are under-specified in that they do not dictate whether the average woman in a population will have ten children in her lifetime, like the Gusii, or less than two, like middle-class Americans, which specific language children will acquire or whether they will be called upon to make a contribution to the household economy, like Gusii children, or not, like middle-class Americans. Furthermore, hardware provides capacities that may not be used by individuals in a given population. Thus the universal capacity for lactation is realized by all Gusii mothers in their infant care practices, due to an ecological setting in which they have no alternative means of promoting child survival (as well as to their conception that breast-feeding is natural, normal, and morally correct); but the same capacity goes unused by many middle-class American mothers, who have alternatives that do not jeopardize survival and whose feelings about breast-feeding have been influenced by cultural conceptions in which the female breast is endowed with erotic meanings. The extent to which species-wide hardware will be used in child care and development, and *how* it will be used, are conditioned by the ecological firmware and cultural software of a specific population.[21]

Similarly, parent–child interaction begins with the universal hardware of child care, that is, innate capacities for communicating and responding, but the child is born in a social environment into which the local conventions of interpersonal communication and kin relationship have been preinstalled as scripts for interactive performance. In attempting to understand parental behavior, then, our first task is to find out what script is being followed and what each action means in terms of that script; later we can learn how performance based on this script represents a choice among organic and economic possibilities.

A cultural script is a highly directive software program, prescribing the content and sequence of interaction as well as the code for interpreting performance, but it is nevertheless another *underdetermining* influence on parental behavior, as indicated by the final white arrow on Figure 1.1. Operating under diverse constraints and pressures, parents within the same community vary in their realization of the cultural scripts to which they may all subscribe. Their actual performance should be seen as a compromise between the demands of the script and those of their individual situations. Thus the influence of cultural scripts on parental behavior is to create central tendencies rather than uniformities in a population. The central tendencies of Gusii parents and their middle-class American counterparts, and the scripts that motivate and influence them, are the focus of our attention in this book.[22]

This chapter has presented a conceptual framework for our case study of child care and the point of view we take in interpreting parental behavior. The cultural mediation model emphasizes parental practices and the cultural scripts that influence them as starting points for understanding child care in its local context. We do not ignore the biological, developmental, and economic contexts, however, but assess them independently of the parental perspective as well as through it. In analyzing the results, we take account of biopsychological universals and consider both utilitarian and semiotic interpretations of Gusii parental behavior, as we search for answers to some basic questions of child development.

# 2

## Infant care in sub-Saharan Africa

The conditions under which infants are raised in sub-Saharan Africa have been explored by anthropologists, demographers, and developmental psychologists.[1] Despite the large size of the continent and the diversity of its inhabitants, the sub-Saharan agricultural peoples are connected by history as well as geography and constitute a distinct cultural region in comparison with other regions of the world. Many Gusii customs are shared with other peoples in the region. This chapter sets the stage for our consideration of the Gusii case by describing similarities and variations in African practices of infant care, beginning with the goal of survival and proceeding to the organizational and relational contexts of caregiving, its characteristic activities and interactions, and patterns of early development.

### SURVIVAL AS A GOAL OF INFANT CARE

African customs of infant care have been described in the anthropological literature since at least the beginning of the 20th century. The earliest observers were Protestant missionaries who worked among Bantu peoples in southern Africa before 1920.[2] Their published accounts are not focused on childhood but include descriptions of customs in which babies are breast-fed for 2 or 3 years, carried on their mothers' backs, and often taken care of by young girls – whose photographs with babies bound to their backs appear in some of the books. The great frequency of infant death is mentioned, often as an aside. Birth rituals, naming ceremonies, and vernacular terms for the early stages of childhood are described, usually with no interpretation. One exception is the Swiss missionary Henri Junod, whose two-volume work on the Thonga of Mozambique first appeared in 1912. He tells us that when Thonga children are weaned from the breast a ritual called *hondlola* is performed.

> This rite is the ordinary hondlola rite which is performed in this or in a similar way at the close of any serious disease as the conclusion of the treatment, with the view of taking away the defilement of the disease. . . . [This] hondlola reveals to us the true conception of the nursing period held by the Natives. For them the three first years of the child's life are a period of disease; so many perils threaten the little one's well-being that he can hardly be considered healthy. He is during the whole time under the supervision of the physician, who takes leave of the little patient on the day of weaning.[3]

The "physician" referred to is an indigenous healer who performs a number of protective rituals for the baby between birth and weaning. According to Junod, the use of these rituals combined with the performance of *hondlola* at weaning demonstrates that the Thonga conceptualize infancy as a period of special risk, like a chronic disease, presumably reflecting a high rate of infant and child mortality.

Krige[4] later claimed that Junod's interpretation applied more broadly among the peoples of South Africa:

> The amulets worn by infants, the rites performed from time to time during babyhood, the belief of the Shangana-Tonga that "the child grows by medicine," all lend support to Junod's theory that the Bantu [*sic*] look upon babyhood as a marginal period – a period of ill-health ended at weaning . . .[5]

In this view, customary caregiving practices are motivated by a concern for the health and survival of the infant. Where infant mortality is high, as it always has been in sub-Saharan Africa,[6] a folk concept of infants as being particularly vulnerable could promote survival by calling attention to the infants' special needs and justifying their nurturance and protection.

A study by Brazelton, Koslowski, and Tronick[7] provides some contemporary evidence in support of this view. They studied newborn infants in the city of Lusaka, Zambia. Ten Zambian infants and a comparison group of ten American infants were examined on days 1, 5, and 10 after birth, using the Brazelton Neonatal Behavioral Assessment Scale (1973). The urban Zambian infants, who showed pediatric evidence of intrauterine depletion at birth, also showed poor muscle tone and were relatively inactive and unresponsive motorically in their first-day behavioral assessments. By day 5, when the Zambian infants were no longer clinically dehydrated, their activity and responsiveness scores had risen dramatically, and there were few differences between Zambians and Americans. On day 10, the Zambian infants' muscle tone was better than average and their alertness and social interest scores were higher than those of their American counterparts. Brazelton et al. concluded that the dramatic recovery of the Zambian infants was directly attributable to rehydration through breast-feeding and tactile or motoric stimulation by their mothers, and indirectly to the mothers' confidence, based on previous experience and observation, that their efforts during the first days of life would be effective.

According to this interpretation, these African mothers, living in an urban slum under conditions of malnutrition and minimal social support, possessed folk knowledge, presumably based on a cultural model and personal experience, that guided them toward practices promoting the survival and growth of their neonates. They facilitated normal development – physical, behavioral, and social – by concentrating their efforts on feeding and physical nurturance during the first 10 days after birth. This can be seen as efficacious "folk pediatrics," applying traditional beliefs and practices in the treatment of vulnerable newborn infants.

The protection of African infants by customary practices is not limited to the immediate period after birth. Nothing is more characteristic of African patterns of reproduction and infant care than a long (24- to 40-month) birth interval, which drastically reduces the number of children a woman bears during her life. Women could give birth annually, as their high fertility goals might seem to demand, but acting under the guidance of local custom, they actually gave birth about every 3 years until quite recently. This phenomenon has been the subject of interpretation by anthropologists, demographers, and biomedical investigators.

The long birth interval in African societies was accompanied by breast-feeding, which continued into the second or third year of the child's life, and was often maintained by postpartum sexual abstinence lasting as much as 2 years. Whiting[8] first suggested that this arrangement was designed to enhance chances of child survival where the postweaning diet was low in protein, and that polygynous marriage protected the arrangement by providing husbands with alternative sexual partners to their lactating wives – a hypothesis now generally accepted by demographers.[9] Saucier[10] showed that the custom of postpartum abstinence is associated cross-culturally not only with polygyny but also with a number of other customs frequent in the sub-Saharan region, including bride-wealth, unilineal descent groups, virilocal residence, and shifting cultivation carried out by women. He argued that customary control of land, women, and political authority by older, more frequently polygynous men in the kin-based community made possible enforcement of abstinence among the younger, largely monogamous husbands, on whom it imposes the greatest hardship.

The conclusion that emerges from these comparative studies is that the desire for numerous progeny in indigenous Africa was qualified by a socially organized concern for their survival. The goal of African parents was to maximize the number of *surviving* children. The long birth interval represents a parental strategy for child survival through prolonged lactation, implemented as custom on a community-wide basis by a gerontocratic and polygynous social order.

The biomedical view of the long birth interval has been summarized by Lestaeghe et al.,[11] who emphasize the importance of prolonged breast-feeding for the health of both mother and child in tropical Africa: It provides the infant with protein where diets are often protein-deficient, with antibodies against prevalent infections, and with a contraceptive effect that permits the mother to recover and "pay undivided attention to the infant." An African mother is considered ready for the next pregnancy only after she has weaned her youngest child.

African parents – in virtually every society for which there is recorded information – are aware that the long birth interval minimizes risks to the child's survival. An interval of at least 2 years is generally normative in rural communities, and women who bear children more often are socially stigmatized. The Sukuma of Tanzania, for example, are described by Varkevisser as trying to space their children by an interval of 24 to 30 months:

> When a woman breeds more rapidly, people say, "Wapon-dekeja" ("She piles children on top of each other") or, with more scorn, "She gives birth like a chicken."[12]

Beliefs regarding the importance of lactation to child health are the basis for this normative attitude. Varkevisser reports that Sukuma mothers consider breast milk the best nutrient for children; when a child is sick, the lactating mother will postpone weaning to extend the period of breast-feeding.[13]

Furthermore, the Sukuma "protect their youngest against competition for the infant's most important source of food, his mother's breast, by attempting to postpone pregnancy until the infant is capable of managing a standard diet,"[14] that is, about 12 to 13 months of age in their view. Thus local belief connects infant health with maintenance of a long birth interval (in this case only 21 to 22 months) during which nothing interferes with access to mother's milk. Furthermore, the beliefs of some peoples connect infant disease and death with abbreviated birth intervals: Southwold reports that, among the Baganda (of Uganda), mothers were "traditionally" forbidden to engage in coitus when they were pregnant or lactating; they knew that weaning too early led to kwashiorkor, an often fatal disorder due to protein-calorie malnutrition, and "their name for the sickness, *obwosi,* is derived from the verb *okwosa,* to be next in order."[15]

Prolonged and intensive breast-feeding itself plays an important role in maintaining long birth intervals. Postpartum amenorrhea, which is only 2 months long on average for women who do not breast-feed, increases to 60% to 75% of the average duration of breast-feeding in populations in which breast-feeding is universal.[16] When infants are not weaned from the breast until 18 months on the average, their mothers are unlikely to become pregnant for the first year, and when the average duration of breast-feeding is 24 months, mothers are protected from pregnancy for about 17 months on average. After 24 months, lactation by itself does not extend the average period of amenorrhea in a population. Average birth intervals longer than 33 months in African populations reflect the effects of postpartum sexual abstinence.

The evidence on customs of postpartum abstinence in sub-Saharan Africa reviewed by Schoenmakers et al.[17] indicates that they were universal in the entire region until the 20th century, when they eroded rapidly in eastern and southern Africa, Ruanda, and Burundi, and the northern Sahel. In West Africa and much of central Africa, norms of postpartum abstinence were retained in close to their original form, though they underwent some erosion associated with Western influence, urbanization, and economic development. The reasons why abstinence eroded much more rapidly in some places than in others are not clear. It virtually disappeared in those parts of Africa where cow's milk was available for the postweaning diet of children (making possible an abbreviation of breast-feeding without additional risk of protein-calorie malnutrition), but it was also eliminated in some other areas, possibly due to the introduction of modern medical services, which might have given mothers greater confidence in the survival chances of their infants.

Thus the second half of the 20th century finds great variation in the maintenance of prolonged postpartum abstinence as a custom among sub-Saharan people who were probably more homogeneous in this respect just a few generations earlier. The longest birth intervals are found among West African peoples who continue the practice of prolonged abstinence. Among peoples of eastern Africa, the average birth interval now depends primarily on the contraceptive effect of prolonged lactation and on the influence of unevenly distributed patterns like polygyny and labor migration, which tend to separate wives from their husbands. But even where they have declined from 3 to 2 years, the birth intervals of rural populations in Africa are consistently long by world standards, giving African patterns of infant care a special character that is readily apparent in the Gusii case.

The close connection between birth interval and infant care in African folklore is illustrated by the status of the child who follows its mother's last birth interval, namely, the lastborn. In diverse cultures of the sub-Saharan region, there is a special word designating a lastborn, who is described as being breast-fed longer, weaned more gradually, and subject to fewer of the deprivations and disciplines imposed on other children during the period between weaning and birth of the next sibling.[18] The mother is often described as making this child her favorite. This treatment is usually characterized as a form of "spoiling," that is, inducing long-lasting expectations of privilege. There is usually a special kin and/or ritual status attached to this sibling position in adulthood, involving particular responsibilities or entitlements. These social and psychological sequelae are linked to the unique place of this child in the mother's reproductive history, particularly to the absence of a "follower" in a birth succession that is assumed (in local thought) to constitute the primary organizer of child care during the first years of life.

We conclude from this overview of the evidence that the customs of infant care most widespread in sub-Saharan Africa – intensive and prolonged breast-feeding and exclusive maternal attention during a long birth interval, often lengthened by a period of mandatory sexual abstinence – evolved culturally to promote the survival of young children in the face of extremely high mortality. African mothers recognize that these customs protect the health of their infants, but many have nevertheless reduced the period of protection in recent decades, perhaps as a consequence of the introduction of modern medical care.

## THE SOCIOLOGY OF INFANT CARE: ORGANIZATIONAL AND RELATIONAL CONTEXTS

Patterns of family life vary widely across African populations, each of which has recognized norms for the formation, maintenance, and dissolution of reproductive unions and the organization of domestic life. There are also local cultural prescriptions for house design, relationships within the domestic group, and the fertility schedules of wives (including maintenance of the birth interval, as illustrated earlier). This intensely scripted quality of domestic life reflects the family's functions as an economic, political, and religious institution, within a local community organized by descent (patrilineal or matrilineal), age and neighborhood, following a public code of conduct that has spiritual as well as social significance. The African family is not a private haven of consumption and informal recreation separated from a public world of economic production and formal relationships, as the modern Euroamerican family has been characterized; it is, on the contrary, part of a public world in which economic production is domestically organized and kinship often constitutes the formal basis for local governance. In reviewing features of family life broadly shared among the agricultural and pastoral societies of the sub-Saharan region, we describe marriage, living arrangements, fertility goals, and domestic authority patterns, and then consider some dimensions of variation that affect the contexts of child care.

### Marital rights

When two people marry, their respective descent groups are involved in the mandatory symbolic and economic transactions, notably the transfer of bridewealth to the wife's family, and in the enforcement of recognized rights and obligations governing their union, including the specifics of residential arrangements, interpersonal relationships, work, sexuality, widowhood, divorce, and custody of children. Marriage typically gives the husband and his kin rights over the wife – that is, over her labor and/or the children she bears – in exchange for a bridewealth in cattle or other goods transferred to her parents. Because married women do most of the cultivation in most African agricultural societies, as well as bearing and rearing the children, this exchange is the most momentous transaction in family life.

In African societies with a substantial bridewealth (e.g., ten or more head of cattle), the prospect of having to return it if their daughter fails to fulfill her conjugal obligations leads the bride's parents to pressure their daughter toward conformity with the expectations of her husband's kin. Where control over the bride's labor is part of the customary agreement, she usually lives with her husband's family, cultivating his share of the land under the supervision of her mother-in-law, and contributing to the labor force of her father-in-law's extended family. Where rights to a woman's children are part of the customary agreement, such as in the patrilineal societies of Africa, then even if she leaves the husband, he can claim custody of the children after weaning. These are "jural," that is, sociolegal, rights enforceable through local dispute settlement procedures that are under the authority of elders, chiefs, and spirits.

### Polygyny and the mother–child household

The basic residential unit in African families is the mother–child household, where a married woman lives with the children she bears and raises to maturity. This household is usually a separate hut, in some cases a room within a larger dwelling, but it is always socially identified with the woman, who is responsible for the care and early training of her children as well as providing their food through cultivation or trade. She is married to a man who either has other wives already, living in adjacent or nearby households, or who hopes to acquire additional wives in the future, in order to enhance his prestige and status in the community and add to the workforce of the domestic group.

Polygyny is the ideal form of marriage for agricultural peoples throughout the region. To make it possible for a majority of men, the pool of marriageable women is expanded through norms of early marriage for females (under age 20), while the number of marriageable males is constricted through the bridewealth requirement. In other words, women must marry by a given age such as 15 to 16 or suffer social stigma, but men marry when they can afford to. Some men cannot afford to marry the first time until they are over 30, thus making more women available for secondary marriages to older men, who have accumulated the resources to afford them. Even men who are able to marry before 30 usually cannot afford a second wife until they are a good deal older. Therefore a minority of married men in a given population may be polygynous at any time, with the monogamists being younger men, most of whom will eventually become polygynists when they obtain the resources to pay bridewealth for additional wives.

What this means from the child's point of view is: (1) Most children are born to men who are eventually polygynists. (2) Some children are raised in initially monogamous homes in which their father takes a second wife at some point during their childhood or after they grow up. (3) Other children are raised in domestic groups that are polygynous from the start, in which they grow up with the reality of another wife and her children – or five other wives and their children. (4) Polygyny reinforces the formality of domestic interaction, because the need to contain competition among co-wives leads to an explicit set of rules for the husband's interaction with the several mother–child units – for example, a rotational schedule for the husband's visitations or a ranking of the co-wives, meaning that fathers are distant socially as well as physically from some, if not all, of their children.

Thus polygny as an institution creates a wide variety of social environments in which children are raised. Common to children in all of these environments, however, is the expectation that the father will take another wife, the sense that it is legitimate for him to do so, and the understanding that it will enhance his prestige and status in the community while posing a threat to the position

of their mother and the security of their inheritance (in a patrilineal society).

### The value of children

No rules reveal more about African parenthood than those concerning the social placement of children. In many African societies, bridewealth marriage confers upon a man the privilege of
claiming all a woman's children, even those conceived after his
death, as his own; they become members of his lineage and are
known as the children of the deceased man. Hence a widow is
obliged to go on bearing children – through the *levirate,* in which
a specially designated kinsman of her husband impregnates her –
for her deceased husband. Fatherhood is thus socially defined as
being associated with legitimate marriage rather than with biological paternity. African societies distinguish between pater and geni-
tor, as the ancient Romans did, so that the man who paid
bridewealth for a wife will reap the benefit of her reproductive
performance.

The underlying assumption is that children do indeed constitute
a benefit to a man, even when he is dead, and to his kin group.
This assumption is also embodied in the customs of *ghost marriage,* in which a wife bears children in the name of a husband who
had not even consummated their union before his death, and
*woman marriage,* in which a postmenopausal widow without sons
"marries" a woman to bear sons who will bear her deceased husband's name, inherit his property, and continue his line.[19] Indeed,
most Africans of both sexes assume that children are an unmixed
blessing to their parents and their kin groups. The high value set
on children and fertility is not limited to those African societies in
which men can claim all of their wives' offspring as their own, nor
is it limited to men. Among the agrarian societies of sub-Saharan
Africa, children of legitimate marital unions are universally
wanted.

The desire for children in Africa has its roots in the economic,
social, and spiritual goals of parents. African agriculture and animal husbandry are labor intensive, and there are many tasks that
can be performed by children, to the benefit of the family. In
adulthood, children are expected to provide their aging parents
with a level of security and protection that could not be expected

from others. Furthermore, kin groups based on descent can survive only if they acquire new members in each generation, and the
defense of their collective resources (usually land and cattle) requires able-bodied men. The rules of custody reflect this need for
recruitment to the descent group. But there is also an overriding
desire for personal and social continuity reflected in the concern
for parenthood after death. Children are necessary to provide
their parents with a proper burial and to perform appropriate
mortuary rituals long after death. As customs like the levirate
suggest, Africans feel enhanced by the sense that their progeny
will continue to expand after they have died. Indigenous conceptions of parenthood do not distinguish sharply among economic,
social, and spiritual reasons for reproduction; one type of reason
implies the others in local thought. Childbearing becomes the
final common pathway for diverse human motives, conferring
wealth, security, prestige, and immortality – virtually everything
valuable – on parents.

The personal salience of these cultural conceptions is best illustrated by how Africans feel about childlessness. A barren woman
or childless man is their image of the worst possible fate: an
incomplete person who has not attained the foothold necessary
for full adulthood and spiritual continuity.[20] In some African societies, such people are pitied and feared, on the assumption that
their thwarted strivings for reproductive competence will make
them jealous of and eventually destructive to those around them.
In others, particularly in West Africa, childless women are entitled to request children from their kin, and they have a socially
accepted role as foster parents.[21] Thus everyone in an African
community wants to be a parent, not once, but many times.

Francis Mading Deng[22] writes of his own Dinka people in southern Sudan:

> For a Dinka, where he comes from and where he goes to are
> points in the cycle of life revitalized and continued through
> procreation. Despite the anxieties birth provokes, it is a cause
> for joy: but death is an end from which procreational immortal-
> ity is the only salvation.
>
> Every Dinka fears dying without a son "to stand his head": to
> continue his name and revitalize his influence in this world. . . .
> When a man dies leaving children behind, people mourn but are

quick to add this is not "the bad death." But a man who dies without issue is truly dead.[23]

[The] goal of procreation . . . being a means to other values, pervades the social system. It creates a web of values and institutions crowned by the overall goal of immortality through children, preferably sons. Just as immortality is a lineage-concept and therefore of group-interest, marriage and all that it entails is group oriented as well as individually motivated.[24]

In virtually all the social and cultural contexts of indigenous Africa, then, childbearing is necessary for moral virtue, spiritual continuity, and material well-being; the more descendants one has, the better off one is considered to be.

### Domestic hierarchy

As economic units, rural families living by agriculture and animal husbandry in sub-Saharan Africa are hierarchically organized, and age and gender are the primary principles of hierarchy. Women as a whole are usually subordinate to men, but each gender has its own age hierarchy, through which a person can expect to pass by becoming older and meeting local standards of maturity. The age-gender hierarchy is symbolically celebrated in the rules of deference for everyday family interaction and in the cultural scripts for rituals and other public occasions, which provide dramatic support for males and elders as sources of authority.

The domestic group operates as a hierarchy of labor, in which the most onerous and least desirable work is delegated downward to women and children, and as a hierarchy of consumption, in which privileges are distributed upward to male elders. The youngest children, after weaning, do the most menial tasks, such as fetching and carrying, and have the least claim on valued goods, such as meat, to eat.[25] Although infants are not yet part of this hierarchy because their survival is considered a goal equal in importance to productive work, mothers are keenly aware of the need to train them for their future roles in it as soon as they are deemed capable of understanding instructions. In precolonial times, when birth intervals were longer and children were not weaned until after 24 months, there must have been more overlap between the period of breast-feeding and the early learning of productive tasks. Then and now, the daytime care of infants when the mother is otherwise occupied is a task delegated by the mother to her children according to norms of the domestic hierarchy, and many of the childrens' earliest social experiences are in an age-ranked group of siblings that introduces them to the norms operative in the domestic setting as a whole.

Relief from the pressures of a subordinate place in the hierarchy is achieved not only by ascending to a higher position as one gets older but also through legitimate forms of escape. A mature married woman who is theoretically under the control of her husband, for example, normally has the autonomy to manage her household without his supervision, so long as she fulfills the basic obligations involved in childbearing and cultivation. After menopause, her relationship with the husband might become quite distant, particularly if they do not enjoy each other's company or he has taken younger wives. Having borne and raised children of both sexes, a wife has fulfilled the reproductive obligations imposed by bridewealth marriage, and though she may still be responsible for cultivating her husband's land (or arranging for others to do so), she is liberated in many other respects from the control of those above her in the domestic hierarchy. To a lesser degree, a similar situation pertains to older children: They are obliged to be deferential in interaction and to act according to the commands of parents and others older than themselves, but they have freedom of action when they are outside the range of adult supervision. Thus the apparently rigid hierarchy of the domestic group, subordinating wives to husbands and elders and children to adults, is mitigated by operating rules that often permit subordinates considerable autonomy, distance from regulation, and relative freedom in unsupervised situations. The hierarchical norms constitute a public structure requiring conformity, and they are rarely challenged or (in the long run) evaded, but they are not expected to be a constant, permanent, or defining part of the person.

### Variations

Within these broadly common characteristics of African family life, there are many population-level variations in domestic arrangements and marital stability that affect patterns of child care.

Among the Yoruba and Hausa of Nigeria, for example, the mother–child household is embedded in a walled compound, in close proximity to and sharing facilities with many other such households, whereas in much of eastern Africa, the mother–child household stands by itself on the land cultivated by the mother, at a distance from other households that is significant for child care and the early experience of children. In parts of West and central Africa, divorce is very frequent, meaning that women leave their husbands and are sometimes separated from weaned children, while taking the babies to a new home; in other parts of the sub-Saharan region, divorce is rare. Among matrilineal peoples, children can sometimes choose whether to live with their mother's or father's kin, whereas in the more common patrilineal situation, children have no choice and live with the father's kin. Finally, in much of West Africa there is the practice of kinship fostering, in which children are sent to live with their parents' kin, often at a distance and for a long period of time. In many places children are sent only when they are over 5 years of age, but among the Mende of Sierra Leone, fosterage of children under 2 is quite common.[26]

The "house-property complex," as formulated by Max Gluckman[27] and comparatively analyzed for East Africa by Thomas Hakansson,[28] is a pattern of family life widespread among cattle-keeping peoples of eastern Africa (both agropastoral like the Gusii and purely pastoral), from the southern Sudan to South Africa. In this pattern, patrilineal descent, bridewealth marriage, virilocal residence (i.e., living at the husband's home), polygyny, and the mother–child household are standard, divorce tends to be rare, and the domestic group of a polygynist is conceptualized as divided into "houses," each consisting of a mother and her sons; they are treated as units for purposes of inheritance and the use of cattle and land. The mother manages the property that will be inherited by her sons, acting as their trustee until they are adults, when the sons and mother cooperate in using the property and protecting it from possible appropriation by the father or others in the family. This situation fosters the loyalty of sons to their mother and generates competition between the half-brothers (i.e., the sons of the several co-wives) in the task of preserving their property to be used as bridewealth in their marriages and inherited after the father dies. The father's role in containing the conflict among co-wives and their sons, while pursuing his own interests in marrying more wives, is a precarious one and usually leads to his being resented by the "houses," who blame him for favoring himself or their competitors. The resultant distrust tends to diminish the cooperation of women from different houses in child care and other tasks and to increase their social distance from each other and from their husband. The house-property complex can be seen as a pattern of economic adaptation in the context of cattle-keeping families in eastern Africa, but its tensions over property rights can result in isolating childbearing women from each other.

### CAREGIVERS, INTERACTION, AND SOCIAL CHANGE

Considering African patterns of infant care from the infant's perspective, two factors stand out: the mother's workload in tasks other than infant care (i.e., her time-energy budget), and the number of women and children available to assist the mother in caring for the infant (the supply of caregivers). In most of the sub-Saharan region, the heavy subsistence burden carried by women during their childbearing years means they must have some assistance in infant care. This need can be minimized when the mother carries the baby on her back when she is trading in the market, grinding grain at home, or weeding certain crops in the fields, but back-carrying is not possible, or at least safe, when the mother is carrying a heavy load on her head or breaking up the earth with a short-handled hoe. Thus there are bound to be periods in the day, in at least some seasons, when mothers everywhere in Africa need help with infant care.

The availability of substitute caregivers is highly variable. Mothers can almost always get their older children to provide daytime care; thus sibling caregiving is found throughout the region,[29] but the amount of care by other children and adult women depends on the demography and social organization of domestic life. In populations characterized by relatively low fertility and high child mortality, for example, every rural locality has middle-aged women with no living children at home, who take an interest in the children of others and make themselves available for child care. In such populations, furthermore, older women – the grandmothers – tend to dote on infants and want to participate in their care.[30] This contrasts with African populations of very high fertility and relatively low child mortality, in which babies are plentiful and taking care of them seems more of a burden than a privilege.

Domestic organization makes an even more obvious impact on infant care. In some African societies, the basic domestic group is a multihousehold compound (often an extended polygynous family), with married women sharing cooking facilities and yards or verandas, often within walls setting off the compound from its neighbors. The women collaborate in processing and preparing food and other tasks and have a cooperative relationship that enables them to call on each other for infant care. Furthermore, the density of women and children in these shared spaces creates a gregarious atmosphere in which older children are likely to interact with infants who are not their siblings, and infants have access to a varied range of persons who take care of them or at least take an interest in them. We have observed this among the Yoruba and Hausa of Nigeria, and it is described in the literature by Wenger[31] for the Giryama of the Kenya coast and Riesman[32] for the Fulani of Burkina Faso.

The Hausa of northwestern Nigeria, for example, had at the time of our 1969 study[33] the demographic profile that favors adult caregiving (high child mortality and relatively low fertility) as well as walled compounds (median number of residents = 10) within which married women shared tasks. The seclusion of these Muslim women, which excluded them from working in the fields and (during their childbearing years) from trading outside the compound, gave them more time for infant care. But cultural norms mandated avoidance between a mother and her firstborn such that the mother must not use the infant's name, show an affectionate interest in the infant, and or even look at the child insofar as possible. Sarah LeVine conducted home observations of 19 Hausa infants aged 6 to 14 months old (mean = 43 weeks), 9 of whom were firstborns, in Malumfashi, Katsina Province. She followed a schedule based on Ainsworth's Uganda study, recording her observations in narrative form for 1 hour during three visits to each infant's compound.

Analysis of these observations showed that all but one of the mothers took virtually complete responsibility for feeding, bathing, and other routine physical care, but the average infant had

3.8 other adult females (over 14 years of age) who ministered to him in the following ways at least twice during at least two of the three visits: comforting the infant, keeping him away from dangerous objects, vocalizing to him, playing with him, encouraging him in vocal and motor skills. Much of the time the mother was present. Half of the mothers interacted with their own infants in these ways *less* than others in the same compound. Of the 173 cries recorded, 92% brought a response, in all but two cases within 30 seconds; 53% were responded to by the biological mother, the remainder by an average of four other caregivers.

In such a dense caregiving environment, the mothers of first-borns, in accordance with the avoidance norms, can and do have less contact with their infants than mothers of laterborns, as the maternal grandmother and other adult women in the compound provide additional care and social interaction for the firstborns. This kind of substitution is possible when adult women are available for infant care within the cooperative and gregarious atmosphere of a compound.

Such a pattern contrasts sharply with the relatively isolated mother–child households of the Gusii and some other East African peoples, where the infant may see few adults other than its mother and few children other than its own siblings.[34] Even in these East African settings, the density of the household may influence the infant's access to care. Munroe and Munroe[35] studied 12 infants ranging from 7 to 13 months of age among the Logoli of western Kenya and found that the frequency with which the infant was held and the rapidity of response to its crying were strongly dependent on the number of people living in the household – for the most part, older siblings who held and soothed the baby when the mother was absent or otherwise occupied. In a later study of 12 infants 11 to 15 months old conducted among the Kipsigis of western Kenya 15 years after the Munroes' research, Borgerhoff Mulder[36] found that the number of household residents did *not* predict the same measures of infant care. Because the Kipsigis babies were about 3 months older on average, drawn from a culturally distinct population, and possibly living under conditions of more prevalent schoolgoing among the older siblings (this last point is not clear), the second study did not constitute a genuine attempt at replication of the first. It nevertheless suggests that the recruitment of household members (especially children) for infant care might be affected by cultural differences and historical change and also that infant care practices in East African societies might be so age-sensitive during the transition between the first and second years of life that conclusions about the relationship of household density and composition to observed caregiving will have to await the results of larger and longer studies.

The care of infants by siblings and other children is extremely widespread in rural Africa, even where adult women are willing and able to provide surrogate care for mothers.[37] More precisely, children 5 to 11 years old (though occasionally younger and older), usually girls, are regularly assigned the task of providing daytime care for their infant siblings, particularly after the infants reach 5 months of age, when their mothers are working outside the home or attending to household tasks. The babies are usually carried on the child caregiver's back, but there are variations in the amount of care, the activities involved, and the extent of adult supervision. It is not surprising that Western investigators have called attention to this pattern, because it is not found in Western countries, where (if no adult is present) it would be considered a form of maternal neglect punishable under the law. Its institutionalization in Africa suggests that parents there consider it to be compatible with the survival, growth, and development of their infants, and this raises a number of questions: What kinds of care do children give infants? Is it differentiated from the care given by mothers; if so, what are its effects on the infant's subsequent behavioral development, and is it better or worse than maternal care? What are its effects on the child caregiver's behavioral development?

Theoretical and empirical discussions of sibling caregiving have generated a diverse set of answers to these questions. On the negative side, there is the skepticism, based on contemporary Western conceptions of infants' needs, that children under 10 years of age could possibly possess sufficient social and emotional maturity to provide "good quality" care for infants without close supervision. On the positive side, it has been argued that children assigned this responsibility can perform effectively with a minimum of training and that it has beneficial effects on their own prosocial skills and values, helping to prepare them for becoming parents.[38] Furthermore, sibling care is said to be beneficial to

African babies in providing early social stimulation and easily imitated models of competence.[39] Two studies in Kenya – one of Kikuyu infants during the first 12 months, the other of Embu toddlers at 15 to 30 months, have examined developmental performance on the Bayley test and concluded that sibling and child caregiving enhances social and cognitive development.

In the first of these studies, Leiderman and Leiderman[40] investigated socioeconomic variations in infant care and development within an economically heterogeneous Kikuyu village on the outskirts of Nairobi, Kenya, with a focus on the impact of nonmaternal care for infants on attachment as well as cognitive performance. They monitored 67 Kikuyu infants by spot observations[41] during the first 12 months of life and administered Bayley Scales and a series of structured attachment situations to find out what developmental outcomes followed from more and less frequent care by mother and child nurse and how these are affected by the family's economic resources. Mothers were interviewed about their socioeconomic background and current household resources. It was found that mothers at all economic levels act as their babies' primary daytime caregivers during the first 5 months and are the persons most frequently near their babies throughout the first year. Mothers of wealthier households spend less time with their infants, relying more on child and adolescent caregivers than poor women, but they more frequently hire adolescents or young adults in their late teens or early twenties rather than using their own preadolescent daughters to look after the infants without pay. The child caregivers engage babies in social interaction more frequently than the mothers do, indicating a possible complementarity in which the mother provides physical care and the child nurse social stimulation. Infants of wealthier families and those who had older adolescents as caregivers perform better on the Bayley Mental Scale at 7 to 12 months of age.

The age of the caregiver proved to be particularly interesting, both in its relation to the economic level of the family and as a factor contributing independently to cognitive performance. Leiderman and Leiderman divided the families into three economic levels. The poorest tended to be unable to afford school fees and had older siblings at home to help in infant care; the average age of the caregiver in these families was 13.9 years. The middle group sent their girls to school but could not afford to hire nursemaids for their infants, so they pressed their own younger (largely preschool) children, with an average age of 10.6 years, into service. The families at the highest economic level hired older girls from outside the family, at an average age of 20.2 years – far beyond the age of child nurses in more traditional rural settings, where a 20-year-old would be married and caring for her own babies. There were nevertheless such wide variations within each economic level that the correlation between the family's level and caregiver age was only .35 ($p < .01$), making it possible to disentangle their separate effects on test performance. The age of the caregiver was positively related to the infant's Bayley mental test score at 7 to 12 months ($p = .35$, $p < .01$), and with economic level controlled, remained significantly correlated (partial $r = .25$, $p < .05$). Thus caregiver age has an independent effect on infant performance, for reasons that are not clear, because the caregiver's social interaction with the baby was most frequent for the middle economic group, which had the youngest caregivers on average. This study nevertheless suggests that when the age range of nonmaternal caregivers is extended to include adolescents and young adults, their age, perhaps as an indicator of social maturity in caregiving, influences cognitive performance during infancy.

The second Kenya study, conducted by Sigman et al.[42] among the Embu of central Kenya, is the largest observational study to date of African children during the second and third years of life. They report that, for 110 toddlers aged 15 to 30 months, sustained social interaction almost always occurred with other children (age range unspecified), and that frequency of social interaction was correlated ($r = .29$, $p < .05$) with the child's performance on the Bayley Mental Scale at 30 months. Regressions controlling for parental literacy and the child's verbal score at 18 months showed that the correlation was not due to these factors. The authors conclude:

> The influence of siblings and peers appeared to be quite important for the Embu toddlers' development. Older sisters were frequently the caregivers who listened to and talked to their younger sibling. Furthermore, those toddlers most involved in sustained social interaction developed the most rapidly, and social interactions almost always involved other children rather than adults.[43]

As Sigman et al. imply, this pattern probably reflects a communicative relationship between siblings established during the first year, before their first observations at 15 months. Thus their study provides at least indirect evidence that sibling caregiving during infancy can be beneficial to infants, as measured by the infants' performance at 30 months on the Bayley Mental Scale. (The generalizability of their finding to other African populations may be limited by having confined their Embu sample to children from monogamous homes, and by the apparent prevalence of nuclear families, parental schooling, and a highly verbal domestic atmosphere in rural Embu in the 1980s, suggesting greater divergence from indigenous patterns than in populations studied earlier.)

Although research seeking to discover whether sibling care in Africa is better or worse, in attention and responsiveness to the infant, than maternal care has not produced definitive answers, it can be stated that care by children has not been proved inadequate and has been shown to have a positive impact on frequency of social interaction and the cognitive skills measured by Western tests. Furthermore, we have been told, by Hausa as well as Gusii, that child caregiving becomes the basis for lifelong emotional attachments between siblings. On the whole, African research has uncovered a variety of benefits from the sibling care of infants and few, if any, drawbacks, though many questions about it have not yet been answered.[44]

The social ecology of the African infant varies not only cross-culturally with the density and internal organization of the domestic group but also historically with the influence of large-scale institutional change. The effects on infant care can be identified by comparing the practices of subgroups of parents within a population who have been differentially exposed to social change. This was the approach adopted by Robert LeVine and Barbara Lloyd in their study of the Yoruba of Ibadan, Nigeria, from 1961 to 1963.[45] Maternal schooling was chosen, on the basis of earlier social research in non-Western as well as Western settings, as the characteristic most likely to mediate between a changing institutional structure and the care of young children. The urban Yoruba population, known to include a larger proportion of women with high levels of schooling than most peoples in sub-Saharan Africa, permitted a comparison of mothers along educational lines. Largely illiterate Yoruba mothers of infants drawn from the walled compounds of a 19th-century neighborhood in the city (the "traditional" group) were compared to Yoruba mothers with secondary schooling or more education who were married to Yoruba men, and lived in new suburban-style housing estates in Ibadan (the "elite" group). Samples of 200 children from each of these groups were weighed and measured repeatedly between birth and 4 years of age. Those from the traditional group fell below the elite sample in height and weight after 3 months of age and remained lower, whereas the elite children approximated the measurements of a reference sample in London, England.[46] This reflects wide differences between the two groups in child mortality and morbidity, health care, family wealth in general, and specific resources devoted to children through nutrition and health care.

Thirty mothers from each group were interviewed. The elite women, contrary to initial expectation, showed no sign of fertility decline; on the contrary, they were more likely to bear five or more children than their traditional counterparts. Thus the more educated mothers shared the high-fertility goals of the traditional mothers but, given improved health and shorter birth intervals, were better able to attain them. On the other hand, the traditional mothers reported more frequent use of Yoruba customary practices of infant care such as female circumcision, molding the skulls and hips and stretching the limbs of infants, and force-feeding by blocking the nostrils. The traditional mothers also adhered closely to practices that help preserve a long birth interval, weaning their children from the breast at an average age of 22.2 months and universally reporting that they practiced postpartum sexual abstinence; the elite mothers, only half of whom said they practiced abstinence, weaned their infants at a mean age of 7.4 months. In accordance with their breast-feeding practices, more than two-thirds of the traditional mothers reported that they were the primary (daytime) caretakers of their infants, whereas less than a fourth of the elite mothers, most of whom had bureaucratic positions as teachers, nurses, and librarians, did so.[47] Despite their busy professional lives outside the home, however, 50% of the elite mothers reported talking to their babies, whereas only 20% of the traditional women did so.[48]

The overall picture is one in which the Yoruba elite women – with secondary schooling, professional husbands, and affluent, Westernized, suburban life styles – had abandoned many traditional Yoruba infant care practices, including those that prolong the birth interval, favored Western medicine and nutrition, which gave their children an advantage in health and growth, and leaned toward a more verbal and less physical style of interaction. Like traditional Yoruba women (who were market traders), they tried to make the best of their economic opportunities, but in their case this meant bureaucratic employment that separated them from their infants during the daytime. Though the economic and reproductive goals of the elite women had not diverged from Yoruba tradition, their means of getting wealth and children had been enhanced, and their style of infant care was distinctively different.

In most of sub-Saharan Africa until recently, the residents of cities (unlike the indigenous Yoruba of Ibadan) have been recent migrants from the countryside; but like the traditional Yoruba mothers, the women with little schooling have not been substantially influenced by Western concepts or practices of infant care. For example, Goldberg[49] studied infant care and development among residents of Matero, a high-density suburb of Lusaka, Zambia, in 1968–1970. Sixteen different ethnic groups were represented among the 40 families studied, who had lived in the city for an average of 8.3 years; most of the fathers had completed primary school and were in manual or clerical occupations. Infants were carried on their mothers' backs in the daytime, breast-fed on demand, and slept with their mothers at night; most were still being breast-fed and sleeping with their mothers at 1 year of age. The majority of mothers, who had attended school for 1 to 3 years, did not attempt to stimulate their babies with toys or play, and expressions of positive or negative emotion to the infant were reported to be rare. Home observations at 4 months of age showed that mothers rarely vocalized to their infants; holding, touching, and looking were the most frequent maternal behaviors. These findings indicate little Western influence and suggest that indigenous patterns had been retained in the urban setting, though the lack of contextual description makes it difficult to say more. Without later urban studies of infant care, it is not known how much this situation has changed.

## DEVELOPMENTAL PATTERNS AND ISSUES

What difference does it make to a child's behavioral development to be raised in the infant environments of sub-Saharan Africa? This question has interested Western observers, professional and amateur, for many years. Most had been influenced by Margaret Mead's notion that in the radical differentness of non-Western practices one could discover the secrets by which child rearing forms personality. How such discoveries were to be made was not clear, however, and the topic invited undisciplined speculation as well as systematic observation. Results from the more systematic studies have been illuminating, largely in dispelling stereotypes about African infancy and in providing detail about some African caregiving environments, but we are still a long way from understanding the processes of infant development in Africa. In this section, we consider the findings in three areas: effects of breast-feeding and weaning, the cultural shape of social and emotional development, and infant attachment.

### Effects of breast-feeding and weaning

Two of the earliest observational studies of African infants, carried out in the 1950s by Albino and Thompson[50] among the Zulu of South Africa and by Ainsworth[51] among the Ganda of Uganda, attacked the validity of speculations based on Freudian theory concerning the psychological effects of prolonged breast-feeding and abrupt weaning in African populations. Ritchie,[52] among others, had characterized these practices as a period of overindulgence terminated with traumatic suddenness, which jeopardized normal ego development in the child. Albino and Thompson, working among the Zulu, whose practice of weaning on a single day set in advance fulfilled the criterion of suddenness,[53] observed 19 children before, during, and after weaning. They found that some but not all of the children were distressed on the day of weaning and shortly afterward, but that their manifest distress soon disappeared and was replaced by social activity and positive emotional states that indicated no traumatic impact. They conclude that the sudden weaning of the Zulu children promotes their social development in general and independence in particular, that it does not overwhelm them or constitute a trauma, and that it is not prognostic of psychological disorder.

Ainsworth, studying 28 Ganda infants over a period of months, noted that they became attached to those who interacted with them regardless of whether those persons fed them or not. Thus the social attachments of infants during the first year of life were

not a product of the oral gratification involved in a feeding relationship, as Freud's psychosexual theory would have it, but were
a function of social communication, as Bowlby claimed. Ainsworth also found that children who were weaned when they were
close to 2 years old showed distress if they had been fed on
demand in accordance with indigenous custom but not if they had
been breast-fed on the time schedule imposed by several mothers
influenced by Western advice, which she explains as resulting
from disruption of the (demand-fed) infant's expected communicative control over feeding. Those children weaned after 24
months were not distressed, even if demand-fed. Ainsworth concludes that breast-feeding will become part of the organization of
infant–mother attachment if babies are fed whenever they cry, in
which case weaning will precipitate observable distress if it occurs
during the second year of life but not if it occurs either earlier
(before attachment to the mother has reached its peak) or later
(when the child has achieved more social autonomy). Like Albino
and Thompson, Ainsworth finds her observations incompatible
with hypotheses based on the Freudian concept of an oral stage,
thus requiring a concept of infants as capable of social relations
based on communicative experience with or without feeding.

### The cultural shape of social and emotional development

Before it was understood in the child development field how
capable infants are of social relations, research into how children's behavior is shaped by their social environment tended to
begin when they were no younger than 3; this was true of the Six
Cultures Study of Socialization, although its field guide also included a section on the description of infant care beliefs and
practices.[54] (The descriptive material for the Gusii provides the
baseline for the present study.) Yet there were signs from Africa
as well as elsewhere that by the age of 3, children had already
gone through a process of socialization or enculturation.

When Robert LeVine arrived in a rural Gusii community in
1955, toddlers, some of them screaming, fled in fear from his path,
a reaction they gradually relinquished as he became a familiar
figure there.[55] But when he first visited a Yoruba neighborhood
in the city of Ibadan, Nigeria, in 1961, children of the same age
greeted him boldly in cheerful giggling groups, embraced his legs,

dogged his steps, and could not be discouraged from their extreme friendliness – though they were no more accustomed to white visitors than their Gusii counterparts were.[56] How is it that the reactions of children to a strange-looking visitor had become so strikingly divergent in these two populations by the time they were about 3 years old or even younger? The answer had to be in their prior social experience, perhaps taking place as early as infancy, when socialization or enculturation must already be going on.

The domestic settings in which Gusii and Yoruba infants were raised seemed to tell part of the story: Young children lived with their mothers in both societies, but a Gusii mother and her children occupied a separate hut with its own front yard, where other adults and children came only as occasional visitors, whereas the Yoruba mothers lived in a bustling compound sharing hearth, yard, and veranda with other mothers and children and having frequent encounters with visitors. In other words, the sheer density of Yoruba domestic social life was much greater than that of the Gusii, and the Yoruba child grew up associating with many more people of all ages. Furthermore, although infant care by siblings or other children was known in both communities, Yoruba babies were more frequently cared for by adult women – grandmothers, childless aunts, and older women living in the compound. Thus the social ecology of the two communities favored greater gregariousness among the Yoruba children and more wariness and fear of strange adults among the relatively isolated Gusii children.

An equally important part of the story, however, was the invisible environment of cultural norms: Yoruba adults adhered to a cultural ideal of sociability and gregariousness[57] in which extended greeting, cheerful interaction, lengthy and hilarious conversations, and expressions of concern for the welfare of others were mandatory as well as commonplace; no child could escape this kind of upbeat interpersonal performance and would begin to learn the script. The Gusii, however, were reticent about interpersonal encounters outside the domestic group, believing excessive sociability to be dangerous for a person of any age, and their conversational interaction was governed largely by a code of restraint (described in the next chapter). Even young children were warned against too much mingling with strangers. Thus the social development of Yoruba and Gusii children was propelled in diver-

Table 2.1. *Acts observed of children 3 to 11 years of age:
Gusii compared with the United States and pooled sample from
the Six Cultures Study*

| Act | Gusii sample ("Nyansongo") frequencies: % | U.S. sample ("Orchardtown") frequencies: % | Mean for the Six Cultures frequencies: % |
|---|---|---|---|
| 1. Acts sociably | 20.4 | 36.1 | 29.1 |
| 2. Insults | 11.9 | 8.6 | 12.0 |
| 3. Offers help | 11.6 | 5.6 | 8.6 |
| 4. Reprimands | 16.5 | 6.6 | 7.8 |
| 5. Offers support | 7.9 | 2.4 | 6.4 |
| 6. Seeks dominance | 2.2 | 8.1 | 6.4 |
| 7. Seeks help | 2.1 | 9.6 | 6.3 |
| 8. Seeks attention | 4.6 | 14.6 | 6.3 |
| 9. Suggests responsibly | 12.7 | 2.5 | 5.8 |
| 10. Assaults sociably | 3.6 | 3.8 | 5.5 |
| 11. Touches | 1.6 | 0.1 | 3.0 |
| 12. Assaults | 4.9 | 1.4 | 2.7 |
| Total | 100.00 | 99.4 | 99.9 |

*Source:* Whiting and Whiting, *Children of Six Cultures* (1975), Table 14,
p. 64.

gent directions by their socially and culturally organized environments, which made an observable impact during the children's
early years.

The results of this early socialization of the Gusii children are
shown in the comparative data analyzed by Beatrice and John
Whiting.[58] Systematic observations in the original Gusii study of
1955–1957 and the Six Cultures Study[59] of which it was part, were
made only on children 3 to 11 years of age, whose actions were
aggregated for analysis.

Table 2.1 shows the relative frequencies of twelve types of acts
in observations of Gusii and American children and for the Six
Cultures samples as a whole (including children from India, Mex-
ico, the Phillipines, and Okinawa). Half of the U.S. children's
acts fall into two of the twelve categories, *acts sociably* (row 1)
and *seeks attention* (row 8), and they are also high on *seeks help*
(row 7) and *seeks dominance* (row 6) relative to the means for the
sample as a whole. The Gusii children displayed these four acts
much less frequently and were much higher than the whole sam-

ple mean and particularly the U.S. children on *reprimands* (row 4), *suggests responsibly* (row 9), *offers help* (row 3), and *offers support* (row 5). In comparison with the U.S. sample, the Gusii profile reflects a more hierarchical situation in which older children, put in charge by their parents, dominate and take care of younger children, who generally accept their place without seeking dominance, help, or attention for themselves.

How do the young Gusii children come to be so much less demanding of attention and more compliant than children of the same age in the United States? Once again, the answer seemed to reside in the cultural models of social interaction of the communities being compared, and in the prior experience of young children with those cultural and social contexts, beginning in the infancy period.

The question of what the early experience of Africans consisted of was explored from the late 1960s onward in studies of infant care and development conducted largely, though not exclusively, in East Africa. Many of these studies were limited in focus, examining a particular behavior during early infancy, that is, the first 3 or 6 months after birth, but they showed how behavior patterns related to a culture-specific parental agenda might arise in the course of infant development. Rural East African parents, for example, encouraged early sitting, standing, and walking, and led their infants to precocity in motor development compared to Western norms,[60] but infant sleeping was unimportant as a specific goal, and Super and Harkness[61] found that at 4 months of age, the average Kipsigis infant slept only 12 hours a day, with the longest episode at 4.5 hours, compared with the average American infant in a comparison group, who slept 15 hours a day, with the longest episode at 8. Ganda parents, bearers of a culture in which gregariousness is highly valued, fostered early smiling and greeting in their infants.[62] Kipsigis parents, studied by Harkness and Super, train their children, during the critical period for language socialization (18–36 months), to comprehend parental commands and comments but not to respond verbally – thus fostering the obedience that is valued in the Kipsigis context but is not compatible with the interactive style of Western tests and interviews.[63] Super and Harkness have argued that Kipsigis parents create a "developmental niche" for the infant, comprised of physical, social, and cultural features that permit the normal growth and development of the baby within the constraints of adult settings and work demands and also encourage the acquisition of culturally valued capacities and behaviors during the first and second years.[64] These studies, taken as a whole, suggest that African parents are sensitive to the capacities of infants and young children at different ages as they implement a culturally based agenda for behavioral development during the first years of the child's life. Infant behaviors reflect the cultural priorities and conceptions of parents.

Trevarthen[65] takes a distinctly different position, claiming that mother and child share innately given meanings that are invariant across cultures, though his study of mother–infant interaction reveals cultural variations in observable behavior. Comparing Scottish mothers and babies from Edinburgh with a Yoruba sample from Lagos, Nigeria, videotaped in the laboratory, Trevarthen finds

> [A] clear difference in maternal playfulness and the amount of time that the infants look at their mothers after three months of age. This reflects a considerable difference in style of cooperative interaction in the two communities. In general the Lagos interactions were more coercive, mothers expecting to be ordered what to do and generally being very manipulative and instructive with their infants, overriding them when they were angry and fretting. This forceful and direct quality of communication was usually full of good humor and not unkind, but it contrasted with the response of the Edinburgh mothers who were more inclined to let their infants express themselves spontaneously.[66]

Trevarthen nevertheless concludes that communication and cooperative awareness among the Scottish and Yoruba children "developed along the same lines" and provide support to his theory that there is a "universal emotional code in mother–infant interaction."[67] Thus he tends to discount the importance of cultural variation in mother–infant behavior and to assume a universal infant psychology. The problem of identifying what is universal and what is culture-specific in mother–infant interaction remains unresolved and is addressed in Chapter 10 of this volume.

### Infant attachment

The first systematic field observations of infant–mother attachment were carried out by Mary Ainsworth in the rural area surrounding the city of Kampala, Uganda, in 1954–55.[68] This intensive study of Ganda mothers and their babies provided the basis for her model of the stages in the infant's development of attachment, which later had a profound influence on child development research. It was not a contextual study, however, and its purpose was not to relate the behavioral development of the infant to indigenous family life and cultural values among the Ganda but rather to discover what was potentially universal in the age-related social development of 28 African children. Thus although some culturally distinctive features are mentioned – for example, prolonged breast-feeding, brief separations when mothers work in the fields, the rarity of face-to-face interaction and other Western conventions of mother–child interaction – these receive little analytic attention, and there is limited information on how Ganda mothers themselves think about them. Ainsworth's study, in conjunction with Bowlby's theoretical model[69] that inspired it, created a new focus for research on the social development of the human child. It also showed that infants raised under conditions broadly similar to those found throughout East Africa grow up "normally" according to Western measures, develop socially in what we know now to be generally the same way as Western children develop, and become observably attached to their mothers and others who communicate with them. But it was left to subsequent research to relate maternal behavior and attachment patterns to distinctive features of African environments.

In 1969, two studies based on Ainsworth's Uganda research were carried out on different sides of the African continent by Sarah LeVine among the Hausa of northwestern Nigeria[70] and by the Leidermans among the Kikuyu of South Kiambu, outside of Nairobi in central Kenya;[71] their descriptive findings on patterns of caregiving have been summarized in the previous section. Both studies sought to discover whether the infant's attachments were affected by being cared for by more than one person, but they used different measures of attachment: For the Hausa data, Robert Marvin devised a measure based on frequency of both positive (e.g., approach) and negative (e.g., crying at separation) attachment behaviors in the noninterventive home observations of those (15) infants who were mobile. The Leidermans devised a measure that combined positive and negative responses to mother, caregiver, and a stranger along a single scale of emotional response elicited in a structured situation similar to the Strange Situation[72] (i.e., involving brief separations) but carried out at home and applied to nonmobile as well as mobile infants. It was found in both studies that all children showed behavioral signs of attachment to mother *and* to a caregiver in the second half of the first year; the Hausa infants were reported to show such signs at a relatively low frequency, but some were attached to more than one nonmaternal caregiver. Both analyses had difficulty in determining the relative strength of attachment among the caregivers, maternal and nonmaternal, but this seems to reflect methodological problems rather than the infant's inability to differentiate one caregiver from another. Although both studies were inconclusive in some respects, they confirmed in different African settings Ainsworth's findings that by the time they are a year old infants have become visibly attached to their mothers and to others who have interacted socially with them, regardless of feeding. In African environments, the others are most likely to be other female adults (as among the Hausa) or female children (as in some of the Kikuyu families).

## CONCLUSIONS

In this chapter we have examined the demographic, organizational, and cultural contours of infant care in the agricultural societies of sub-Saharan Africa, indicating how the environments of African families affect parents and the context of early child development. Striving to maximize the number of their surviving children in the face of high child mortality, African families organize infant care around a birth interval of 2 to 3 years, with intensive breast-feeding and maternal care focused on each child during that period. The mother–child household, embedded in a family that is already polygynous or prepared to become so, provides the setting for the married woman as child-bearer, food-producer, caregiver, and supervisor of her children as supplementary daytime caregivers for the infant. Within this general pattern, we have reviewed some of the variations in domestic arrangements affecting infant care – variations due to sociocultural differences and historical change in the sub-Saharan region. That these infant environments as a whole depart quite drastically from those of Western countries can hardly be doubted: Prolonged breast-feeding (up to 2 years) and day care by children are among the

African patterns noted by Western observers that have raised questions for developmental investigation. Research to date has not indicated that these features are detrimental to the growth and development of children, and has shown ways in which they propel the behavioral development of African children in culturally distinctive directions.

*Part II*

## Parenthood among the Gusii of Kenya

# 3

## Gusii culture:
## A person-centered perspective

The Gusii people, now numbering over a million, inhabit the southwestern corner of the Kenya highlands, elevated above the hot coast of Lake Victoria farther to the west (Figure 3.1). They have occupied this territory – with its cool climate, rich soil, and abundant rainfall – for perhaps two centuries, maintaining a distinctive Bantu language and ethnic identity amidst the Nilotic-speaking peoples who surround them. Geographically isolated in 20th-century Kenya, the Gusii nevertheless have become known throughout the country since World War II, first for their productive agriculture, and more recently for their exceptionally high fertility and population growth.

The Gusii were precipitously introduced to Western culture in the first decade of the 20th century when they came under British rule and the first Christian missionaries arrived. Their lives have never been the same, and the pace of social change has increased with each successive decade up to the present. Yet their contemporary survival strategies, family life, and patterns of child care can only be understood in terms of traditions inherited from their ancestors. Here we present an overview of Gusii culture and institutions in precolonial times and how they changed between 1907 and 1974, of the Gusii life course as experienced by adults and learned by children, and of the community in which we studied Gusii young children and their parents from 1974 to 1976.

The precolonial Gusii – seven contiguous but politically autonomous groups speaking one language (Ekegusii) and recognizing a common patrilineal ancestor named Mogusii – were a mobile people, migrating from the north in their eighteenth century to their present location, then migrating within their territory in response to external military threats from neighboring peoples, internal divisions among Gusii clans, and opportunities for expansion in

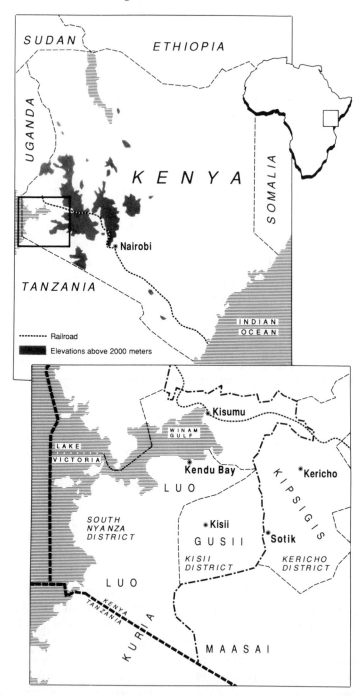

3.1 Map of Gusii within Kenya and Africa.

open land. Their culture was not static; on the contrary, they absorbed immigrants and customs from the surrounding Nilotic-speaking peoples (Luo and Kipsigis and, to a lesser extent, the Maasai). Nevertheless, despite some internal variations, there was not only a common language but also a common culture and social organization among the people who called themselves Abagusii.

The western Kenya-northern Tanzania region was one of politically uncentralized peoples who engaged each other in trade and alliance as well as cattle raids and retaliatory warfare. Like other peoples in the region, the Gusii lived in homesteads dispersed across the countryside rather than in clustered villages, produced food through cattle husbandry mixed with agriculture, were organized by patrilineal descent, practiced polygyny, and used cattle in bridewealth. Like the Luo (but in contrast with the Kipsigis and Maasai), the Gusii had localized patrilineages, within clan territories, as their primary form of social organization, without a cross-cutting age group organization. Like the Kipsigis and Maasai (but in contrast with the Luo), the Gusii practiced ceremonial circumcision for boys and girls, and considered it the prime requisite for adulthood. Many other customs and institutions were shared with one or all of the surrounding peoples, but precolonial Gusii culture can be seen as a unique amalgam of characteristics found widely in the region.

One way in which the Gusii differed from their neighbors was in their greater reliance on agriculture and correspondingly less dependence on cattle for subsistence. This stood the Gusii in good stead during the 1890s when herds were decimated by the great rinderpest epidemic as it swept westward through East Africa. The famine-stricken Kipsigis to the east traded their women for Gusii grain. They also raided Gusii border clans with such ferocity that the Gusii had to build walled settlements for protection; but the Gusii eventually forged a broad military alliance (which included Luo groups) and inflicted a decisive defeat on the Kipsigis, shortly after the turn of the century. Thus the Gusii entered the colonial period with a history of economic and military success over serious challenges to their survival.

In their fertile and abundant territory, the Gusii lived like frontiersmen – on the defensive, in dispersed and mobile homesteads, and with a portable culture. Their lives were organized around three priorities: food production, military defense, and childbearing. Food production was achieved through the shifting cultivation of indigenous millets (eleusine and sorghum) and the raising of cattle for milk, goats and sheep for meat. Local defense was necessary in the absence of a central authority to protect against cattle raids and other military actions, requiring all able-bodied men to be prepared for a spear-fight and the young warriors to act as a militia. Bearing children was necessary to maintain both food production and defense. Gusii institutions were not differentiated into political, economic, and religious spheres. Their social order, based on patrilineal kinship, included a division of labor by age and gender in which both sexes contributed in agriculture: Men were responsible for defense, governance, and animal husbandry, and women for food-processing and the rearing of children.

The Gusii saw themselves as morally superior to their Nilotic-speaking neighbors. They were particularly proud of their code of prescribed conduct for everyday social life, which emphasized sexual modesty and restraint in intergenerational and marital relationships. To them, the Luo, Kipsigis, and Maasai peoples seemed immodest and loose, defective in their concern for sexual morality. The Gusii code was enforced by a cycle of rituals involving sacrifice to the ancestors and symbolic rebirth in the ceremonial management of predictable life transitions and disruptive life events. Initiation, wedding, and funeral ceremonies brought kin and neighbors together and mobilized the energies of men and women in support of the social order and its goals.

## THE DOMESTIC MODEL OF SOCIAL ORDER AND PERSONAL SUCCESS

Precolonial Gusii culture, as a set of ideals and prototypes that continue to influence the experience and behavior of Gusii parents and children, can be characterized by its domestic model of social order and its concept of avoidance as essential to morality. The homestead (*omochie*), that is, the domestic group as a set of familial relationships spatially organized for daily life in uniformly designed and clustered houses, represented a pervasive blueprint for living, a built environment that embodied for Gusii adults not only the locus of their productive and reproductive activities but also the rules, roles, and symbols by which their lives were governed and their activities motivated. Children were born into and grew up in a physical environment rich in the norms and models that would guide them throughout the life course.

The domestic group consisted of its owner (*omonyenye*), who was the elder or patriarch (*omogaaka*) of the homestead, his several wives and unmarried children, his married sons and their wives and children. Each wife had her own house, yard, and cultivated fields assigned to her; there were also children's and bachelor's houses (*chisaiga,* sing. *esaiga*). The initiated men who were unmarried or recently married spent much of their time away from the homestead, along with young men from neighboring homesteads of the same *riiga* (localized patrilineage), in a cattle camp (*egesaraati*), where they jointly grazed their fathers' herds and defended them against raids by other Gusii clans. The patriarch himself, head of the homestead, would normally rotate his residence among the houses of his wives, but a particularly wealthy and powerful man might have another house called *etureti* in which to entertain his friends and followers from the neighborhood. This, in broadest outline, was the spatial context for Gusii domestic life.

Within this basic context, however, the interior spaces and external placement of Gusii houses (Figure 3.2) conformed to a design in which every detail was endowed with significance for social interaction and ritual.[1] Each role, each stage and transition in life was defined by assigned and forbidden spaces and by customary actions performed in those spaces using traditional objects. The domestic organization of life constituted a heavily prescribed (and proscribed) world for residents of the homestead and for their guests as well, who were treated according to equally detailed normative prescriptions.

Each homestead was autonomous in many respects; it occupied a hillside, fed and governed itself, answered to no higher authority than its owner for its internal affairs. Neighboring homesteads of the same patrilineage cooperated in herding, cultivation, mutual defense, ritual performance, and governance at the suprahomestead level, but operated without permanent organizations or leaders specializing in work, warfare, religion, or law. It was possible for a homestead head, in a dispute with his neighboring kinsmen, to move his people elsewhere, providing they were

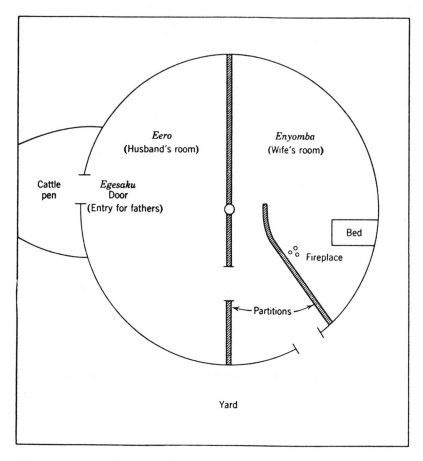

3.2 Traditional Gusii house.

numerous enough to defend themselves and their cattle without help or could persuade other kin to move with them. Abundant land of high quality made this type of expansion frequent and seems to have prevented the development of stable chieftainships or groupings based on criteria other than patrilineal kinship.

In this frontier situation, there were no real public spaces devoted to community activities: no plazas, markets, temples, graveyards, or shrines. All events of public and private significance took place at home, if not at everyone's, at least at someone's home. Disputes between domestic groups were settled at the homestead of an important man, with an informal assembly of elders participating. Divination took place at the house of a diviner, and circumcision at the home of the circumciser. Virtually all other rituals were domestic and were conducted in the settings of each family's everyday life. The dead were buried in specified locations just outside their own houses. Most remarkable is that the seclusion of newly circumcised boys, constituting their initiation into warriorhood, was located at the paternal homestead. In most East African groups, such as the neighboring Kipsigis, boys are secluded in large groups away from anyone's home, and the period of seclusion establishes lifelong bonds among men of differing descent and locality. Among the Gusii, however, two or three boys of adjacent homesteads and patrilineal relationships, usually the sons of brothers, were secluded together in the homestead of one of them. The domestic setting remained the scene of all significant action.

The code of conduct for the homestead served as the prototype for social norms outside the homestead. The domestic group itself was divided into generations, such that one acted in a restrained manner prescribed by the avoidance taboos (*chinsoni*), with one's own parents and children, but in a more relaxed and familiar manner with one's brothers and sisters and grandparents and grandchildren; this applied to others of their generation who were more distantly related. Outside the homestead, kinship terms established equivalence with these primary kin according to their generation and carried with them the appropriate norms of restraint or familiarity. The terms, and the norms associated with them, applied through one's clan, which could number in the thousands, and in other clans to which one was related by marriage. Gusii who had not met each other before would establish which norms applied to their interaction by recalling how someone of known genealogical relationship to one behaved toward a known kinsman of the other.[2] In precolonial times, then, the code of domestic conduct served as a universal guide to social interaction.

Gusii domestic organization, as a model of and guide for social order, provided a conception that gave purpose and meaning to individual lives. Each Gusii patrilineage was seen as the homestead of its founding ancestor extended to the present in genealogical continuity from each of his wives and their sons. This genealogical perspective provided not only a framework for contemporary social relationships but also an ideal image of domestic success, centered on the proliferation of wives, children, herds, and cultivated fields – in a mutually reinforcing cycle: The cattle reproduced themselves and provided bridewealth with which the founder acquired more wives, who cultivated more fields (producing more food), and bore more sons (who defended the herds) and more daughters (whose marriages brought in more cattle). Providing that additional land was available, and it was, each increment in the production of food and the reproduction of humans and animals was beneficial to the entire cycle. The founder's success stemmed from the resources he had to start the cycle and from the entrepreneurial and managerial skill to keep it going, particularly in containing conflict among his wives (and their grown sons) and using his sons as a small army to prevent homestead property from getting into the hands of outsiders. Each genealogy had to contain such a success story for men, for if the founder had not been successful, he would not have had a lineage named after him. The success of women, too, was there, for lineage segments were named after women who had a number of loyal and relatively prosperous sons, and whose stories were told and retold. Thus Gusii images of goals worth pursuing and of how to pursue them in precolonial times were based on the domestic experience of recent ancestors. Like concepts of proper conduct in social interaction, concepts of individual success and failure were framed in a domestic context.

The Gusii ancestor cult is part of the same cultural model. The sacrifices to placate long-dead ancestors are nothing more than a completion of the funeral rites performed by surviving members of the deceased's homestead, and the emotions and intentions attributed to an ancestral spirit portray him as a homestead member vis-à-vis his survivors there.[3] The ancestor cult, from a Gusii point of view, is literally the intergenerational and marital relations of the domestic group continued after the death of one of its members. The precolonial Gusii conceptualized themselves as genealogical links between the homesteads of their ancestors and those of their descendants, constrained by the past and seeking to provide for the future, but in the same context of domestic ideals.

Gusii ethnosociology, their indigenous discourse about social groups, relationships, and processes, drew heavily on domestic idioms. *Enyomba,* the Gusii word for house (and for the wife's room in the house), also means the group constituted by a mother and her sons in a polygynous homestead, and a segment or faction within any larger group. The word *riiga,* hearthstone, also referred to the largest lineage unit that normally cooperated in cattle-herding and mutual defense; because a Gusii hearth has three stones, segmentation is understood here, too. *Egesaku,* literally the small doorway from the men's room of the house to the cattle-pen – symbolizing the elders of one's father's generation who (because of avoidance rules) may enter one's house only through that door – was used to refer to a lineage at any level, an ethnic group such as the Gusii, and (later) a nation-state such as Kenya. Each *egesaku* was conceptualized as comprising several *chinyomba* (plural of *enyomba*) or segments like the domestic group; hence the potential for divisiveness and eventual segmentation was explicit in Gusii social thought.[4]

The Gusii model of social order, however, was largely implicit. Some of its most basic assumptions were simply taken for granted, for example, the absolute necessity of a command hierarchy in which those of high status made decisions and gave commands, and those below unquestioningly followed. In the domestic context, the homestead head was the top of such a hierarchy and small children were at the bottom. Although there were checks on his power, which gave a significant measure of autonomy to the *chinyomba,* the elder gave orders to his wives and adult sons and expected obedience. They in turn did the same to those below them – the wives to their children, the adult sons to their wives and children. Delegation was the rule: Those of higher status delegated to those below such tasks as the latter were capable of so that the superior could turn his or her attention to other tasks and to supervising and managing the subordinates. It was a cardinal sin to challenge the command of someone higher in the age-gender hierarchy of the homestead, and disobedience and insubordination were severely punished, particularly in children. The parent–child avoidance system and rituals such as the father's curse (of his adult son) supported the hierarchy and discouraged insubordination among the adults.

This hierarchical model of social order was, in Gusii thought, essential to the functioning of the domestic group in food production and the defense of the property. Food production was successful because the women and children of the homestead were diligent in cultivation under the supervision of the head, who cleared the fields, initiated the sowing of the eleusine (the staple cereal grain), and left them to do the rest. Animal husbandry was successful because the young warriors faithfully carried out the homestead head's orders in their herding and in their implementation of the bridewealth exchanges he negotiated. The homestead and its property were safe because they operated as an army under his command. Indeed, the success stories of lineage founders embodied in genealogical accounts left no doubt that obedience of sons to their fathers and of wives to their husbands was the sine qua non of a man's achievement.

A successful patriarch exercised influence and authority outside the homestead as well as in it, as a powerful man (*omonguru*) to be feared and as a member of an ad hoc council of elders called to resolve disputes. The homesteads of such men were major landmarks in Gusii geography, and even in recent times, people locate their homes and other places to strangers from within the local area by saying, "I live near Musa's" or "The other side of Ariga's" or "between here and Bichagi's." However important was the lineage and clanship in Gusii social organization, powerful men also defined the subjective landscape in which people lived.

## AVOIDANCE AS THE MODEL OF MORALITY

The Gusii defined themselves as persons and as a people in terms of the moral aspects of their social order. Their morality, based on the concept of *ensoni* or sexual embarrassment and restraint between parents and children, was conventionalist in outlook. A code of avoidance between parents and children, real or classificatory, designed to prevent such embarrassment and maintain conventionally modest appearances in interpersonal conduct, entailed a broad range of rules called *chinsoni* (plural of *ensoni*), which were specified by situation. There was no set of principles that could transcend *chinsoni;* powerful men broke some of the rules when it suited them, but without attempting to justify it in moral terms.

*Chinsoni* amounted to a detailed code of extreme modesty and restraint between parents and children: no touching, seeing each other undressed, or being jointly present when sexual topics were discussed. Even shaking hands (the usual greeting among persons of the same generation) was proscribed, not only with real parents but with parents-in-law and all classificatory parents within the clan. Similar codes of kin avoidance are found among many other Bantu-speaking (and other African) peoples, as well as among the indigenous inhabitants of Oceania and the Americas. For the Gusii, the most salient of these rules was the one prohibiting a father from entering the house of his married son, under any conditions. The central meaning of this custom is avoidance of contact between a man and his son's wife. Barring the homestead head, the "owner" and ruling patriarch of the domestic group, from entering any of the houses in his domain would be dramatic enough in itself, but in the context of the explicit Gusii identification of the house, *enyomba,* with the married woman who cooks on its hearth and sleeps next to its cooking fire, its import as a ban on sexual access to his son's wife is unmistakable.

The Gusii kin-avoidance code was extended through the use of kinship terminology to all adjacent-generation kin and – in its opposite or complementary forms ("familiarity" as opposed to "restraint")[5] – to same-generation and alternate-generation kin as well; thus it provided a comprehensive guide to social interaction in most situations precolonial Gusii faced. In addition to the primary rules concerning avoidance of particular forms of contact and speech, the code included a wide variety of secondary rules regarding avoidance of situations in which the tabooed contacts had a high probability of occurrence. These latter rules included the use of euphemistic vocabulary for sexual and reproductive matters when *abansoni* (persons who should avoid each other) were likely to overhear a conversation. The rules of kin avoidance, primary and secondary, were not isolated conventions of social interaction but were integrated with the norms of marriage in Gusii society: For example, father–son avoidance included a prohibition on adult sons taking as leviratic wives the younger widows of their deceased polygynous father, a common practice in many other African societies. The code of kin avoidance thus embodied a model of moral governance, first in the domestic group and then outside it, through the maintenance of social distance between individuals.

The Gusii were proud of their morality, which they saw as superior to that of other Kenya peoples. This pride was symbolized by the *ebitinge,* the iron ankle-rings worn by married women who had undergone the *enyangi* wedding ceremony, an elaborate ritual that publicly and religiously certified the monogamy of a Gusii wife, her lifelong bond to the husband who gave bridewealth for her. Precolonial Gusii, seeing the *ebitinge* as their visible mark of distinction from surrounding people, referred to themselves as *abanyamatinge,* "people of the *ebitinge.*" The implication was that their marriages were permanent, their wives faithful, their communities free of the sexual promiscuity they attributed to other groups.

The Gusii ideal of moral order, then, was one in which an individual could take pride in the restraint and modesty imposed by conformity to a code of prohibitions. Avoidance as a distancing device mandated by that code could also be used for domestic moral purposes other than the control of sexuality. The maintenance of the cattle camps, for example, kept the potentially troublesome young warriors at a distance from their homesteads that protected the elders from their rebelliousness. By the same token, the houses of co-wives in a homestead were separated from each other by a cultivated field – a distance believed to minimize the possibility of disputes between them.[6] When the patriarch had died and brothers quarreled over the inheritance of cattle or land, they moved quickly to divide the homestead as a spatial and social unit and thereby reduce interaction (sometimes by emigration to another area), so that overt conflict could be avoided. Avoidance was used as a general strategy for managing interpersonal conflict in Gusii families and communities, not merely in following the rules of kin-avoidance, thus pragmatically maintaining what was sensed to be the distance necessary to prevent conflict in the domestic group. In the Gusii model of moral order, aggressive and sexual misbehavior was minimized and harmony fostered by the maintenance of optimal distances between potentially offending kin. Given this cultural model, it is hardly surprising that the most vivid Gusii image of evil, namely, the witch (*omorogi*), is that of a neighbor or wife who gets too close to one.[7]

## HISTORICAL CHANGE: 1907–1974

In ways the precolonial Gusii could not imagine, their world began to change in 1902 when the so-called Kenya-Uganda railway was opened, with its western terminus at Kisumu, 75 miles north of Gusiiland. The pace of change was slow at first due to the isolation of Gusiiland from the railroad and from Lake Victoria, the nearest port being located at Kendu Bay, some 28 miles away. The lack of roads and intractable mud during the frequent heavy rains made travel by wheeled vehicles difficult and unreliable. The Gusii first brought themselves to the attention of the British administration by raiding cattle from the Luo in 1905; some British colonial officers entered Gusiiland and took livestock as retribution. In April 1907, a British administrative post was established in what is now Kisii Town, and early in 1908 the District Commissioner, G. A. S. Northcote, was speared and wounded by a Gusii warrior named Otenyo. This brought punishment from the Kenya Police and King's African Rifles, who massacred at least a hundred Gusii and ended armed resistance to British rule. During the next 2 years, the Seventh-Day Adventist and Roman Catholic missions were established in Gusiiland, the former at the Luo border, the latter near Kisii Town. The pacification of the Gusii, however, was not completed until 1913, when the British abolished the cattle camps, dispersing the young warriors to their homesteads so they would not engage in feuding and cattle-raiding. Thus between 1905 and the outbreak of World War I, the Gusii people's first contacts with foreigners suddenly subjected them to foreign rule and introduced new institutions and new policies that would bring about fundamental social change.

British rule ended military activity within Gusiiland and the surrounding region. This brought security to the local communities, the benefits of a centralized state that provided chiefs and courts for the settlement of disputes and the punishment of crimes. The Gusii appreciated this benefit and took full advantage of it. But the new development also deprived young men of their social function as warriors, around which male identities had been built and male initiation ceremonies organized. With no other function available to replace the warrior role, young men tended to become demoralized and disruptive, and an increasing source of violent crime (particularly the abduction of unmarried women in other clans) during the decades that followed. The age at which male circumcision was performed dropped from about 16 in the first decade of the century to 10 by 1946, reflecting the fact that it no longer initiated boys into a warrior status in which they would be called upon to fight but into an ambiguous adulthood in which the symbols of warfare were invoked only as metaphors of masculinity bereft of social utility. Gusii youth became warriors without weapons or a legitimate cause in which to use them. Men were now available to marry at an earlier age, and they demanded to do so; in response, the marriage age of women – and their age at circumcision – apparently dropped precipitously as well in the following decades. Thus Pax Britannica had numerous social consequences, of which the increased fertility resulting from earlier marriage may have been one of long-lasting importance.

The disbanding of the cattle camps also posed new problems of social control in the homestead. Gusii elders cherished the distance between themselves and the young warriors that the *ebisaraati* had maintained. Once the youth were at home, their aggressive energies were no longer automatically directed toward an external enemy, but might affect father–son relations and undermine the authority structure of the homestead. Thus young men were excluded from the beer-drinking gatherings of their elders, on the grounds that when drunk they might attack their own fathers (a spiritual as well as social offense, requiring sacrifice to the ancestors). In other words, an avoidance rule for homestead interaction was erected to replace the residential distance and military distractions of the cattle camps, but it put additional pressure on the patriarch to maintain his own authority in the face of potential threats.

The completion of the road to Kericho by 1928 and of some crucial secondary roads within Kisii District set the stage for several important new developments during the 1930s: The first Gusii youths became labor migrants, working on the nearest European farms, in the Sotik and Kericho areas. Markets and trading centers were established in the rural areas outside of Kisii Town, introducing European consumer goods and providing a market for surplus agricultural produce. Schools were established and some Gusii – a tiny fraction of the population – began attending. The Kisii Hospital was established in 1934, serving as the base for a District Medical Officer responsible for preventing and curtailing epidemics of communicable diseases such as typhoid, cholera, and measles as well as attempting to reduce the spread of malaria. Thus before World War II, the economic, educational, and medical groundwork for modern institutional development had been laid, although most Gusii would not experience its effects until much later.

During and after World War II, the pace of change quickened. Some Gusii men worked for the British Army and traveled as far as Egypt. Increasing numbers worked on the tea estates of Kericho for a few years between circumcision and marriage and brought home cash. European goods – clothes made of imported machine-made cloth, kerosene lanterns, soap, sugar, and tea – became widely available, first in the shops of Indian traders, and increasingly used. The first Gusii youths completed secondary school and by the late 1940s had embarked on careers as school-teachers and policemen. Though few in number, they served as beacons for future cohorts of pupils. Some progressive farmers, Seventh-Day Adventists, began growing tomatoes and cabbages to sell to institutions like the Kisii Prison and the Kericho European Girls' School, then to individuals at the market in Kisii Town. Surplus grain was sold to the local stations of the government's marketing board, as well as on the black market, and coffee was introduced by the government as a cash crop to be grown by Gusii smallholders and marketed through cooperatives. Despite new land settlement near the Maasai boundary in the 1930s, population pressure was being felt and litigation over land – first to establish the boundaries of clan and lineage holdings, then at the homestead level – became intense. Thus the decade of the 1940s saw both the intensification of agriculture and the beginnings of dependence on an external economy for cash and consumer goods, as the Gusii moved beyond subsistence cultivation toward export production and employment. These trends continued and accelerated in the following decades, spurred by mounting land pressure, the introduction of new cash crops (pyrethrum, tea), and the growth in numbers of persons educationally qualified for employment.

The socioeconomic development of Gusiiland after World War II was somewhat different from that of other parts of highland Kenya, partly because of its isolation from the railroad that determined the main pathway of commercial and institutional development.[8] The Gusii were productive and increasingly market-oriented farmers who were beginning to invest in the schooling of their children. But the possibilities of higher incomes from farming at home kept most of them out of the labor market, which was (for the most part) far away in central Kenya, and staying at home kept them less sophisticated about the outside world, more conservative about family and religion, and more politically compliant, than other peoples of Western Kenya.

Gusii colonial chiefs, themselves large-scale polygynists (one chief had 20 wives in the 1940s), used their power to buttress patriarchal authority throughout their domains, for example, by arresting disobedient sons on grounds of poll-tax evasion and confining them in a lock-up at the chief's camp to teach them lessons in filial piety. Bridewealth transactions were similarly reinforced by chiefly authority, despite the tendency of girls (in the 1950s) to elope with men they loved rather than marry those who could pay a large bridewealth to their fathers. The disobedient sons and eloping daughters were, however, signs of the future, and it was possible to forecast from the observations of 1955–1957 how patriarchal authority would be undermined by the increasing economic autonomy of sons.[9]

It was *Uhuru,* the national independence of Kenya in December 1963, that initiated long-distance labor migration among the Gusii. In the first years after *Uhuru,* two Gusii were appointed members of the presidential cabinet and two were civil servants of the highest rank. These four men, and very soon others of less elevated position, sponsored young Gusii from their home areas for both private- and public-sector jobs in Nairobi, Nakuru, and other towns previously unfamiliar to the Gusii. Although few Gusii showed up as living outside their home district in the national census of 1969, a trend had been started that accelerated during the 1970s, when significant numbers of Gusii were to be found working everywhere in Kenya, from Mombasa on the coast to Kitale near the Uganda border, at positions of every level from unskilled worker to professional. During the 1960s, too, many of the more affluent Gusii bought land formerly belonging to European settlers at Sotik and in the Rift Valley. The insularity of Kisii District itself was slowly modified by more contact with the wider national society and by an increasingly educated population that read newspapers, listened to the radio, traveled, and mixed with Kenyans from other places. In 1962, only 34% of the children between ages 5 and 9 had attended school; by the 1979 census, about 95% of boys and girls between 10 and 14 had attended.

Equally significant was the upsurge in secondary school enroll-
ment in Kisii District after 1963, as increasing numbers of Gusii
also went elsewhere to attend secondary school. By 1979, 42% of
males aged 20 to 24 and 20% of females in that age group had
attended secondary school. Those who completed it, some of
whom went on to university and other postsecondary training,
had been visibly changed in their attitudes and lifestyles. Whether
or not they returned to live in the rural areas from which they
came – many were incorporated, as teachers and principals, into
the expanding school system of the district – they became influential vehicles of culture change.

The colonial period in Gusii history lasted 56 years. Eighty-
year-old Gusii of 1975 were 12 years old when the British arrived
and 68 when they left. In between, they had witnessed the introduction of chiefs, courts, Christian missions, roads, literacy,
schools, hospitals, money, markets, cash crops, and consumer
goods, as well as accelerating change in basic socioeconomic conditions and cultural ideals. Pax Britannica made life more secure
but deprived young men of their valued role as warriors. Improved health conditions permitted Gusii parents to maximize the
number of their surviving children, but the resulting population
growth put an end to their possibilities for continued expansion
on the land. Economic opportunities through commercial agriculture, schooling, and employment brought cash and consumer
goods (including better clothing and a more varied diet), but also
increased economic competitiveness and inequality beyond the
threshold that Gusii communities could manage without divisive
conflict. The decline in patriarchal authority made young men
and women freer of the domination of their fathers, but the resultant decay of social norms created marital instability and encouraged the spread of heavy drinking to young mothers and even
children. By 1974, a decade after the end of colonial rule, each
historical trend had resulted in outcomes that were clearly beneficial and others that were obviously damaging or disastrous.

From an external viewpoint, Gusii patterns of population
growth, social conflict, and normative decline observable in the
1970s seemed to promise future problems of potentially disastrous
proportions. But from their own perspective, many Gusii believed their situation at that time to be an enormous improvement
over times past, particularly in economic and reproductive terms,

and were unconcerned about the future. Furthermore, the Gusii frontier spirit – their opportunistic search for new solutions to their resource problems – was still alive, and motivated a variety of adaptive behaviors in the wider field of possibilities offered by Kenya as a whole. And although this meant largely finding new sources of livelihood and enrichment for particular families, the Gusii had by no means abandoned their traditional conceptions of normative order but constantly recognized them as ideals against which to measure and criticize actual behavior.

### "MORONGO": GUSII COMMUNITIES IN A LOCAL CONTEXT

Our field research among the Gusii was conducted in an area centered around an administrative and market center to which we have given the pseudonym "Morongo." This was the headquarters of a powerful chief during the colonial period, when a marketplace and school were also established there. Surrounding the center are the dispersed homesteads of Gusii families, organized as local communities based on clan affiliations but with no formal leaders. Community boundaries are invisible to the untutored eye but are of great significance to the inhabitants as markers of the outer bounds of potential cooperation based on neighborly obligation among the local members of a patrilineal clan. One such community or *risaga* is "Nyansongo" (also a pseudonym), studied in the 1950s as part of the Six Cultures Study of Socialization.[10] Its population at that time was 208; in 1974 it was about 450, despite a certain amount of emigration. For the study of 1974–1976, however, we worked in a set of six communities around Morongo (including Nyansongo), with a total population of about 2,100.

The Morongo area had been virtually uninhabited until 1929, when the building of the road that runs through it (which connects Kisii Town with the road network eastward to Nairobi) and the appointment of a new colonial chief who was determined to exploit its land ended the area's status as a vacant Gusii buffer zone against the Maasai. The chief established his own homestead nearby and permitted settlement by three clans, one of which (his own) was considered politically dominant in the administrative unit he ruled. All three clans have remained in the Morongo area to this day and regard their territories there as permanently identified with their respective groups. The local clan segments have intermarried with each other following the patrilocal rule in accordance with which women move at the time of marriage to their husbands' natal homes and become socially absorbed therein, thus preserving clan boundaries – which remain as salient for their members as they ever were.

Morongo market was, from its beginning in the 1930s, a center of outside influence. Its shops were started by Maragoli people who had gained commercial experience in their homeland 100 miles to the north, where American missionaries had been active. The Maragoli, who speak a Bantu language closely related to Gusii, brought their religion along with their enterprise and commerical skill, starting a Friends primary school and a Church of God congregation. In the vanguard of change during the 1930s, the Maragoli intermarried with local Gusii and eventually melted into the surrounding population. As religious innovators they were overshadowed by the Seventh-Day Adventists – Gusii acting under the guidance of an American mission – who founded a religious commune just south of Morongo market, in one of the subordinate clans. Although the group had lost its collective character as far as property and governance were concerned before 1935, the impact of the commune's Calvinistic ideology remained powerful even in the 1970s. The Seventh-Day Adventists who had been members of the commune were the first "progressive" families to grow vegetables for sale to new institutions in the district and outside it, and they were among the first to accept export agriculture and high-yield dairy cattle of European stock when they were made available to Africans. As members of a clan discriminated against by the chief in the distribution of economic opportunities, they saved and invested their money in shops and crops, sent their children to school before it became fashionable, and turned themselves into something of a privileged elite – a phenomenon that was conspicuous by 1974.

The Seventh-Day Adventists, however, were always a minority in the Morongo area (as among the Gusii generally), and the former collectivists and their descendants constituted a minority within a minority. Most of the other Gusii there became Roman Catholics, a step that conferred a Christian identity without any such break from Gusii tradition as demanded by the Adventists, with their prohibitions on beer, polygyny, dance, sacrifice, and other Gusii rituals. Catholic affiliation during the colonial period also gave Gusii families access to a Catholic school near Morongo market and the Roman Catholic school system of East Africa, enabling boys of demonstrated educational promise to attend Catholic secondary schools outside the district and even in Uganda. The first Gusii university graduate (in 1954) was a Catholic from a subordinate clan in the Morongo area, and his neighborhood, which seemed poor relative to some of the Seventh-Day Adventist neighborhoods in 1974–1976, still produced more university students than the others. The secondary school at Morongo is Catholic and so is Cardinal Otunga High School, also located in Kisii District and widely regarded during the 1970s as one of the best secondary schools in the country. Thus the Catholic orientation toward higher education for the few who can successfully compete seemed to be associated with greater economic inequality in rural neighborhoods, whereas the Seventh-Day Adventist strategy of self-improvement through rural economic development seemed to promote a higher average standard of living, particularly in the neighborhood of the ex-collectivists. But even such guarded generalizations must be treated with caution, for variation was the rule throughout the Morongo area.

The major social divisions in the Morongo area during the 1970s were based on clanship, neighborhood, religion, and socioeconomic status. These divisions were neither completely congruent nor entirely independent. The closest correspondence was between neighborhood and clan membership, for each group residing on a particular hillside (or set of adjacent hills), was a local segment of one of the three clans of the Morongo area, which we shall call clans A, B (the subordinate clans), and C (the chiefly clan). Six of these neighborhood groups or local communities were involved in our study. The main religious division was between the majority Roman Catholics and the Seventh-Day Adventists (SDAs), though there were a handful of members of other Protestant churches (Church of God, Pentecostal, Swedish Lutheran) and a more substantial number of Gusii traditionalists who were unaffiliated with any Christian church. Most SDAs (including ex-collectivists and their descendants) were members of Clan A, the most numerous subordinate clan, but many other members of Clan A were Catholics and some were unaffiliated Gusii traditionalists. Clan B, the other subordinate clan, from which the first university graduate had come, was entirely comprised of Catholic and unaffiliated families. Clan C, the chiefly clan, was largely Catholic but contained some SDAs of the old colonial chief's subclan, since he had been an Adventist, and some unaffiliated traditionalists. Religious affiliations did not entirely determine marriage, and there were numerous Catholic–SDA marriages. Although everyone knew where the SDAs lived and which clan most of them belonged to, there was no sense that religious affiliation necessarily went with clan membership.

Socioeconomic status based on the modern criteria of education, occupation, and income was the least clearly bounded division, with conspicuously rich and poor families living next to one another. As mentioned above, the SDAs tended to be the most prosperous farmers with the largest plots of land, whereas the Catholics produced more university graduates, but this approximation does not do justice to the complexity within both groups. Among the SDAs there had been numerous "backsliders," who in their Calvinistic prosperity had resumed the polygyny and beer-drinking of their forefathers, thus increasing the number of descendants to share their wealth and sometimes dissipating it themselves. Among the Catholics there were industrious farmers, craftsmen, and shopkeepers who managed to achieve affluence without Calvinism or abstinence from alcohol, some of whose sons obtained higher education and important positions in Nairobi. Many of the poorest families were also Catholic. Socioeconomic status in modern terms thus varied from one family to another within each of the religious groups and local clan segments, creating distance and division between neighboring families without pulling together those of like circumstance into solidary groups. Although clan, neighborhood, and religion can be seen as both cohesive *and* divisive, socioeconomic differences were a source of conflict throughout the Morongo area.

Viewed in terms of ideals rather than actual material conditions, the socioeconomic situation of the Morongo area is somewhat more coherent. The Seventh-Day Adventists held ideals of social decorum and self-discipline that set them off from other Gusii and suggested a lifestyle distinctly bourgeois and American, if not sufficiently pious by Adventist standards. They were active entrepreneurs and farm managers, grew floral borders around their houses, were concerned about thrift and nutrition, modified funerals to replace outpourings of grief with eulogies, and maintained an active women's organization. Even many of the backsliders aspired to these ideals: The church could expel them but they bore the imprint of its teachings in their ambitions, personal standards, and the impression of themselves they tried to create. Their Catholic neighbors respected the distinctive qualities of the SDAs, referring to them as "Abakristo" (Christians), a term they could have claimed for themselves but ceded in the face of Adventist zeal.

As for the Catholics, their aspirations for the educational advancement of their children led in a different direction: toward urban employment and involvement in the national society (of which the Catholic Church is an important part) rather than development in the rural home. Those who remained behind might not live according to the modern standards of their educated children but they would be happy in the thought that their children did so, much like first-generation American immigrants who remained in poor ethnic neighborhoods but vicariously enjoyed the social mobility of their offspring. Thus the backsliding of the SDAs and the growing economic inequality of the Catholics, though indisputable realities of life in Morongo during the 1970s, must be seen not simply as symptoms of social disorganization but as concomitants of striving toward ideals that provided meaningful goals for contemporary Gusii.

On an average weekday, the visible signs of community life in the Morongo area are few and far between. The marketplace itself, though a center of activity and sociability, is far from where most people live, and only a small proportion of the population can be found there each day. There are no other public plazas, and sizable gatherings for any purpose other than funerals or weekly church services are rare. Cooperative work groups (*omogesangio, risaga*), though still recognized as potential obligations, are infrequently activated nowadays. Some people live particularly isolated lives, for example, the woman who gave birth alone in her own house (Chapter 5), children we observed who seemed to have had no contact with any other children but their own siblings before going to school. Yet it would be a serious mistake to conclude from such evidence that there is no community life in the neighborhoods of Morongo.

The area's community life is located in the pervasive processes of interpersonal communication among its residents. Only through understanding these processes were we able to discover the ways in which the Gusii of Morongo are not as isolated as they seemed but tightly integrated into a functioning social order. First, most resident adults know most of their neighbors and many others in the area by sight, name, residential location, and kin relationship. The men were born and raised in their current homes (as were their fathers). Their wives, though necessarily coming from other clans, were either raised near Morongo themselves or had visited there as children, and they usually had sisters, aunts, and other female kin who had married into the same clan segment or an adjoining one. Thus, despite the absence of residential clustering and the rarity of large gatherings, the neighborhoods of Morongo are not anonymous settlements of people to their inhabitants but the opposite: communities of familiar, known people related by blood, marriage, and long neighborly association. Strangers to the area stand out against this background of familiar people.

Second, adults in the area know a great deal about one another, particularly within their own neighborhood, but even beyond it: their past histories, current routines, debts, disputes, relationships, misdemeanors, strivings. Social conventions preclude asking a person to make personal disclosures, but gossip makes detailed information about each life known to all, and everyone knows that what he or she does will become public knowledge. When anyone deviates from established routines or relationships, it will be known. Third, people observe each other closely, looking across the hills and down the footpaths to see who is going where at what time and with what apparent purpose. Although they do not appear to be looking and might deny it if asked, they quickly notice anything new or striking, particularly departures from expectations that might indicate something remarkable going on. With so much background knowledge of their neighbors' habits and routines, they can usually detect something of interest immediately and store the information for future checking or discussion with others. And again, people are aware that they are being watched as well as watching others. Fourth, interesting information about neighbors that has been noticed is soon disclosed in private conversations to others, and through the gossip network it is disseminated across the area as effectively as if it had been broadcast on the radio. This sharing of information and the sense it generates of mutual, if clandestine, involvement in each other's lives must be counted as a fundamental aspect of community in the Morongo area.

Finally, there are gatherings and public occasions. Although the settlement of disputes by local elders was not as frequent in the 1970s as in the 1950s, it did occur and the drinking of millet-beer and *changaa* (illegally distilled corn spirits) brought together groups of elders, women, and others at bars near the market and in ordinary homesteads virtually every day. The chief, who was not as prominent as in the colonial period, held weekly meetings of local leaders and elders in the *baraza* (assembly) hall next to our clinic. Roman Catholic and SDA religious services on Sunday and Saturday, respectively, were the largest weekly gatherings. Gusii ceremonies were not as frequent, but in the course of a year they brought together neighbors and kin to celebrate birth, death, circumcision, and marriage and to heal afflictions frequently enough to renew bonds among those who lived apart from one another most of the time. In other words, the expressions and reaffirmations of community in public association were far from absent.

All of this does not deny the low level of trust and cooperation we found among kin and neighbors in Morongo, nor their preoccupation with each other's jealousy and potential ill will. The neighborhoods of Morongo would not rank high among agrarian peoples in terms of social solidarity, but their relative stability of residence and mutual involvement with each other (albeit at a distance and with few overt signs) were very great indeed.

## GUSII LIVES AT MORONGO: THE DILEMMAS OF CHANGE

The Gusii parents with whom we worked experienced their lives in the changing environment of Morongo during the mid-1970s in ways that reflect both their continued adherence to precolonial models of social and moral order and their reactions to the options and stresses of contemporary life. To portray this experience concisely, we have gone beyond the terms in which Gusii adults themselves talk about it, to distinguish their reproductive, economic, and spiritual careers, indicating the domains in which they

Table 3.1. *Gusii life stages*

| Female | Male |
|---|---|
| 1. Infant (*ekengwerere*) | 1. Infant (*ekengwerere*) |
| 2. Uncircumcised girl (*egasagaane*) | 2. Uncircumcised boy (*omoisia*) |
| 3. Circumcised girl (*omoiseke, enyaroka*) | 3. Circumcised boy warrior (*omomura*) |
| 4. Married woman (*omosubaati*) | 4. Male elder (*omogaaka*) |
| 5. Female elder (*omongina*) | |

seek goals and measure their progress according to culturally defined standards.[11]

There is a "life plan" for each sex, that is, a prescribed set of stages of maturity for adulthood (Table 3.1) and a trajectory of purposive behavior. Men and women want children, worldly goods, and spiritual safety and immortality. There is a timetable for their attainment of these goals and social recognition for being on time or ahead of time as well as social stigma for being behind. A person expects to reach certain levels at certain times of life and experiences anxiety if he or she does not.

The reproductive career is clearest in the Gusii context, for there are gradations of adult status that require specific levels of reproductive performance. To reach the age grade of elder, for example, a man or woman must have married children, and steps toward that goal (such as the circumcision of one's first son) are publicly celebrated. Falling behind one's local age peers in such steps is inevitably a source of concern. The reproductive career includes not only one's own role in procreation, but also that of one's children, particularly the sons.

The economic career, though not clearly defined in terms of steps or stages, is no less important to an adult, involving as it does access to vital resources. For Gusii men, their inherited shares in the land and livestock owned by their fathers is the critical goal; for women, in accordance with the house-property complex,[12] it is their sons's shares. (All sons are theoretically entitled to inherit equal shares, but as members of the "house" established by their mother they have the strongest claim to land cultivated by her and cattle resulting from the marriages of her daughters, their full sisters; there is much strategic positioning before the father's death and litigation after it, particularly between different "houses," i.e., the sons of different co-wives.) Nowadays, money, shops, and jobs are also involved, especially for men, and the concern is with debts, occupational success and failure, and invidious comparison with those in the local reference group who have less or more. The Gusii have always distinguished between rich and poor men, but commercial and educational development have sharpened these distinctions and made them more salient points of self-evaluation. The poor lack the money for school fees that would guarantee their children's futures, or at least prevent them from falling farther behind; the rich are able to lend money to their poor kin and to dominate them to some extent – as well as gain modern advantages for themselves and their children.

The spiritual career is partly – and most importantly – a reflection of the other two, because men and women frequently seek spiritual remedies from diviners, healers, and in domestic rituals for serious reproductive and economic failures. But there is more to the spiritual career, in that one's own career includes the sacrifices neglected by one's father and grandfather that return to haunt one (literally) as omens and afflictions. Furthermore, such afflictions (including reproductive and economic failures) do not affect oneself alone but threaten the survival of the entire family, and will become worse if the correct spiritual remedy is not found. There are many healers in the Morongo area, all of whom once had seriously threatened reproductive careers and health problems that were cured before they undertook training to heal others.

These careers – reproductive, economic, and spiritual – though not formulated as such in Gusii thought, constitute the contexts in which Gusii adults evaluate themselves and their neighbors as they move through the gender-specific phases of the life course. These contexts depend a great deal on one's birth cohort, for social change has been so rapid that members of precolonial cohorts and their progeny in cohorts that increasingly took schooling, consumer goods, modern medicine, and national politics for granted, lived side by side in the Morongo of 1974–1976. Rather than document this in full detail, which would take us too far from the topic of this volume, we present some vignettes from our fieldwork in Morongo of the terms in which Gusii experienced their lives, particularly their family lives, and the dilemmas and paradoxes of their existence at that time.

## THE OLDER GENERATION

Agostino, a grizzled, ailing man of 68 in a tattered mackintosh topcoat, lived near our pediatric clinic and could be found most mornings talking to his cronies at the millet-beer shop between the clinic and his homestead. His impoverished appearance, his inability to afford simple medication for his heart condition, and the stories of violent clashes among his adult sons living at his homestead might have led one to classify him as a pauper, someone at the lowest level of Gusii society. But 20 years earlier, he had been an important man in the Morongo area, the government agricultural officer who had introduced coffee cultivation to the local farmers, giving them their first experience with an export crop grown solely for cash. He had lived in a modern bungalow erected on the boundary between his home and the chief's camp, and he was a familiar and respected figure at the marketplace in his neat khaki uniform. Agostino was the official representative of agricultural innovation as it came to the Gusii during the colonial period. Born when British administration was just established, Agostino grew up in a Kisii that had been pacified but hardly exposed to the outside world. He managed to acquire sufficient literacy and the right connections to become one of the first agricultural officers, at a time when few Gusii had government jobs. Like other prosperous Gusii, Agostino married three wives who bore him many children and produced crops on his land. The daughters moved to their husbands' homes, leaving their father with cattle from their bridewealth. The sons brought their wives home and begat grandchildren for Agostino. Though the sons went to school and some were employed, by 1975 they and their wives and children had exceeded the carrying capacity of the homestead land and they quarreled and conspired over dwindling resources. Economic success had turned to failure in 20 years.

Did Agostino experience his career as a failure? No doubt the poverty and divisiveness of his family caused him suffering, but there is reason to believe that he was deeply satisfied with his life in some respects. Agostino said he liked to sit at the top of his land and count his children and grandchildren. Rather than wringing his hands at the poverty inflicted by fertility, he could comfort himself with the large number of his descendants. (This numerical emphasis was also brought home to us at the funeral of a woman about Agostino's age, where a tabulation of her descendants, with a total at the bottom, was handed around for all to admire.) Agostino was anticipating his own funeral, soon to come, where all his offspring and their spouses and children would attend and pay him their respects, with his sons' sons digging his grave and burying his corpse in accordance with Gusii custom. This is the way a Gusii man wants to go, guaranteed a place as the founder of an expanding lineage, its reproductive continuity a certain sign that, no matter what the material and psychological circumstances of its members, their spiritual well-being is assured.

Agostino's situation and his attitudes were in no way exceptional. In fact, the children and grandchildren of once-prosperous older men with three or more wives – some had as many as eight – accounted for a large proportion of Gusii children in the 1970s as in earlier years. As they grew older and less able to cope with the bitter quarrels of their wives and sons, the patriarchs (including Agostino) withdrew from family life to tend a few milch cows on whom (as they saw it) they could depend for sustenance, and live an existence uncomplicated by human vengefulness. Their wives lived autonomous lives, each in her own house or on her own plot of land, close to her unmarried children, her daughters-in-law, and her sons' children, working the land, running a small business like the brewing of millet-beer, pursuing a spiritual career as a Gusii diviner or healer in a Christian church, and worrying about whether the husband would take a new wife to divide her sons' patrimony further.

As strong and resourceful as these women were, they regarded their place in life and their basic well-being as contingent on that of their sons. So long as they had sons who were married and begetting offspring, their primary goal was achieved. Women who bore only daughters or whose sons had proved incapable of reproduction went to enormous lengths for remediation, as detailed in Chapter 4. The next goal, however, was to provide the son and his family with resources for survival, which pitted the woman against her co-wives and made her suspicious that the husband would unduly favor their sons. Each woman, like her husband, became the founder of a lineage segment, *enyomba* – literally, a "house" – which was both a source of fundamental satisfaction to its living ancestress and a source of division within the homestead – particularly with a diminishing land base.

The more children a woman had, the more secure she felt in her embattled world, the more junior hands to help out at home, the more diversified her social connections in the later decades of her life. Children were a mixed blessing in the 1970s, but it was the blessing most salient for Gusii women as well as men of the older generation – the authors, as it were, of the Gusii population crisis.

## MORALITY IN POPULAR SONG

A short distance from Agostino's homestead lived Samson, a toddler when Robert LeVine knew him in the 1950s, but by 1974 he was the 21-year-old leader of a local band that made popular recordings with original Gusii songs. Samson, who had completed primary school, wrote the songs himself, and their popularity was due to the pungent social criticism he injected into them. Their lyrics, translated into English, reflect the conflicts Gusii faced in their lives during the mid-1970s. For example, "Lazy Flora":

> Before I married Flora I was longing for the day we'd wed;
> Flora, now that you're in my house you want tight dresses
> [i.e., impractical modern clothes] and you don't want to
> dig [i.e., cultivate fields];
> My problem is that I married a lazy girl who only wants tight
> dresses but not to dig;
> Surely Flora, I married you so we could work in the fields
> and from *that* you would get tight dresses.

Flora's deviance from traditional virtue has its male counterpart in that of Micah in "Respect Parents":

> Micah, you're so famous in fighting with your homestead;
> When you drink beer, Micah, you beat your parents;
> All the money you get, Micah, you use on beer;
> You don't have a house, Micah, you live in the granary;
> At dawn, Micah, you set off for beer;

When you're drunk, Micah, you return to start fighting with
   your parents;
Micah, please stop drinking so much beer, build a house and
   don't fight with your parents;
Some boys I see around respect their parents, but you,
   Micah, you're spoiled and you beat your parents.

Both of these songs defend traditional domestic morality against
the threats of tempting consumer goods by arguing that yielding to
temptation is impractical as well as immoral. In other songs, Samson proposes modern solutions:

### "Abandon Beer, Educate Your Children"

Many people I see around inflict problems on themselves;
The money they get they spend on beer;
Their children don't go to school, leaving the straight path,
   they become beer drinkers;
Their agemates have completed school, are employed, their
   homes are peaceful;
Those who didn't attend school steal and quarrel . . .

Schooling is seen not only as a contemporary alternative to
drinking but also as a means of restoring harmony and morality in
the family and community. Yet progress is not without its risks, as
indicated in "Witchcraft is Poverty":

Around eleven in the morning at Morongo market I heard
   people say a witch had been caught near my home;
A crowd gathered to see the witch and we were surprised to
   find it was a respected elder woman of the homestead;
When the witches see a child progressing, they try to stop
   him;
When they see a merchant doing well, they feel jealous and
   try to interfere;
This world isn't ours, though we live in it, for God alone
   takes care of all humans.

Jealousy, personified in the image of a witch, is presented as the
enemy of academic and economic progress. Thus the modern
conditions that offer new responsibilities for personal advancement to the Gusii are fraught with potentials for antagonism as
well as profligacy. Young Samson, rooted in conventional piety,
identified the problems afflicting Gusii families in 1974–1976 and
supported the solutions in which they believed. Armed with a

guitar rather than the spear his grandfather carried at the same age, Samson defended the Gusii moral order by publicly criticizing immorality, giving hope that the Gusii of the late 20th century would prove as adaptable in dealing with their problems as their ancestors had been in coping with theirs.

## GUSII SOCIETY AS A
## LEARNING ENVIRONMENT

How do Gusii children become adults who pursue their economic, reproductive, and spiritual careers according to the standards of competence and virtue of a Gusii community? This is one of the questions that motivates our study of Gusii children in the earliest phases of their lives, and in that context it is a topic of this entire book. But in this chapter about the institutional environment of Gusii individuals, the problem of education must be addressed in a more general way: What was the provision for educating the young in Gusii society, what goals and processes of learning were entailed, and how has this changed in the course of the 20th century? We have already mentioned the numerical rise of primary school attendance from 1962, when it was rare (1 in 3 children), to 1979, when it was virtually universal, but that is only one part of the educational story. The other parts can be summarized as follows:

### *Learning without teaching*

In precolonial Gusii society, like most of indigenous Africa, there were no schools, that is, no institutions dedicated to instruction. Only the annual male and female initiation ceremonies, specifically the period of several weeks during which newly circumcised boys and girls were secluded (separately), provided an occasion dedicated to training: Older teenagers instructed the novice in the code of gender-appropriate adult conduct, with an emphasis on sexual information that could not be publicly discussed. This event, happening once in a person's life (during puberty in precolonial times and somewhat earlier – 7 to 8 for girls, 10 to 11 for boys – from the 1940s onward), constituted a dramatic personal transition, but it was regarded as the *completion* of his or her education, on the assumption that the person had already been educated at home. So the question is: What did this earlier education consist of?

### The domestic setting

The setting of Gusii children's learning was the domestic group, that is, the household and the homestead of which it was part, which served as the omnibus location for virtually all the activities in Gusii life: food production and processing, child care, social interaction, ritual, dispute settlement, and so forth. Children had observational access to these activities and participated in many of them, often as part of a sibling group. Participants were age-heterogeneous, and activities were hierarchically organized, with older participants delegating certain tasks to younger ones and often giving them commands.

### Goals

In the context of a child's growing up at home, parents had age-differentiated expectations related to the attainment of culturally defined goals at each stage in the child's life (Table 3.2). As the child became older, he or she was expected to approximate culturally valued forms of virtue and competence. Skills and moral virtues were not sharply distinguished from each other, as skilled performance was considered to indicate moral maturity, and it was inconceivable that one could be morally virtuous without the willingness to acquire and perform skills of value to the home.

### Attainment

Children often did attain the expected skills, sometimes at remarkably young ages: Two 6-year-old girls were observed in 1956 to have cultivated a small field of maize by themselves, from sowing to harvesting; most girls by age 8 could perform most of the household tasks done by married women. Boys were slower, particularly in attaining what most concerned Gusii parents, namely, mature restraint and modesty that were taken as signs of readiness for the initiation rites, a reason given for postponing their initiation to a later age.

Table 3.2. *Gusii child rearing: Implicit goals and norms*

| Age/Stage | Culturally defined goal | Cultural script |
| --- | --- | --- |
| First 15 to 17 months (before weaning) | Healthy infant: Normal physical growth and motor development | Feed, hold, monitor growth and distress, respond to negative signals, promote motor development |
| | Quiescent infant: Easily calmed, inactive motorically | Soothing: Rapid response to crying with lulling and feeding; comfort through body contact day and night |
| Second and third years (after weaning, 18 to 36 months) | Compliant and safe child: Comprehends maternal commands, obeys, makes few demands | Keep expectation for maternal attention low; put toddler with other children; instruct in following commands |
| Infancy and early childhood as a whole | Maximize number of surviving offspring and optimize labor contribution of child to family (Utilitarian perspective) | Maintain regular birth succession, giving each child concentrated physical care during period of greatest risk, while minimizing demands on maternal attention |
| | Child to learn Gusii scripts for respect and obedience: *ogosika, okoigweera* (Semiotic perspective) | Avoid mother–infant emotional equality of verbal interaction; sociability with other children |
| School-aged child | Respectful, obedient, responsible, competent in tasks, contributing to home production | Apprenticeship in domestic work; corrective feedback |
| Initiation | Preparation for marriage and adult relationships; self-control | Gender-specific ritual graduation to mature status |

## Processes of learning

Gusii children learned largely through what Lave and Wenger[13] call "legitimate peripheral participation," that is, by being co-participants in domestic activities to which they were at first expected to contribute little or nothing and then gradually being absorbed into fuller participation in the activities they had observed many times. Gusii boys 3 to 4 years old in the 1950s tagged along as their older brothers herded cattle, holding switches with which they would imitate their brothers' motions in beating the cows' rumps; soon they would be expected to herd the sheep and goats in this way, and by 8 or 9 to herd the cattle themselves. If a boy were the eldest in a family and there were no older boys around, the father would intervene to provide instruction, particularly if he himself were a labor migrant who was rarely at home. Normally, however, participatory learning involved little parental intervention. Parents expected learning to take place in the context of the group of siblings and cousins. This applied not only to the acquisition of economic skills but also to language learning, acquiring respect, becoming an appropriate girl or boy.

## Learning sequences

Gusii children learned by observing, imitating, and receiving corrective feedback, some of it harsh. Neither parents nor older siblings provided praise, approval, or other rewards for correct performance of desired tasks. To Gusii parents, their giving praise would undermine the domestic hierarchy on which subsistence activity and social regulation depend, introducing the risk that children would become conceited and disregard commands. They knew that children could learn through participation, without positive reinforcement, and they were counting on this in the case of their own children.

Thus Gusii education took place through children's participation in the productive work and other activities of a hierarchically organized domestic group. Parents, including mothers, acted primarily as managers, protectors, and disciplinarians, rarely as teachers, and never as playmates. So long as the traditional Gusii family we have described persisted as a productive organization with a clear authority structure, parents could assume that the education of their children would be assured in that environment, without their own constant involvement. This conception of parenthood in relation to childhood education should be borne in mind as we consider, in the next chapter, the outcome of parental reproductive careers, namely, the high fertility of Gusii families.

# 4

## Gusii fertility, marriage, and family

For Gusii infants and their parents, high fertility is a pervasive condition of family life and child development. Like parents elsewhere in Africa, the Gusii fervently desire the maximum number of surviving offspring, but they have been exceptionally successful in achieving this goal: Their fertility ranks near the top among human populations. The population of Kisii District, that is, Gusiiland, grew from under 300,000 in 1948 to well over a million in 1979, with the highest population growth rate in Kenya (which has the highest national growth rate in the world) and it also became, as of the 1979 census, the most densely populated district in the country. Thus fertility, though highly valued by the Gusii, had resulted in a serious ecological problem by the last quarter of the 20th century.

This situation was evident in Morongo, where the 1956 population density of 450 per square mile had risen to about 1,000 by 1976. Robert LeVine, who lived at Morongo in the 1950s, was unable to recognize the Nyansongo locality in 1974 because of the number of houses filling up the cow pastures, which had been its most visible internal boundaries. Homesteads, and houses within homesteads, were closer together than they had been – too close for comfort, by Gusii standards.

Ombese, a 60-year-old father in our sample, exemplifies the consequences of population growth for family life. His father, one of the original settlers of Morongo, had owned a large hillside of 75 acres, and Ombese, as one of three sons, had inherited about 20 acres. But he married six wives, who had given him (by 1975) more than 50 children, of which 25 were sons – each entitled to inherit a share of the land. Some of his older sons pursued modern occupational careers – one was a local school principal, others worked in Nairobi – and Ombese himself was a businessman actively involved in wholesale and retail trade. But they all still looked to the land for a sustenance and security it could not adequately provide its 61 residents, as of 1975, or its potential inheritors.

Not content to sink into poverty, most of Ombese's wives and sons supplemented the cultivation that had formerly been the mainstay of their lives with other remunerative activities. For example, his fifth wife, the mother of our sample child, sold *chang'aa* (distilled corn spirits) from her house, the yard of which served as an informal (and illegal) bar. Thus, in 40 years, Ombese had populated his abundant land with too many people to maintain an agricultural livelihood. As they turned to other pursuits, their frustrations about land led to conflict between the several "houses" of the homestead and the dissolution of family trust. Ombese tended to isolate himself from the family he had spawned, devoting himself to business and often neglecting all but his sixth and youngest wife. Reproductive success on a limited land base had in his case – and those of countless other Gusii – turned prosperity into tension in one generation.

In this chapter we examine the Gusii fertility predicament in detail, attempting to explain *how* their fertility reached and remained at such a high level, *why* parents want to bear so many children, and what consequences their successful fertility has for infant development. Later sections describe the state of marriage in Morongo and the socioeconomic conditions of our sample families.

## THE GUSII DEMOGRAPHIC SITUATION

The Gusii demographic profile is parallel to that of Kenya as a whole. Kenya's national birthrate was the highest in the world at the time of our study, but its death rate and infant mortality rate were intermediate on a world scale (see Table 4.1). Gusii women had a completed (i.e., lifetime) fertility of more than 8.7 children and a child mortality close to the national average (see Table 4.2). For both Kenya and Gusiiland, the excess of births over deaths each year yielded natural increase rates of roughly 4%, which means a doubling of the population in 17 years.

Table 4.2 shows how Gusii fertility and mortality compared with those of their neighbors (Luo, Kuria, Kipsigis) and Kenya peoples

Table 4.1. *Birth and death rates for Kenya and selected other countries, 1983*

|         | Crude birth rate | Crude death rate | Infant mortality rate |
|---------|------------------|------------------|-----------------------|
| Kenya   | 54               | 13               | 91                    |
| Nigeria | 50               | 16               | 109                   |
| India   | 33               | 12               | 89                    |
| U.S.A.  | 16               | 9                | 11                    |

*Note:* Crude birth and death rates are the annual number of births and deaths per 1,000 population; infant mortality rates are the number of deaths during the first year per 1,000 live births.
*Source:* The World Bank, *World Development Report 1987* (New York: Oxford University Press, 1987).

in other regions (Kikuyu in the central highlands, Giryama at the Indian Ocean coast) in 1969 and 1979. Although infant and child mortality varied widely across these groups, their completed fertility was largely restricted to a range between seven and nine children per woman, with the Giryama as the only exception. Gusii fertility was the highest, but it was quite close to that of other peoples of the interior. Reported mortality of children under 2 years of age among mothers 20 to 24 years old in 1979, however, varied from 4.8% in Nyeri to 21.8% in South Nyanza, with the Gusii intermediate at 9.8%.

Some important historical trends are visible in Table 4.2. Changes in fertility from 1969 to 1979 were generally small and not consistent in direction across districts, though for Kenya as a whole the general drift has been upward.[1] Although Gusii fertility appears on Table 4.2 to have declined slightly, the following table (4.3) shows that Gusii women *under* 45 years of age reported more births in 1979 than those of the same age 10 years earlier. (The bottom row on Table 4.3 shows separate means for *rural* Gusii women, including 9.04 children ever born for the 45 to 49 age group.) In other words, Gusii fertility, like that of the Kenya population as a whole, increased between 1969 and 1979.

The decline in infant and child mortality during the same period was dramatic.[2] Table 4.2 shows a sharp drop in every district except Kericho and Kilifi. The proportion of child deaths under

Table 4.2. *Estimates of fertility and child mortality for selected districts, Kenya Census, 1969 and 1979*

| | Completed fertility: Mean no. of children ever born to women 45–49 years old | | Child mortality: Percentage of children dead by age 2, reported by mothers 20–24 years old | |
|---|---|---|---|---|
| | 1969 | 1979[a] | 1969 | 1979 |
| Kenya (National) | 6.69 | 7.17 | 14.7 | 12.5 |
| Kisii (Gusii) | 8.82 | 8.74 | 12.7 | 9.8 |
| South Nyanza (Luo, Kuria) | 7.81 | 7.71 | 24.3 | 21.6 |
| Kericho (Kipsigis) | 6.83 | 7.93 | 8.1 | 9.0 |
| Nyeri (Kikuyu) | 6.83 | 7.02 | 5.3 | 4.6 |
| Kiambu (Kikuyu) | 7.62 | 7.44 | 9.2 | 6.7 |
| Kilifi (Giryama) | 4.82 | 5.86 | 21.6 | 21.1 |

[a]For most districts, the rural means (excluding small urban populations) are slightly higher than these district totals.
*Source: 1979 Population Census of Kenya,* Vol. II, Analytical Report, p. 70.


2 years of age reported by Gusii women aged 20 to 24 dropped from 12.7% to 9.8% in that decade. Demographic evidence for the entire country strongly suggests that this was part of a long-term decline beginning in the 1950s as the result of public health measures as well as increased income and education, and continuing to the present. The infant mortality rate in Kenya (i.e., the number of children who died in the first year of life for every thousand live births) decreased from 120 in 1969 to 87 in 1978; it is estimated to have been as high as 160 in 1950 and was undoubtedly much higher earlier in the century. This massive shift in the basic conditions of child development, then, took place in a single generation. Though many of her siblings might have died in infancy or early childhood, an average Gusii mother of 1975 could reasonably expect that most of her own children would survive to maturity.

Table 4.3. *Mean number of children ever born to Gusii women aged 15 to 49, Kenya Census, 1969 and 1979*

|        | Age categories | | | | | | |
|--------|-------|-------|-------|-------|-------|-------|-------|
|        | 15–19 | 20–24 | 25–29 | 30–34 | 35–39 | 40–44 | 45–49 |
| 1969   | .29   | 1.94  | 4.19  | 6.17  | 7.48  | 8.48  | 8.82  |
| 1979   | .38   | 2.08  | 4.34  | 6.49  | 7.82  | 8.58  | 8.74  |
| 1979[a]| .39   | 2.16  | 4.49  | 6.72  | 8.09  | 8.87  | 9.04  |

[a](Rural only)

Table 4.3 shows the upward trend in births reported by Gusii women under 45 years of age between 1969 and 1979. The differences are small but consistent, suggesting that Gusii women in 1979 were giving birth somewhat earlier and more frequently than their age counterparts of 1969. Given the high fertility of 1969, this was a remarkable feat, but it is expectable from other demographic evidence showing reductions in the birth interval and age at marriage under the impact of modernization.[3]

The demographic context of Gusii family life in the 1970s can now be clarified. Like the national population of which it was part, the Gusii population was characterized by extremely high and increasing fertility combined with moderate, but rapidly decreasing, child mortality. The decline in child mortality created an unprecedented situation in which women were not only bearing 10 or more children (half of the 33 Morongo women past menopause we interviewed in 1976 had done so), but seeing close to that number become adults. The pace of change, particularly in mortality, was so great that our sample mothers who were over 40 in 1975 had begun their reproductive lives when infant death was probably 50% more frequent than for mothers under 25 in 1975.

The recency of these changes suggests the likelihood that the Gusii system of reproduction and infant care as we observed it from 1974 to 1976 represents a response to earlier demographic realities in which the demand for children always exceeded the supply and survival was the central goal of infant care. Although some modifications in infant care practices occurred during the decades of mortality decline and are described in this book, the basic assumptions and structure of the system are best interpreted as cultural adaptations evolved over centuries in a situation of high infant and child mortality.

## FROM MARRIAGE TO MENOPAUSE: THE SOCIAL DETERMINANTS OF FERTILITY

The Gusii maintain their high level of fertility through the presence of some conditions highly favorable to childbearing and the absence of conditions that reduce fertility in other populations. In reviewing these direct or proximate determinants of fertility[4] for the Gusii, we are exposing a social organization dedicated to maximizing the number of offspring, as it operates in a permissive environment.

### *Proportion of women in reproductively active unions*

Virtually all Gusii women marry, and the few who do not bear children out of wedlock. Seriously disabled women, for example, those with limbs damaged by polio, though considered less attractive mates, can and do become the secondary wives of older polygynists, so long as they are able to ambulate in some fashion. The small number of blind women and others with more severe ambulatory disabilities may not marry but usually bear numerous children in any case. In the 1950s a girl normally married at 15 years of age. (If she were not married by 17, people would wonder why: Had the families of prospective husbands discovered that her mother was a witch?) This was probably a reduction of several years from the precolonial age at marriage. The decrease seems to have begun between 1913, when the warriors were sent home from the cattle camps, and the 1930s, when fathers were demanding large amounts of bridewealth for their daughters. The elimination of the warrior role and consequent reduction in the age of male circumcision permitted men to marry earlier and created a greater demand for marriageable girls. Fathers raised the bridewealth to a point that abduction threatened to become prevalent, particularly in 1937, and we assume that the increasing difficulty of protecting girls from abduction combined with the anticipated benefit of a higher bridewealth motivated fathers to marry off their daughters at an earlier age. This decline in the age at marriage, placing subsequent cohorts of girls in reproductive unions earlier than before, probably set the stage for the surge in population growth that followed. By the 1970s, however, schoolgoing, the declining frequency of polygyny, and the decay in the bridewealth system had raised the average age at marriage again.

Gusii norms facilitate the childbearing of married women who might otherwise stop reproducing before menopause, namely, widows and women whose husbands have reproductive difficulties. The widow in a normal bridewealth marriage remains the wife of her deceased husband in terms of social status but undergoes a ritual transition less than a year after the husband's death[5] in which she chooses one of his collateral kinsmen (brother or patrilateral cousin) as a levir (in Gusii, *omochinyomba*) to impregnate her regularly so she can go on bearing children "for" the deceased husband. The wife whose husband has reproductive difficulties can appeal to his brothers, who will sanction her taking a collateral kinsman in the neighborhood as a clandestine mate for the purpose of continuing her childbearing career at home rather than seeking her reproductive fortune elsewhere. (It is assumed that a wife whose husband does not "give" her children will be tempted to run away with another man who is reproductively competent, and this had happened among families with whom we worked.) Taken as a whole, these customs legitimize the maintenance of marital fertility even under circumstances that might otherwise prevent it, and the affected – the widowed or those with reproductively incompetent husbands – take advantage of them in order to realize their personal reproductive potential. In short, most Gusii women marry, and once married, bear children legitimately until menopause even if their husbands die or cannot serve as fertile mates.

### Lack of pathological infertility

There are very few childless Gusii women of childbearing age (we found only 2 in the Morongo population of 2,100), and secondary infertility is also extremely rare. Because many African populations are afflicted by diseases, primarily gonorrhea, that terminate fecundity and reduce fertility rates,[6] this must be counted as a condition unfavorable to fertility that is virtually absent among the Gusii, as among other peoples of highland Kenya. Table 4.2 suggests, in agreement with Frank's findings,[7] that it is only on the coast (represented by Kilifi District) that such a reduction exists in Kenya. The protection of the Gusii from venereal disease is probably attributable to three factors: (1) Their isolation, that is, the very small proportion of Gusii who had traveled to areas where gonorrhea was more prevalent (before the 1970s, when labor migration became more widespread among Gusii) and the small number of non-Gusii traveling to Kisii District; (2) their restrictions on the nonmarital sexual behavior of women, making casual liaisons difficult and effectively confining most women's sexual contacts to a relatively narrow circle of neighboring Gusii; and (3) their lack of a norm requiring the prolonged postpartum abstinence found in other parts of Africa, which Frank[8] identifies as a factor promoting the spread of gonorrhea because it motivates men to find sexual alternatives to their wives during the long period of abstinence following each birth. In the Gusii case, husband and wife are free to resume coitus as soon after birth as they agree to do so. In the 1950s, prostitution was almost unknown in Gusiiland, and the only Gusii prostitute one heard of was a figure much gossiped about who consorted with foreigners. By 1974, however, prostitution existed in bars at the rural markets, and Gusii isolation and restrictions on women had also declined markedly. The presumed rise in sexual mobility resulting from these changes during the 1970s did not, however, lead to lower fertility as measured by the national census of 1979 (see Table 4.3).

### Lack of deliberate fertility control

Despite widespread knowledge of contraception among younger Gusii and reports by some married women that they had used birth control pills for a limited period, deliberate fertility control aimed at bearing a specific number of children (i.e., parity-dependent fertility control) was virtually nonexistent in the 1970s. The proportion of Gusii women reported to be using effective contraceptive methods in the Kenya National Fertility Survey (KNFS) of 1977 was 1.4%, which was the lowest among ethnic groups in Kenya.[9] (Surveys of 1985 and 1989 showed contraceptive use in Kisii District had grown to about 15%.)[10] The reasons for this, apart from the lack of intense effort by the Government of Kenya's family planning program, have to do with the reproductive attitudes of men and women, described in the next section.

### Frequency of coitus

It has already been mentioned that the Gusii lack a formal period of abstinence after birth, thus precluding the very long birth
intervals found in African societies that practice postpartum abstinence. What needs to be added, however, is that Gusii women
deliberately pursue reproductive goals in their marital sexual
behavior, rather than considering reproduction as merely a by-
product of routine sexual encounters. A woman who has been
legitimately married with bridewealth is *entitled* to become pregnant on a regular basis that maintains a birth interval of no more
than 3 years, even if her husband does not have sexual intercourse with her frequently. If, as occasionally happened in the
1950s, a husband lost interest in one of his wives and did not
visit her regularly, she would go to the chief to complain of his
neglect on the grounds that she had not given birth for too long,
and the chief would order the husband to attend to her demands
for more offspring. In the 1970s, a man who became a labor
migrant in a distant place, leaving his wife and children on his
land, might fail to visit his wife in time for her to conceive on
schedule; she would then raise the money to visit him where he
worked, staying until she believed herself to be pregnant and
then returning to Gusii. A more responsible husband would manage, even if he had lost interest in a wife or migrated to work far
away, to impregnate her on schedule even without having sexual
intercourse with her frequently. The intent to conceive children
and the enforceable obligation to maintain reproductive continuity assumed primacy over sexual interest and motivation, so that
marital coitus between spouses separated by physical or emotional distance was designed to produce offspring even when
intercourse was infrequent. This strong tendency in the absence
of postpartum abstinence probably accounts for the fact that the
Gusii showed the lowest mean duration of menstruating interval
(between resumption of menses and conception), namely, 4
months, of all ethnic groups in the KNFS.[11]

This pattern has roots in precolonial Gusii culture. A wife could
use nonverbal signals to let her husband know it was time for him
to impregnate her again. If he was a young married warrior living
in the cattle camp, she would send the recently weaned youngest
child, accompanied by an older child, to bring a calabash of milk

to the father; this was understood to mean she was ready to conceive the next child. If the husband was an older man living at his homestead with several wives (having been replaced at the cattle camp by his circumcised son), then his wife would send a child to the co-wife to get her husband's stool (*ekerogo*); every man had a particular stool, identified with him personally, which would be put on his grave when he died. He would sit on this stool at the house of the wife with whom he was currently living (and having sexual relations), when eating, or warming himself at her hearth. Returning to the co-wife that evening, he would find his *ekerogo* missing and locate it at the house of the wife who wanted to resume her reproductive schedule. He had to respect this unspoken but emphatic demand because it was understood to be an obligation of marriage. This custom legitimized the wife's initiative, albeit nonverbally, in resuming sexual relations after a child was weaned, and women who went to see the chief during the colonial period were invoking this generally recognized right. By the same token, she was responsible for protecting the birth interval by keeping the husband away before she considered the child ready to be weaned, and this was probably the reason for the marital conflict over sexuality that was reported during the colonial period.[12] A wife would be blamed if her children were born too close together; thus it was her responsibility to regulate the birth interval.

### Lactational amenorrhea

The KNFS reports, for 357 currently married Gusii women aged 15 to 44 in 1977, breast-feeding for 17 months on average, with 12 months of lactational amenorrhea and a live birth interval of 28 months, which was below the average for the Kenya population as a whole.[13] Our own samples (from Nyansongo in 1955–1957 and from the larger Morongo area in 1974–1976), having been recruited as mothers of young children, are skewed toward younger women,[14] who tend to have shorter and more regular birth intervals. Furthermore, Morongo is probably more affected by outside influences and likely to have a shorter average interval than many other rural areas in Kisii District. Thus the average birth interval we found in 1976 was 23 months, 5 months less than the KNFS and down from about 27 months recorded in Nyansongo 20 years earlier, but the mean duration of breast-feeding was 17 months in 1976 (identical to the KNFS), down from 20.7 in the earlier Nyansongo study. Ignoring the discrepancy in average birth interval between the KNFS and our 1976 studies as due to a greater proportion of older women in the former (and greater sophistication in Morongo), we can conclude that the duration of breast-feeding and the length of the birth interval among younger Gusii mothers have declined by 3 to 4 months over the 20-year period of 1956–1976.

That Gusii women were generally successful in maintaining a healthy interval through lactational amenorrhea is indisputable, but the briefer length of the interval among monogamists in 1955–1957[15] and its decline in average length between 1956 and 1976 in Morongo suggests that changing conditions (abbreviation of breast-feeding and decreasing frequency of polygyny) have favored a shorter birth interval – and hence higher fertility.

This brief review of proximate fertility determinants leads to several conclusions: First, Gusii marriage norms have been applied among all living cohorts of women in such a way as to guarantee almost universal entry into reproductive unions and to assure reproductive continuity until women in such unions reach menopause, even when their husbands are no longer able to impregnate them. Second, the factors preventing Gusii women from reaching the biological maximum of fertility are age at marriage and birth-spacing rather than health conditions affecting their fecundity. In other words, acting in accordance with the norms of their culture, Gusii women have not begun bearing children as early as they could have and have not given birth as frequently as was biologically possible (though they have done so more frequently than many other Kenyans). Among cohorts living in 1975, both factors have changed toward higher fertility: Women probably began marrying at an earlier age after World War I (though age at marriage has increased more recently) and reduced the intervals between births after Kenya's independence in 1963 to a point lower than the Kenya national average. These reductions in marital age and birth-spacing probably increased fertility (Table 4.3).

Finally, the maintenance of the natural fertility schedule, that is, the bearing of a child every 2 to 3 years from marriage to menopause, was dependent on the voluntary activity of Gusii wives, often in the face of a husband's absence, death, or loss of interest, and was carried out with such determination and efficiency as to produce an average interval of only 4 months between resumption of menses and conception. Thus high marital fertility among the Gusii cannot be attributed simply to the pressures of duty and obligation on Gusii women but must also be understood as a reflection of their personal intentions.

### THE PARENTAL IMPERATIVE: WHAT MOTIVATES GUSII FERTILITY?

What explains the maintenance of high fertility among the Gusii? In the foregoing section we showed that the norms of Gusii marriage and family life support each woman in realizing her reproductive potential, within certain limits on marriage age and birth intervals, and that Gusii women and their husbands – in pursuing their reproductive careers – take full advantage of this situation, resulting in their high level of fertility. The Gusii population could well be described as mobilized for the realization of its reproductive potential, with social organization and voluntary activity operating in concert to achieve this demographic outcome. Having described the social organization of fertility, we need to explain its voluntary basis. Norms can be violated, and in fact many of the norms of Gusii marriage and family life *were* being violated in the Morongo area during 1974–1976. Rules governing bridewealth, family violence, even incest, were broken, not once but many times and often without punishment. Yet we never heard of anyone there who deliberately avoided bearing children; when it came to fertility, perfect conformity was the rule.

From the Gusii point of view, of course, maximizing fertility is a means of pursuing one's own interests through a reproductive career rather than conforming to social dictates, and what needs to be understood is the benefit expected from reproduction. For most Gusii the benefit is self-evident, as is the deprivation associated with childlessness.[16] Yet it is possible to explicate both conscious and unconscious benefits that parents anticipate from childbearing.

On the conscious side, there are three classes of benefits: (1) returns expected from the activities of children during childhood and adulthood; (2) parental progress on the status ladder of reproductive maturity; and (3) the signal value of reproductive continuity as a confirmation of personal and family well-being.

### Returns from children's activities

Children are considered valuable for their labor contributions to domestic production, either directly in cultivation and herding or (more frequently in the 1970s) indirectly in the performance of household tasks – particularly infant care – that free the mother for agricultural production and commercial activity. As they grow up, they (especially sons, who remain members of the parental homestead) are valued for the safety they provide in a community where violence is frequent, and for their cash contributions – for example, paying the school fees of their younger siblings when the parents cannot do so, and for marrying women who provide companionship and assistance to the mother. Finally, Gusii parents emphasize the role of descendants (sons and grandsons) in giving them a proper burial. Girls are more useful to the mother in the short run, before they marry, and boys in the long run, but Gusii parents see their utilitarian benefits expanded with each additional child.

### Advancement in the life course

Each parent's progress in the local age-sex hierarchy is dependent on reproductive accomplishment (Figure 3.2). Each man and woman gains recognition and respect for the birth of a child, the circumcision of a son, the marriage of a son, the birth of a grandchild, and so on. Within the reference group comprised of local agemates of the same sex, these reproductive events are what count most for status and prestige. Without them, a Gusii is "nothing." Both men and women are highly motivated by the desire to become a respected elder, which is impossible without keeping up with the others in one's reproductive career.

### Safety and health

In Gusii belief, reproductive disruption is a sign of growing disaster visited by the ancestor spirits, usually for omission of sacrifices. Once the compensatory sacrifices and other rituals have been performed, the only way a man and his wife can know that they are free of future affliction is by the resumption of normal reproductive function. Twins, breech delivery, prematurity, and albinism are birth anomalies interpreted as caused by spirits and requiring not only elaborate ritual remediation but also a succeeding normal birth to prove that the rituals worked. Because numerous other personal and family troubles are also diagnosed by diviners as attributable to ancestor spirits and requiring sacrifice, many couples find themselves in the position of continuing their childbearing with a special urgency to obtain the signal that they are safe from disaster. If the wife becomes infertile after giving birth to five or six children, she will interpret it as an intentional event, caused either by an ancestor spirit or by a jealous co-wife who has resorted to witchcraft, that presages a greater disaster if it is not dealt with and effectively cured. This quest for spiritual safety and health leads inevitably to the maintenance of normal fertility until menopause.

These are the benefits from fertility most frequently mentioned by the Gusii, usually in contexts in which it is assumed that fertility represents the highest value. From the point of view of Gusii parents, childbearing enhances their economic and spiritual careers. Other considerations, for example, the possibility that wives might indulge in extramarital affairs if they are not always pregnant or lactating, emerged in male discussions of hypothetical proposals for birth control. In a society dedicated to fertility, there seems to be no end to the reasons supporting it. Yet some of its strongest support may come from unconsciously experienced benefits.

Our inferences regarding unconscious benefits to reproduction are based on Gusii rituals, which give metaphors of birth and gestation a central place in their dramas. In Gusii rituals of transition (notably the annual male and female initiation ceremonies) and of healing (particularly following anomalous births), the afflicted person – that is, the novice who has just been circumcised or the mother with her abnormal offspring – is led into a protective seclusion in a house where she is warmed by a permanent fire, fed in order to strengthen the body, and kept from the sight of any potentially hostile persons.[17] After several

weeks, a ritual of emergence is performed, involving animal sacrifice and the administration of protective medicine in cuts made
on the healed person's body as a final strengthening before facing the hostile world. Although the Gusii do not call this a
rebirth, there is no doubt that they experience it as a symbolic
gestation-birth process.

Some of the evidence for this interpretation includes the fact
that when twins are born, which happened twice in Morongo in
1975–1976, the placenta is kept near them in a bowl as protection
until their seclusion from the view of outsiders is complete. In
other words, the placenta that once fed and protected them in the
womb is seen as giving them temporary magical protection until
they are fully secluded in the house. This metaphorical continuity
between the placenta and house as protective structures is facilitated by the Gusii word for placenta, *omogoye* (plural, *emegoye*),
literally referring to the bark strips that kept together the frame of
a Gusii house before the advent of nails. Furthermore, the term
for a newborn child is *mosamba mwaye,* "he/she who has burnt
his home," implying that the baby has lost his housing. Thus the
womb of normal gestation is represented as a home that protects
and nurtures the fetus. In ritual seclusion, the person enters a real
house for a drama of protection and nurturance that symbolically
imitates the gestation process.

In these ritual dramas, the reproductive process is interpreted
as a source of strength to which a person can, indeed must,
return when weakened and vulnerable in order to gain through
spiritual means the renewed bodily capacity to face a dangerous
world. Social life is dangerous, but gestation is equated with
safety. This has its counterpart in the Gusii adult's quest for
spiritual and somatic safety through continued reproduction,
which we have just described. The ceremonies that contain these
dramatic celebrations of the reproductive process occur with sufficient frequency – annually in the case of circumcision, irregu-
larly but perhaps once a year for birth anomalies, in the ordinary
person's experience – to provide public, though implicit, valida-
tion for the sense that fertility is the route to personal security.
Thus the symbolic world of Gusii ritual gives indirect but unmistakable support to high fertility in Morongo.

To recapitulate our analysis: Fertility was maintained through the operations of a kinship system that continued to place every woman in a marital union, restrict her extramarital sexual activity, and guarantee her reproductive continuity until menopause – even if her husband died or became unavailable sexually. Child survival was improved by preserving practices favorable to infant health (marital stability during the childbearing years, universal and prolonged breast-feeding, a birth interval of 2 years), while taking advantage of newly available medical services for the treatment and prevention of disease (see Chapter 7). Social organization and cultural symbols alike favored fertility and child survival, giving them a central place in the public life of Gusii families and communities. These factors worked in the absence of legal enforcement or coercive pressures because they were consistent with the motivation of Gusii parents, who believed their own interests would be advanced by maximizing the number of their surviving offspring.

We have argued that Gusii adults use their own and their children's fertility as signs of well-being, and they experience reproductive discontinuity (including infant mortality) as an omen menacing personal and family welfare. When disaster threatens, they take recourse in rituals that dramatize gestation and birth as symbols of comfort and renewed strength. Thus, their emotional well-being depends on the pursuit of a reproductive career in which childbearing (as a sign and symbol of personal safety and continuity) is an end in itself, an end we have termed the spiritual career, as well as a social obligation and a public virtue.

The reproductive career of each man and woman is united with the expansion of the patriarchal homestead in the imagery that motivates childbearing among Gusii adults (including the genealogical success stories of named ancestors who bore many children), making high fertility subjectively desirable as well as socially compulsory. This may appear irrational in terms of the increasingly unfavorable ratio of people to land and the increasing costs of children, but Gusii parents remain preoccupied with the possibility that those with *fewer* children will be unable to protect their own interests in the competition for scarce resources. It is not that Gusii parents lack a rationale for high fertility, but that *all* their rationales are predicated on reproduction as an adaptive strategy and have no place for birth limitation as anything but a sign of failure.[18]

## FERTILITY AND THE INFANT ENVIRONMENT IN MORONGO

The consequences of Gusii fertility, like its determinants, are socially organized. The 2,100 people surveyed in the Morongo area lived in 144 homesteads dispersed across 6 localities each of which was homogeneous in clan membership. The average number of residents in a homestead was 15.4, but there was a wide range – from 4 (in cases where homesteads had recently been divided among young brothers) to 61 (where Ombese, the 60-year-old polygynist with six wives and dozens of descendants occupied 20 acres). Both large homesteads (with over 30 residents) and small ones (with under 7) were found in all of the localities; the median homestead size for localities ranged from 9 to 15.

Most babies in Morongo are born to women in reproductive unions living at their conjugal partners' homesteads in houses assigned exclusively to them and their children.[19] They give birth regularly; in our sample, the years a woman had been married was highly correlated with the number of children she had borne. By the time they are 30 years old, women have an average of 4 to 5 children living with them. When they reach 40, they have about 7 children at home, after which the number declines as the daughters marry and move out, the sons build new houses in the homestead for their wives to occupy, and the mother herself reaches menopause. About a quarter of the women between 50 and 70, and 90% of those older, are widows.

A typical Morongo household, then, consists simply of a married woman and her children. The most difficult time for a woman is when she is in her 20s and has two children who need care and are too young to help her. Later, although she has more mouths to feed, the older children assist their mother in infant care, fetching water, cooking, doing errands and other household tasks. She has some of her own children in the household until she is well into her 50s, by which time her sons' children should be there to give her occasional help and provide companionship. The average mother is involved in infant care of her own offspring over more than 20, and often 30, years.

Given the large number of children and the burden of agricultural as well as household tasks, Gusii women organize the routine care of their babies according to a definite plan, described in

Chapter 6, that is attuned to the normal developmental schedule of infants and the expected duration of the birth interval. The average birth interval in Morongo, as mentioned above, declined in duration between the 1950s and 1970s and was probably one determinant of increased fertility during that time. Another contributor to the rise in fertility may have been a drop in the frequency of polygynous marriages.

In 1956, 44.4% of the married men and 55.8% of the married women in Nyansongo were polygynously married; by 1975, only 8.9% of the married men and 27.9% of the married women were. This extremely steep decline reflects the scarcities of land and cattle that made polygyny virtually impossible in the 1970s, except for men over 50 who had accumulated some wealth. (For Morongo as a whole in 1975, 32.1% of the men over 50, but only 5.4% of the men 25 to 50 years old, were polygynists.) At the later period, Nyansongo was intermediate among Morongo localities in frequency of polygyny, which was more frequent in the more prosperous neighborhoods, particularly the one with the most Seventh-Day Adventists, who (paradoxically, given their church's prohibition) were not only better able to afford plural wives but had large enough land holdings for them to cultivate. Thus polygyny remained a possibility for affluent men over 50 years of age, but the majority of Morongo children (84.5% of those under 5) were now being raised in monogamous homes.

An analysis of the number of children living with married women under 40 shows that polygynously married women have fewer children, although the difference is not a large one. For example, among the 35 Morongo women between 31 and 35 years of age, monogamous wives had borne an average of 6.2 children and polygynous wives 4.7; among the 37 who were 36 to 40 years old, the monogamous wives had borne 6.6 children and the polygynists 5.8. (These comparisons probably underestimate the difference that polygyny makes, because some of the women classified as polygynous were first wives who had borne some of their children under monogamous conditions.) The KNFS results show the same gap in a different way: The marital fertility rate was lower for the whole Gusii sample (361 per thousand) than for the monogamous woman separately (375 per thousand).[20] This higher fertility of monogamists was statistically significant for the Kenya sample as a whole in the 1977 survey, but – contrary to theoretical

expectation – there was no concomitant difference in average duration of breast-feeding or the birth interval. After a multivariate
analysis, Pebly and Mbugua[21] conclude that the lower fertility of
polygynous wives in Kenya must be due to the reduced fecundity
of their older husbands (rather than to reduced duration of
breast-feeding or frequency of coitus).

Thus the difference in childbearing between monogamists and
polygynists may not help explain the abbreviation of the birth
interval over the 20-year period of our studies. In any event, the
abbreviation meant that the Gusii mother had to turn her primary
attention to a newborn infant when the previous child was younger than had formerly been the case.

Though the birth interval had declined in duration, its significance in Gusii infant care remained as great in the 1970s as it had
been 20 years earlier. The succession of births, spaced by regular
intervals, is the Gusii version of the "natural fertility schedule"
found in populations where there is no deliberate limitation of the
number of offspring,[22] which is widespread in tropical Africa.[23]
Growing up among women who have given birth 10 or more
times, the young Gusii mother expects that each infant is one in a
long and regular sequence of offspring she will bear – until
*omokogooti,* the lastborn, whose care will differ from the rest in
being breast-fed longer and "spoiled" by extended maternal attention. Each previous infant must be replaced by a "follower," so its
unique place in the mother's attention has a clear and expected
endpoint – the birth of the next child. The cultural stereotype of
the lastborn infant as being exceptional in receiving more maternal resources *because* there will be no successor indicates how
strongly the concept of a birth succession figures in Gusii mothers'
assumptions about the care of the other 90% of their infants. In
studying Gusii infant care and development, we were observing
the lives of children during an interval between births in their
mothers' reproductive careers.

## MARRIAGES AND CONSENSUAL UNIONS

The traditional rules of Gusii marriage were still, during 1974–
1976, regarded as fundamental to the formation of reproductive
unions: Bridewealth in cattle was to be paid to the bride's father,
she was to move to the bridegroom's homestead and live in his

house, men were free to marry as many wives as they could afford, all children were considered the legal offspring of the man who paid bridewealth for their mother, divorce was difficult and gave the father custody of the children. These were recognized as the standards for proper marriage, but many were frequently honored in the breach, as a new set of socioeconomic realities altered practice and in effect created new norms that would have been considered outrageously deviant only 17 years earlier.

Nothing illustrates the tension between ideal and reality – and its effects on mothers and children – better than elopement as the means of forming a household. The decline in the bridewealth system between 1957 and 1974 resulted in new conditions for reproduction and child care in Morongo. In 1957, a negotiated bridewealth of some 10 or 12 cows would be transferred to the bride's home, and after a month – if none of the cattle died and if no derogatory information about the bride or groom undermined the agreement – the young woman would be released to take up residence at her husband's homestead.[24] The local chief virtually guaranteed these arrangements by assigning his constables to enforce them if one party deviated from a publicly negotiated settlement. The system was nevertheless showing signs of erosion even then: Four of the 51 legitimately married women living in Nyansongo were known to have lived in consensual unions elsewhere prior to their marriages, and at least 5 women were living in consensual unions in the community at one time or another during 1956–1957. Furthermore, several Nyansongo girls eloped with men from other clans, and one of them had done so more than once, thus acquiring a reputation that would make it difficult for her to contract a legitimate marriage later on.[25]

By 1974 it was so common as to be expectable that a young woman would take up residence with a man of her own choice, at his homestead, without the consent of her parents. The latter were nevertheless outraged, on the grounds that they had been cheated of the bridewealth payment (which should have been made before the bride was released), and they could be placated only to some extent by the young man's seeking an agreement and promising to pay in the future. But they would not engage in customary affinal (in-law) relations until an acceptable bridewealth had been paid, as much as 10 years later.

During the prebridewealth limbo, a woman's mother usually

would not visit her at her new home, even if it were nearby, and would not make the ritual greeting of the first baby (*ogokwania omwana*) borne by her daughter – despite the importance of this ritual as a celebration of her daughter's fertility and (through the expensive gifts of food involved) of respect and friendly relations with the family of the daughter's husband. Once the bridewealth had been paid and the daughter was considered married, the ritual greeting would be performed with all the gifts and other formalities – even though, as in one such event we witnessed in Nyansongo in 1976, the firstborn child was 9 years old rather than an infant and there were already two younger children of this "new" marriage.

More serious difficulties attended the social placement of children from consensual unions that did not last. When a union was terminated after a woman had become pregnant or had given birth, the child was not regarded as belonging to the biological father's lineage since no bridewealth had been paid. The young mother returned to her parents' home temporarily, while seeking another union, but her child could not belong to her father's lineage either, according to Gusii custom. If the child were a daughter, the young woman could bring her into a new union, where – though considered *ekerantane,* "a brought one" rather than someone who belongs to a place – a girl would be welcome as someone who would leave at marriage, make no inheritance claims, and might even bring in bridewealth. A son, however, would not be welcome because of male rights to permanent residence and a share in the homestead estate; yet the boy would have no right elsewhere either. In Gusii eyes this is a particularly pitiable position, posing a lifelong dilemma for which there is no conventional solution, but it was still a relatively unusual situation in the 1970s: Our 1975 census of Morongo indicated no more than 3% of children were born outside of a union that could become fully legitimate – in effect, outside of the homestead of a man who assumed the role of father.

Women often remained in consensual unions they would have terminated but for the birth of a son who might be legitimized by the biological father's payment of bridewealth but who had no chance of permanent affiliation at another man's homestead. The only alternative was to leave the boy with her own mother, where he might well be subject to neglect (see Chapter 7). As of 1976, the number of young women who did not raise their own children and give them the best available chance for legitimacy was still small. But the consensual union had introduced a new problem in the raising of Gusii children, namely, that of providing them stable and caring environments in the early years and permanent group membership for the future – benefits guaranteed in the days when bridewealth preceded cohabitation.

A bridewealth debt – representing the gap between old ideals and contemporary realities – hangs over Gusii women in consensual unions like a thick cloud. The young woman eloping with the man of her choice faces the same tasks as a bride married in the traditional way. First she must fit into her husband's home. This involves presenting herself as deferential, compliant, and industrious to senior members of her husband's lineage, particularly her mother-in-law. This relationship is problematic, for she and her mother-in-law can become competitive over her husband's emotional allegiance and economic resources. If her mother-in-law is not amenable to a warm and cooperative relationship, the bride sometimes finds a substitute in a senior sister-in-law (i.e., her husband's brother's wife).

The most significant factor facilitating acceptance in her husband's home is a young wife's success in producing a male child. Once she has a son there is pressure from within the homestead for her to remain with her husband. Until this point the relationship is in a sense a private concern between two young persons, but the birth of a son to the couple makes their union the concern of the lineage as a whole: They now have male issue, a link to the future. Although men sometimes cast off women who have borne them sons, they encounter strong criticism from the lineage elders for doing so. For her part, the Gusii woman who has lived as his wife and borne a son is not easily denied access to her husband's property.

By 1974, Morongo fathers rarely paid bridewealth for a woman until she had proven herself by giving birth to at least one son. A woman who had lived as a man's wife for perhaps a decade and borne him only daughters tended to appear downcast, knowing that his kin were probably urging him to drive her out or take a second wife. Given the ambiguity of the situation, she was likely to have remained in close contact with her family of origin, especially her mother.

With or without bridewealth, a young woman had to forge a relationship with her husband's mother, for whom she worked at first and in whose fields she might work for many years. In better-off families a woman was assigned her own plot to farm, but the majority in our sample still shared land with their mothers-in-law or sisters-in-law. One-third of the sample mothers viewed their mothers-in-law as a main source of social support, but another third named them as the chief obstruction to gaining support in the homestead. This variation was related to the position of the younger woman: Those for whom bridewealth had not yet been paid *all* cited relations with their mothers-in-law as their main difficulty, yet even some of those whose marriages had been legitimized by the transfer of cattle complained about their mothers-in-law. Thus the payment of bridewealth cattle was a necessary but not sufficient condition for the young woman's smooth adjustment at her husband's homestead. Many women in Morongo were raising their first three or four children under unprecedented conditions of social and psychological insecurity.

## THE LONGITUDINAL SAMPLE OF INFANTS AND PARENTS

To study the family environments and developmental patterns of Morongo children from birth to 30 months of age, we selected a sample of 28 infants, divided into 3 cohorts for observation and assessment: Cohort I, 12 children followed from birth; Cohort II, 8 children followed from 6 months of age; Cohort III, 8 children followed from 12 months of age. Each cohort had an equal number of males and females, and when there was more than one possible child in an age-sex category we chose the one from a hitherto underrepresented neighborhood of Morongo, in order to achieve maximum spread through the area described in the previous chapter. Background data were collected on the parents and families of each child enrolled in the sample, who was followed for about 17 months with the program of observations, tests, and measurements reported in subsequent chapters.

Table 4.4 shows some standard characteristics of the parents and infants in the longitudinal sample. The average mother was about 29 years old (but they ranged from 20 to 41), had attended school for less than 3 years (but some had not attended school and

Table 4.4. *Gusii longitudinal sample (n = 28):*
*Family characteristics*

|                        | Mean | S.D. | Range |
|------------------------|------|------|-------|
| Mother's age           | 29.2 | 6.4  | 20–41 |
| Mother's school level  | 2.9  | 3.3  | 0–10  |
| Father's age           | 37.4 | 11.5 | 20–66 |
| Father's school level  | 5.6  | 3.5  | 0–11  |
| Birth order of infant  | 4.3  | 2.5  | 1–10  |

one had gone to school for 10 years), and was married to a man about 8 years older with less than 6 years of school attendance (also highly variable). The large standard deviations in relation to the means show how varied they were in age and education; the older members of the sample tended to have had less schooling, for both husbands and wives, reflecting the historical period in which they grew up.

## THE ECONOMICS OF PARENTHOOD: DIVERGENT PATHWAYS

Several distinct economic adaptations characterized the 28 sample families, and they are most simply classified by their membership in the Roman Catholic or Seventh-Day Adventist churches or their lack of a church affiliation. The Roman Catholic couples showed the strongest involvement with the urban world of education, employment, monetary economy, and the mass media. The husbands had finished primary school and were employed outside the community, often in clerical jobs. They earned a higher cash income than the Seventh-Day Adventist and Unaffiliated husbands and tended to rent land for their wives to cultivate, making up for their smaller holdings of inherited land. They owned more consumer goods like radios and also drank alcoholic beverages frequently by local standards.

The Seventh-Day Adventists, on the other hand, tended to follow a model of rural economy involving intensive agriculture, thrift, and sobriety, as advocated by the SDA Church. The husbands were less educated, and less frequently employed outside the community. Though their cash incomes were lower than those of the Catholics, they spent less on alcoholic beverages and other consumer goods and thus probably had as much or more money available to spend on child nutrition and health. More owned cows or purchased cow's milk for their young children to drink.

The Unaffiliated parents in our sample were the oldest and least educated and had the smallest cash incomes but lived in homesteads with relatively large landholdings. Few of the fathers were employed outside the community and their drinking frequency was above average but slightly less than that of the Catholics. Although access to inherited land and membership in an older cohort made their lifestyle more like that of their forefathers, their lower cash income must count as a contemporary disadvantage, particularly with respect to school fees and supplementary foods for infants and young children.

Examination of Table 4.5 shows that these characterizations are qualified by considerable variation within each of the three groups and thus there are few statistically significant differences. They nevertheless represent divergent pathways of economic adaptation in Morongo the significance of which is only partly indicated by the numbers.

Choices concerning how to make a living and how to spend money are pervasive for married couples. Husbands must decide whether to seek employment in a distant place or attempt to make a living locally through small-scale commercial agriculture and other commercial activities. If they have completed primary school, they are likely to leave in search of an urban job, particularly if they have little access to homestead land. Many married men, about 40% to 50% of the adult male population of Morongo at any time, are working outside the district. Although all married women cultivate the soil, they and their husbands have to decide how much will be devoted to food crops and how much to the cash crops of tea and pyrethrum. If they harvest a good crop of maize but are short of cash, they must decide whether to sell some of it at Morongo market or keep it all for the family's food.

Religious affiliation helped to make many of these domestic decisions for Morongo couples in the cohorts represented by our sample parents. The Catholic Church offered an extensive primary and secondary school system connecting the rural area with the outside world through academically based employment, whereas

Table 4.5. Differences in parental characteristics by religious affiliation

| | Seventh-Day Adventists (n = 9) | | Roman Catholics (n = 10) | | Unaffiliated (n = 9) | | Total Sample | | Differences by religious categories[a] |
|---|---|---|---|---|---|---|---|---|---|
| | Mean | S.D. | Mean | S.D. | Mean | S.D. | Mean | S.D. | |
| Mother's age (in yrs.) | 27.1 | 3.8 | 29.1 | 3.4 | 31.3 | 3.0 | 29.2 | 3.3 | N.S. |
| Father's age (in yrs.) | 34.3 | 4.2 | 34.0 | 1.8 | 40.7 | 3.0 | 36.4 | 3.5 | N.S. |
| Mother's education (in yrs.) | 3.4 | | 3.2 | | 2.0 | | 2.9 | | N.S. |
| Father's education (in yrs.) | 5.8 | 1.4 | 7.5 | 1.5 | 3.3 | 1.3 | 5.6 | 1.6 | Catholic vs. all others, $\chi^2 = 4.12$, $p < .05$<br>Unaffl. vs. all others, $\chi^2 = 6.03$, $p < .05$ |
| Father's occupational status | 2.4 | | 4.0 | | 2.6 | | 3.0 | | Catholics vs. all others, $\chi^2 = 6.27$, $p < .05$ |
| Cash income (per mo. U.S. $) | 95 | 59.9 | 109 | 58.4 | 82 | 95.2 | 96 | 70.8 | N.S. |
| Homestead land | 6.0 | 6.0 | 5.5 | 5.6 | 9.9 | 12.0 | 7.1 | 8.2 | N.S. |
| Total land cultivated | 6.1 | 5.9 | 9.5 | 7.3 | 9.9 | 12.0 | 8.5 | 8.6 | N.S. |
| Mother's drinking frequency (self-report, means) | 0.44 | 0.53 | 2.40 | 2.0 | 2.25 | 2.0 | 1.70 | 1.8 | SDAs vs. others, $\chi^2 = 6.8$, $p < .01$ |
| Father's drinking frequency (reputational ratings, means) | 1.11 | 1.3 | 2.10 | 1.0 | 2.00 | 1.2 | 1.75 | 1.2 | N.S. |
| Stress on mother (means) | 11.9 | 1.2 | 13.4 | 1.9 | 14.6 | 3.0 | 13.3 | 2.4 | SDAs vs. others, $\chi^2 = 5.54$, $p < .05$ |
| Father employed outside community | 4 | | 8 | | 3 | | N.S. | | N.S. |
| Radio in household | 1 | | 6 | | 2 | | N.S. | | N.S. |

[a]Kruskal–Wallis one-way ANOVA chi-square test

the Seventh-Day Adventists preached scientific agriculture, nutrition, thrift, and abstinence from alcohol. Belonging to one church or the other does not simply determine how one will allocate one's energies and family resources, but it does exert a discernible influence in the aggregate.

The basic economic problem faced by the sample families is that their land holdings are insufficient to meet their needs, especially given their high fertility and their desire for amenities that can be purchased only with cash – including clothing, school fees, and transportation to clinics. The average homestead has less than 3 acres, and some young couples have the use of less than an acre of inherited land. They must find ways of acquiring a reliable cash income, and not only through devoting some of their land to cash crops, which deplete their food supply. Fathers must get jobs outside the district or become small businessmen locally, in addition to their wives' tending the gardens. If possible, they must rent or buy additional land for more food and cash crops. Families who ignore these imperatives take the risk of being unable to provide their children with adequate material conditions for development. Whether they choose the alternatives typified by Catholics or Adventists in our sample, couples must adapt to these economic and demographic realities or neglect their children.

## PARENTAL RESPONSIBILITY AND DRINKING BEHAVIOR

Even if Morongo parents earn enough to take care of their children, there is the question of how they use the income. Temptations to ignore their parental responsibilities and divert resources to immediate pleasures face both mothers and fathers. Alcohol is the biggest problem, but men working away from their wives for long periods are also tempted to spend money on other women, neglecting the support of their wives and children at home. Furthermore, alcohol consumption is more than a drain on the family economy; it can result in personal and familial disorganization that prevents parents from acting responsibly. Given their few acres of land, many children, and unreliable back-up support, a Morongo couple in 1975 had to maintain a high level of organization and discipline to provide adequate material care for their children.

Some parents were clearly inadequate in these terms and were recognized as failing in their parental responsibilities. The mothers who drank most heavily tended to neglect their children's needs, using available cash for alcohol instead of cow's milk or clothing. With less energy for agricultural work, they spent less time in the gardens and produced less staple food. Some of the fathers who drank most heavily tended not only to dissipate family resources to a point that their houses and children were visibly neglected, but also beat their wives and got into trouble with neighbors because of their aggressive behavior when drunk. Some of the excessive drinking among women seemed to be a response to being abandoned by a husband working far away who did not send money home. In such cases the precariousness of the safety net for child care in Morongo was most obvious; if mother and father did not exert themselves effectively for the children, no one else could be counted on to do so. Hence the popular song, "Abandon Beer and Educate your Children" (Chapter 3).

Maternal drinking frequency, assessed through self-reports as well as independently, was associated with religion and education in the sample. The Seventh-Day Adventist mothers, in accordance with the dictates of their church, drank very infrequently compared with the others ($\chi^2 = 6.8$, $p < .01$). Women who had attended school longer also drank less ($r = -.41$, $p < .05$), even with age controlled ($-.41$) and income controlled ($-.33$, $p < .05$). Because SDA women had not attended school longer on the average than the others, the religion and school effects are independent. This suggests that schooling provided mothers with personal resources for adaptation lacking in mothers who had not attended school, or had attended only briefly.

The substantial differences in resources and forms of adaptation among our sample families reflected the beginnings of major divisions between the rich and poor in Morongo, divisions likely to widen with each generation of children raised in affluent or impoverished environments. On the other hand, however, the most prosperous middle-aged men in Morongo (including Seventh-Day Adventists) are most vulnerable to the lure of polygyny, which fragments the resources available to their children and inherited by their sons. Insofar as this pattern continues in succeeding cohorts of men, polygyny – even as a minority phenomenon – will tend to counteract the intergenerational transmission of economic inequality between families.

The Gusii family as a parenting environment, though still remarkably stable, was under stress in the mid-1970s. Household formation was no longer regulated through bridewealth marriages negotiated in advance, and consensual unions involved a period of uncertainty about whether the woman and her children would stay or go. Most unions that had borne children nevertheless became permanent, but they became so in in a homestead lacking the land to support them from agriculture alone. Young parents struggled to make a living for their children, using strategies and resources available to them from their families, their churches, and their educational backgrounds. If the husband's support flagged, the burden on his wife was greater, and some of our sample mothers struggled alone on behalf of their offspring. Heavy drinking by one or both parents was the greatest threat to adequate care for children. Gusii models of family life and parental responsibility were still dominant influences, but their implementation was jeopardized by new conditions of life in Morongo.

# 5

## Pregnancy and birth

Our investigation of Gusii infants began before their birth, to understand not only the family environments into which they were born (Chapter 4), but also to examine the processes of pregnancy and delivery as organized in the Gusii context and experienced by women in the Morongo area. This part of the study focused on 26 pregnant women, who were offered prenatal care at our clinic.[1] Each woman was given an initial physical examination by Constance Keefer, M.D., followed by an interview on aspects of pregnancy and childbirth by a Gusii assistant. During the last month of pregnancy, Sarah LeVine interviewed each woman at home about her domestic activities and social relationships and observed her handling of the toddler who was about to be displaced. The women averaged 29.1 years in age and ranged from an 18-year-old, pregnant for the first time, to a woman over 45 expecting her 13th child.

Clinical examination showed the women to be generally healthy. Their average height and head circumference fell between 85% and 95% of those for adult American women, indicating that previous nutrition and health had been adequate for growth. None were obese, and most were lean and muscular. Despite hunger in the preharvest period and the presence of malaria and intestinal parasites in many of the women, they did not appear debilitated. Sixteen of the 26 women interviewed admitted to drinking alcohol, in small to moderate amounts, and only a few smoked tobacco rarely. None had any chronic illness except one who complained of arthralgias without any evidence of arthritis.

These women's reproductive histories seem to attest to their healthy condition. The number of previous pregnancies and births is given in Table 5.1. Most of the mothers had been pregnant or lactating for virtually all of their reproductive years. One woman

Table 5.1. *Assessment of perinatal risk:Maternal characteristics*

| | Number of subjects | Mean | S.D. | Range |
|---|---|---|---|---|
| [a]Age (years) | 24 | 29.1 | 5.9 | 17–45 |
| [a]Parity | 24 | 5.1 | 2.5 | 1–10 |
| [a]Number of living children | 24 | 4.5 | 2.2 | 1–10 |
| [a]Prior birth interval (mos.) | 22 | 34 mos. | 16 mos. | 24–84 |
| Presentation weight (Kgs, 0.2 Kg) | 24 | 62.92 | 6.59 | 51.52–75.04 |
| Height (cms 1.8 cm) | 15 | 159.8 | 5.6 | 147–166 |
| Head circumference (cms 0.5) | 19 | 55.2 | 1.3 | 53–58 |
| Weight gain (kgs/wk.) | | | | |
| Late second | 15 | 0.44 | – | 2–.75 |
| Early third | 18 | .22 | – | 0–1.0 |
| Late third | 24 | .02 | – | 0–8.0 |

[a]Cross-validated with area census

could remember only two individual menstrual periods in her 9 years of childbearing.

Some of the women with stated prior birth intervals (PBIs) of greater than 36 months had conceived and miscarried. They had not usually regarded the pregnancy as terminated but believed that fetal growth had been slowed down; this process is known as *ekemuma* and is usually attributed to witchcraft. Eventually, however, they had given birth normally, believing the newborn to have been conceived years before. Hence, some women who in fact had PBIs greater than 36 months reported that their pregnancies had lasted "very long" – 18 months and in one case, 3 years.

All women made their first clinic visit in the middle to late part of the second trimester; that is, at a time when their condition had already become readily apparent. During the first visit, a medical history was taken (see Appendix A). Biweekly clinic visits were encouraged in the last trimester, but a majority failed to observe our recommended schedule, feeling generally as well as they expected and not seeing the need for prenatal care.

Few women gained weight during the last half of pregnancy (Table 5.1). In fact, only three gained at a rate accepted as standard by American obstetrical practices of one pound per week. Most stayed the same and a few (3) actually lost weight. We were concerned about this lack of weight gain. Of course, we had not measured prepregnant weights nor those of the first trimester. It might have been that some had gained earlier in the pregnancy and then leveled. The marginal nutritional adequacy of some of these women's diets may in part have explained the lack of weight gain during pregnancy, but we saw no evidence of intrauterine growth retardation, and only one newborn was small for gestational age.

In Gusii tradition pregnant and lactating women eat eleusine porridge (*oboori*), which contains large amounts of calcium and is a rich food. Most of the women craved this food but most had it rarely, especially before the harvest. The older women particularly reported the benefits of "Luo salt," earth from the shores of Lake Victoria (inhabited by the Luo people). This substance contains large amounts of calcium in the fossilized residue of animal life from this inland sea. No other forms of pica were mentioned.

The women suffered from few illnesses during pregnancy, although some cases of malaria (fever and chills) were suspected. Over half of the women reported intestinal parasites, but treatment was deferred until after the birth of the child.

Thus, despite some features that would be considered abnormal in a prenatal clinic in the United States (e.g., low weight gain, febrile illness, parasitic infestation) the medical impression of these pregnant Gusii women is one of health. Most women complained of fatigue, back pain, and general malaise. Their complaints were not presented as serious ones and they continued to carry out their daily activities. The majority of Gusii women in Morongo carried a heavy workload during pregnancy, with only sporadic assistance from husbands and female kin. In the more affluent families, laborers were hired to cultivate the fields, but other strenuous tasks were performed by the pregnant women themselves. Physical labor could be burdensome during pregnancy, especially for women giving birth during the period between April and July, when food stocks were running low. After their maize was exhausted, they would have to purchase grain with which to make *obokima*, the staple porridge that is the main source of carbohydrate for all Gusii, or live entirely on green vegetables and beans. Doing without *obokima* was felt to be a severe deprivation. If they entered their last trimester after the harvest, however, even the poorest women were reasonably well fed.

## RELATIONSHIPS AND EMOTIONAL
## RESPONSES DURING PREGNANCY

In those families where husbands were absent due to labor migration, marital interaction was not directly affected by a wife's pregnancy. Women whose husbands were at home, however, reported an aversion to sex during the last trimester and often starting much earlier. Most indicated that they complied with their husbands' sexual demands for fear of being beaten if they resisted. Those who refused, regardless of the risk, said they did so because intercourse would cause them to vomit.

Although a few men helped their pregnant wives or even substituted for them in the performance of agricultural tasks, and others kept an eye on small children for short periods, we knew of none who undertook domestic tasks such as cooking or fetching water. Gusii men want children but do not feel obliged to be especially supportive of their wives during pregnancy. In fact, several women reported that during pregnancy their marital relationships were more difficult than usual because their husbands would pursue other women, whose attentions the husbands secured with resources their expanding families could ill afford to lose. There were few dramatic changes evident in the relationship between a pregnant mother and her about-to-be-replaced child, primarily because the mother anticipated becoming pregnant again and had prepared the children for it, as described in Chapter 6.

Given the great value placed upon fertility, the ambivalence with which Gusii women treat pregnancy when interviewed comes as a surprise to an outsider. Any pleasure, whether physical or emotional, to be derived from the condition is firmly denied. To volunteer news of one's pregnancy would be regarded as "crazy" behavior. Only seven women said they had announced to their husbands that they were pregnant, and only two said that they had volunteered the news to their best female friend. None had volunteered the information to their children. On being asked about their growing bellies, eleven women said they had acknowledged their pregnancy to their husbands, and nineteen to relatives or friends. When questioned, only four had confirmed their children's suspicions. The others all said they could not speak of such a "shameful" matter to children. In several cases women went through their entire pregnancy without speaking of it to anyone at all. They reported having received all inquiries in silence. "Why bother to confirm what is obvious?" some said; whereas others explained, "No one would talk to me about such a thing. It is not the Gusii way."

This profound reluctance to announce her condition or to confirm it if questioned is explained by the conviction that a pregnant woman is the target of jealousy and malevolence. The only way to avoid the dangers to which pregnancy exposes her is to hide her good fortune for as long as possible and then to deny she experiences it as good. If, in August, a woman obviously far along in her pregnancy is asked, "When are you due?" she will reply, "I must suffer until November." This convinces no one, but she says this because she hopes to avoid being seen as flaunting an advantage. We were told, "No one speaks about her pregnancy. When a woman complains that she is tired and that her back aches, people will know that, although expecting a child, she is not proud; indeed, she is suffering." She is paying dearly for her good fortune and rather than envy her, others should pity her! Furthermore, unless she is in imminent danger of miscarrying, a Gusii woman will not allude to her condition, especially to other women, even those with many healthy children of their own. Only with complaints and symptoms is she permitted to draw attention to herself and thereby attract solicitude and support rather than envy and possibly malevolence.

When women did talk about pregnancy in the interview situation, they talked about it primarily in negative terms. The most common physical symptoms mentioned were food cravings and aversions; nausea was also common. Although a majority had morning sickness for the first 3 months, eight women experienced nausea and vomiting *throughout* pregnancy. Six reported nausea as a specific response to intercourse, and with the sight of their absent husbands' clothes.[2] Of all 26 women, only one, in her early 40s, did not report having any physical symptoms. All said they felt less healthy than normal during pregnancy, and none said she enjoyed giving birth. Indeed, when told that some American women found that the excitement and exhilaration of childbirth more than compensated for the discomfort of pregnancy and pain of delivery, these Gusii women were incredulous.

The negative emotional responses to pregnancy reported by the majority of respondents included shame, fear of the delivery, worry about how to provide for the unborn child and the rest of the family unit, and anxiety about possible miscarriage or physical abnormalities of the infant. Of the 16 who reported a recent dream only one reported a pleasurable dream. Seven of the other dream accounts dealt with difficult childbirths, and five with death of the dreamer's own child, a friend's child, or of an *omogeni* (literally "visitor" or "stranger" but often used to refer to a newborn). It would appear, then, that when asleep as well as awake, Gusii women experience pregnancy with considerable ambivalence and anxiety.

Four women conceded in low voices that it might be all right to be proud of one's pregnancy, especially if one had miscarried the previous time or had been infertile for a long period, so long as that pride was kept to oneself. Three young women, moreover, admitted that, although they were anxious, they were also eager to "meet" this new baby, and again, 16 women reported that, despite some anxiety, they had felt secretly pleased, or even very happy, on feeling the fetus move for the first time.

Most women appeared to have known little about childbirth prior to experiencing it themselves. Gusii conventions of modesty and respect between mothers and daughters, and mothers-in-law and daughters-in-law, preclude conversations about sexual and reproductive matters. Although a child might sneak glimpses of the birth process in her own home, she was not invited to do so and the particulars of the birth would often not be discussed. Nineteen respondents stated that they learned nothing about conception and pregnancy from their own mothers, and five added that at marriage they were still entirely ignorant. Although 17 had actually seen a mother, stepmother, sister, or aunt in labor, 12 had found the experience distressing, and only 5 of the 12 had received any explanation of what they had witnessed. In the other seven instances, Gusii shame about sexual matters apparently barred women of the parental generation from talking about what was happening.

Thus the fear of jealousy and socially unacceptable self-disclosure gave pregnancy a negative emotional tone; in addition, the reluctance of most women to discuss either the physical or emotional aspects of reproduction resulted in pregnancy and childbirth remaining ordeals even for some who had borne several children.

Gusii expectant mothers make no preparations for the new baby, because it is generally believed that purchasing clothes, for example, would be excessively optimistic. "How do you know you aren't going to give birth to a piece of meat or a hyena; how do you know your baby won't be born dead?" we were told. An expectant mother might mention needing a child nurse (*omoreri*) in the future, but she would not locate one before the birth. Thus, in spite of a constant preoccupation with the reproductive process, the Gusii woman bears a child with minimal prior arrangements.

The women were reluctant to reveal daydreams about their unborn children. Indeed, eight said they did not think about the child at all, and only one specified which sex she wanted her child to be. Although several of the younger women were known to need sons in order to establish themselves in their husbands' lineages, they would not admit to hoping for this. Such wishes as they could admit to concerned the physical and economic well-being of the child. Several women said that they wanted their children to be educated as a means of achieving financial security away from the land. Two women, both in their 40s, stated that they hoped their children would be obedient, well-behaved, and respectful; that is, that they would approximate traditional Gusii norms of behavior. Only one woman alluded to the conventional expectation that children care for their aged mothers, by saying that she hoped this child, in his adulthood, "would not forget her."

## LABOR AND DELIVERY

Childbirth usually takes place at home. Only 3 of the 26 women – all of them from better-off families – planned to and actually did give birth in one of the mission-operated clinics in the district, staying 1 or 2 days. Two others resorted to the government hospital, one after a difficult and protracted labor at home, the other after delivery with a retained placenta. The rest delivered at home, where two-thirds were attended by another adult, usually the husband's mother; and one-third were alone or attended only by a child.

Many women reported premature labor pains (Brackson-Hicks contractions) long in advance of delivery. For example, Paula began complaining about labor pains 6 weeks before giving birth to her 13th child. The year before she had lost two children and lived in terror of her sister-in-law's malevolence, which she was convinced had caused her sons' deaths from measles. Thus this new pregnancy was an excessively fearful experience for her. She wanted to replace the children she had lost, but she feared becoming once again a target for jealousy and witchcraft. Paula was convinced that if this woman were present at her delivery – as would normally be the case – she would kill the infant. Accordingly, Paula chose to give birth in the fields all alone. Later we learned that although some women, like Paula, give birth alone out of acknowledged fear, others do so out of a conscious desire to prove themselves. Such a woman makes a point of keeping up with her regular workload throughout her pregnancy; ultimately she will give birth "on the path" or wherever she happens to be working at the time, and very soon after delivery she is back in the fields again, privately delighted with her accomplishment.

The majority of women give birth indoors in the presence of female relatives and neighbors. But just as during her pregnancy a woman will have avoided mentioning her condition, she keeps the realization of being in real labor to herself for as long as possible. Indeed, she is likely to be more anxious now than at any time in the past 9 months about arousing jealousy, so she will wait until she considers herself ready to deliver before summoning help.

When asked about their arrangements ahead of time, most younger women said they expected their mothers-in-law to be present, whereas older women said they would call sisters-in-law, neighbors, or in one case, an adolescent daughter. Only one said she expected to call a woman especially skilled in delivering babies. In each instance, however, these plans were quite vague. Sometimes, when the time came, the pregnant woman found that the person she planned to rely on was not at home, and alternative arrangements had to be made on the spot. This improvised quality of the arrangements for delivery was expected.

Because Gusii rules of kin avoidance, *chinsoni,* forbid a mother from entering her son's house, his wife must give birth in her mother-in-law's house if she wants the latter's assistance. Nowadays, some families interpret these rules less strictly than in the past. Thus, although no mother (in fact, no woman of the parental generation) may enter the *enyomba,* the room where her son sleeps with his wife, it is now acceptable for her to attend the delivery so long as it occurs in *eero,* the man's room for entertaining guests, of her son's house. We saw matting walls torn down dividing *enyomba* from *eero* in order to open up the bedroom (the private sexual space); thereafter, a mother-in-law and other senior female relatives may attend the labor without violating the rules.

A woman well along in her reproductive career may be attended by one or two female neighbors or kin, or often by a single teen-aged daughter. These attendants maintain the fire and minister to the woman in labor by rubbing her abdomen and flanks at the time of the membrane rupture, making a solution of ash and water for her to drink in order to enhance the contractions, and tying a medicine stick around her abdomen. When a younger woman goes into labor, however, the news spreading through the neighborhood may attract as many as 20 post-menopausal women to gather around her. Regardless of their usual feelings, they do not act overtly supportive on this occasion but mock her and chide her, shrieking with laughter among themselves. The young woman in labor tolerates the ordeal stoically, never crying out.

This is a Gusii rite of passage in which the older women of a lineage and locality verbally abuse a younger woman who is in transition to a higher status. Such hazing is customary on three occasions: when a girl undergoes clitoridectomy – an essential part of her initiation into womanhood, although she may be only 7 or 8 years old;[3] when a woman already married with bridewealth undergoes the most formal Gusii marriage ceremony (*enyangi*), in which iron rings (*ebitinge*) are put on her ankles[4] (rare nowadays); and when she gives birth for the first time. On all three occasions, the senior women of the locality – once young, in-marrying strangers themselves – mock the novice, particularly with sexual insults.

The custom of hazing at the first birth has undergone change with the decline in bridewealth practices. In 1956, those few girls who gave birth out of wedlock were subject to the most extreme hazing, as the Gusii believe that a girl who conceives before marriage cannot deliver until she has revealed the real name of her child's father. If the girl had previously refused to name her lover, the old women of her family and neighborhood threatened her during labor: "Talk quickly or die!" and they might pinch and slap her to coerce the confession.[5] For the woman in a bridewealth marriage, the situation was somewhat different: The first time a woman gave birth might attract a crowd of 15 or more older women. On one such occasion in 1956, a middle-aged neighbor was sitting behind the 18-year-old girl in labor and was supporting her in a sitting position identical to that used in the clitoridectomy operation. The women usually told her to be brave and keep her legs apart or she would suffocate the baby. Sometimes they pinched, beat, or slapped her face to force her to aid the contractions, and they often held her legs apart forcibly. To add to the commotion, some women might impatiently urge her to confess adultery in order to ease the delivery.[6]

By 1974, however, the distinction between married and unmarried mothers was much less clear, because bridewealth had not been paid for the majority of women giving birth for the first time (and in many cases, the first three or four times). Thus, although they were living as the wives of men in terms of their social roles in everyday life, the lack of prior bridewealth payment put these women into the category of unmarried mothers by standards that had prevailed only 17 years earlier. This ambiguity in their social status gave rise to a diversity in the practice of hazing: Those women who were on good terms with their husband's family would probably be hazed only at first birth, regardless of whether their bridewealth had been paid; those not on good terms with their husband's family would be hazed even on their third and fourth births if bridewealth had not yet legitimized their unions. Thus, the ritual hazing that had been reserved for the first birth in the 1950s was being directed in the 1970s at women who had already borne children.

The Gusii women we observed in labor endured this hazing without overt response. We never heard a woman cry out during labor, nor did we often hear of this. Having undergone in childhood the pain of clitoridectomy, and the hazing accompanying it, with a precocious courage demanded by the ritual, a Gusii woman has learned to endure impassively the pain of childbirth and the hostile laughter and joking sexual abuse that accompany it. The challenge of childbirth is to prove oneself again by producing a healthy infant with the dignity of silence and restraint that constitutes a moral virtue for a Gusii woman. The parallel with the initiation ceremony is explicit, and informants speak of the woman confined during and after delivery as *omware,* meaning the secluded novice who has just undergone the circumcision or clitoridectomy operation.

When labor begins, a woman paces about the room fully clothed, periodically crouching or reclining in response to her pains. As the contractions accelerate in frequency she undresses and, wrapped in a blanket, sits on a low stool. Grasping its rim on either side, she braces herself, her legs stretched out in front of her. When the baby enters the birth canal, she is held from behind by her mother-in-law or an older woman and exhorted to push the baby out. Around her the other women sing and dance, shouting at her to make haste. Though young children are usually sent away, they often return and are permitted to remain, while no attempt is made to keep older children out of the way.

The Gusii have midwives, but they are usually called upon only in the case of particularly difficult deliveries. They monitor the progress of the delivery, manipulate the fetus, administer medicines to hasten delivery, and retrieve the placenta after birth. If no midwife is present, a woman who is not of the parental generation and therefore not constrained by avoidance rules, monitors the delivery process by parting the woman's legs for a periodic inspection. In one instance we observed that the periodic inspection was omitted because no one of the appropriate generation was present. When no midwife or kinswoman is present, the baby may slip out onto the floor during birth. If any adult female is there to receive the baby, she stimulates the infant to cry, removes mucous from the mouth, and cuts the umbilical cord with a used razor blade. She bathes the baby in cold water while the mother huddles in a blanket on the floor. When the infant has been dried and wrapped in a towel, it is passed among the other women present for greeting and inspection and is finally placed in the mother's arms. The mother is often given bottled orange soda to drink, a luxury not ordinarily available to many families, while the placenta is immediately disposed of in the latrine to prevent its use in witchcraft against the mother.

Although firewood was at a premium in the 1970s, the immediate postpartum period remained one of the few occasions on which families saw to it that a fire was kept burning around the clock. Once she has washed and dressed herself, the new mother lies on a makeshift bed beside the cooking fire on which her mother-in-law prepares the porridge and green vegetable, *chinsaga,* which Gusii believe to be essential for the release of the mother's milk supply. The mothers took *chinsaga* in the first 2 or 3 days after delivery to stimulate milk production; they also acknowledged that hydration was helpful to milk production. They did not, however, believe milk production was related to the infant's suck, nor did they believe that colostrum was of any value, although they did not consider it as harmful. In all cases, infants slept with the mother, and nursing was reported to be very frequent.

Nursing was not started immediately after birth but at 12 hours of age with a "practice suck." (This delay in breast-feeding, which is customary, puts the Gusii in the category of those peoples who do not take full advantage of colostrum as a means of rehydrating the neonate and providing antigens to fight infection.)[7] By 24 hours of age, the baby was offered the breast "on demand" in response to even minimal physical or vocal fussing. This type of demand schedule led to an almost continuous nursing pattern when the infant was awake.

## THE POSTPARTUM PERIOD

In the past, women enjoyed a few weeks of rest after they gave birth. They relied on sisters-in-law or even co-wives to perform their domestic and agricultural functions while they recovered from childbirth. In the 1970s, however, few women were able to enjoy this luxury. If they were fortunate, a neighbor or relative might cook for them the first day, but thereafter most women were on their own again. In the weeding season, a conscientious new mother would force herself out into the fields a few days after childbirth, and although a few took pride in their rapid resumption of chores, most complained bitterly and appeared very tired.

In the days and weeks after the birth a new mother is likely to receive many visitors. During the first day or so, as she lies by the kitchen fire in her own house or in her mother-in-law's, depending on where the delivery took place, neighborhood women will come to greet the new baby. He is passed around to be admired, and everyone has an opinion about whom he resembles. News of the birth will have reached the woman's natal home and soon members of her family will appear to pay their respects. The woman's mother, however, must come with certain gifts, including flour, sugar, tea, and meat. If she is poor, she may have to wait many months or even years to save the money to purchase these things. If bridewealth has not been transferred, the maternal grandmother will come without the customary presents or not at all. A Gusii marriage is a reciprocal relationship between two families, and thus a woman cannot expect to receive gifts from her parents until her husband has paid bridewealth for her. When her own mother fails to celebrate the birth in the traditional manner, a Gusii woman feels rejected, regardless of her expectation. Similarly, if her father-in-law delays coming to greet the child, or if her absent husband fails, on learning of the birth, to send the baby clothes (considered the father's responsibility to supply), a woman will be exceedingly hurt and fearful of her status within the family.

Because the Gusii have no prescribed period of sexual abstinence after birth, husbands may insist on resuming sexual relations within a week or 10 days. Polygynists tend to stay away from their wives for much longer, and some fathers working out of the district may not even return home for weeks to months following the birth of a child.

Our investigation of Gusii pregnancy and childbirth, then, resulted in several paradoxical findings: Gusii women are exposed to tropical parasites, hunger, and hard physical labor during pregnancy (as during most of their lives), but the mothers examined at Morongo were generally healthy. They gained little weight during pregnancy – usually interpreted as a sign of risk for the fetus – but most of the babies they delivered were normal, healthy, and of good size. Gusii women want to bear children and are highly successful at it, but their experience of pregnancy is avowedly unpleasant and accompanied by fear and censorship. Their labor and delivery, though taking place in a community that values fertility above all, elicits little interpersonal support, as many give birth while being hazed or in complete isolation. Thus the mothers of Morongo, in beginning their reproductive careers, experienced biological success in a context of psychosocial stress during the 1970s.

## RITUAL PROTECTION FOR
## VULNERABLE NEWBORNS

Gusii culture provides parents with means of protecting babies who are believed to be particularly fragile at birth, specifically twins and those delivered prematurely or in a breech presentation – many of whom are in fact fragile due to low birth weight. These children and their mothers are subjected to a lengthy postpartum seclusion designed to protect and strengthen them and to restore the mother's normal reproductive career and permit the baby to survive despite small size at birth. This ritual reveals Gusii assumptions about health, reproduction, and physical growth and development, illuminating the Gusii system of infant care as parents conceptualize it. We were able to observe the ritual in full on three occasions during 1975, twice when twins were born to Morongo mothers and once when there was a breech delivery.

The Gusii response to abnormal births is distinctive. Some African peoples (Kikuyu, Igbo) are reported to consider twins in particular such a serious sign of spiritual danger that they must be killed at birth; others such as the Yoruba of southwestern Nigeria, although sharing the sense of danger represented by a twin birth, recognize a sacred obligation to protect twins through specific religious activities (connected with the wooden figurines called *ibeji*). In the Gusii case, the sense of danger is also present but the spiritual peril is symbolically embodied in the physical vulnerability of the mother–child unit, which requires procedures to enhance physical strength and foster healthy growth. The explicit prototype for abnormal birth among the Gusii is their initiation ritual, in which a wound is inflicted on the preadolescent by circumcision or clitoridectomy, requiring a protective seclusion for healing and the nurturing of the individual to regain strength and growth.

Some of the rituals for abnormal birth in the 1970s had been performed for every Gusii newborn, but had been discontinued in the Morongo area before our initial fieldwork in 1955. When the infant mortality rate was much higher, perhaps every child was considered to be in almost as much jeopardy at birth as those born abnormally. However we interpret this change in custom, it shows the continuity in conceptualization of those born normally and abnormally, for both were thought of as needing perinatal protection and nurturance. Thus by examining the treatment of twins, prematures, and breech deliveries, we can learn more about the Gusii conception of normal birth and perinatal care.

When an abnormal birth occurs, Gusii see it first of all as a threat to the mother's reproductive career, a sign that death and destruction – or at least reproductive failure – will follow if a ritual is not performed to repair the relationship with her husband's deceased ancestors. This belief motivates Gusii parents to undertake an expensive and inconvenient ritual. Once the ritual has been completed, the test of its efficacy is whether the mother's next birth is a normal one, which would show that the family has nothing more to fear. In this context, the primary meaning of abnormal birth is its place in the mother's reproductive life and the spiritual life of the whole family; the welfare of the newborn child is not in focus. As the ritual unfolds, however, it becomes clear that the survival of the child or children is equally important and is the goal of many measures taken. Were the abnormally born child to die, this would be a disaster in itself. But the interests of the mother and her offspring are not separated in Gusii thought; it is rather the mother–infant unit that is the focus of ritual action.

The ritual (*enyangi*) can be divided into three phases: confinement with the placenta, seclusion after the placenta has been buried, and emergence (*ekiarokio*) from seclusion.

### Confinement with the placenta

As soon as the birth takes place, the mother and newborn(s) are seated next to her cooking fire and begin receiving visitors inside the house. With normal births, the placenta is buried immediately (or thrown into the latrine), whereas in a case of twins, breech delivery, or premature birth, the placenta is placed in a metal bowl and covered with leaves called *emesabakwa*, which are used in other Gusii transition rituals, notably initiation. Mother and newborn must remain inside the house (near the placenta) while there are visitors present who might see them, though the mother may emerge briefly under cover of darkness, when no one would be visiting. Neighbors and kin who visit may hold the babies, in the Gusii courtesy known as *ogokwania omwana*, "greeting the baby," so long as they are in the room with the mother and the placenta.

The father, meanwhile, has been notified of the abnormal birth and his arrival is awaited before the placenta is buried. If he is a migrant laborer who must come from a distance, the placenta is kept there for a day or more. Those who visit and greet the baby during this time may visit in the next phase, that is, after the placenta has been buried, *but no one else may.* The placenta covered by *emesabakwa* is understood to continue the protection previously afforded by the mother's womb, during a period of new risks presented by neighbors who might wish the babies ill and harm the babies simply by seeing them. These babies are more vulnerable to such ill will than those born normally, but the potential danger of specific persons is neutralized by their visitation during the period of placental protection, so that they may visit later on.

There is an unmistakable symbolic equivalence between the warm and protective house in which the mother and neonates are confined and the womb they have previously shared. The word for placenta in Gusii, *omogoye* (plural, *emegoye*) can be translated as "a binding" and is the word that denotes the bark strips that held together Gusii house frames before the advent of nails. The newborn is referred to as *mosamba mwaye,* "he who has burnt his own home," indicating that the baby cannot go back into the womb, but in the ritual drama the vulnerable baby does return to a symbolic womb in domestic confinement with his mother. The danger that forces this return is that of a potentially hostile interpersonal environment to which a small and abnormally delivered newborn would be even more susceptible than a large and normal one.

### Seclusion

After the placenta is buried, mother and infant(s) remain in the house as before, forbidden to emerge or to be seen in the house by anyone who was not there during the period of placental protection. The fire is to be kept going for their warmth, as in the initiation seclusion, and the mother is to be fed good food for her health and protection. She holds the babies most of the time and breast-feeds them frequently.

The father is now searching for an appropriate *omokorerani,* that is, a ritual officiant who herself has given birth to a child with the same abnormality and who has gone through training in performing ceremonies for others. Following her advice, he also procures a goat to be sacrificed in the next phase and the millet-beer that is to be drunk at that time. If he is poor, he will contact kinsmen for a loan for these expenditures. All this takes time and prolongs the period of seclusion, which in the three cases we observed lasted from 3 to 6 weeks. This length of time was not regarded as unusual, and it appears that about a month is an expectable period for the seclusion of a mother with her abnormally delivered newborn(s).

### Emergence

Once the father and the *omokorerani* have made all the necessary preparations, the ceremony of emergence can be performed. This is called *ekiarokio*, the ceremonial emergence from any ritual seclusion in the Gusii ritual system. It takes most of a day and involves a sacrifice to the ancestors, libations of millet-beer, and administration of protective medicines to mother and infants before their emergence. The mother must also hold up the babies to the sun, asking for protection, on the morning of the ceremony. A grass ring must encircle the house before the actual emergence. Every one of these elements is designed to strengthen mother and newborns physically as well as neutralize the interpersonal dangers that might threaten them when they are no longer in seclusion. The mood at the end of an *ekiarokio* is a cheerful one, indicating an ordeal that is over and a sense of relief that the infants have survived.

Informants said that in the past mothers were confined for a few days after normal births and held up their babies to the sun on emergence, as in the ritual for abnormal births. Thus twins, prematures, and breech presentations were not seen as anomalies totally discontinuous with normally born children, but simply as more vulnerable and requiring more ritual strengthening and protection, along with their mothers, whose reproductive careers were in jeopardy. The ritual for abnormal birth is a drama in which mother and newborns are strengthened bodily and spiritually against risks to their health from social and spiritual sources. Following the cultural script for this drama, Gusii parents provide an incubation – that is, a 1-month period of continuous holding and breast-feeding in a warm place – for small and vulnerable neonates that helps to safeguard the infant against postpartum risks to health and growth. Thus a Western pediatric assessment of Gusii care for babies of low birth weight suggests that, except for the withholding of colostrum for 12 hours, their rituals tend to enhance the likelihood of survival in the neonatal period.

## NAMING

According to Gusii tradition, the baby is given a personal name on the fourth day after birth, or when the umbilical cord falls off, after which it is no longer called *mosamba mwaye.* During the four days before naming, the mother is considered *omware,* a novice, thereby likening her situation to that of the newly circumcised girl or boy who is also confined in a house near a warm fire and fed good food to heal a genital wound from which blood has been lost. Some informants likened the naming ceremony to the *ekiarokio,* the ceremony of emergence from seclusion for initiated youth and mothers of twins. Early in the morning, the paternal grandmother holds the newborn child, shaves its head (or cuts the hair with scissors, by the 1970s), and then names it. Both parents are present as well as other women in the family, who hold the baby in turn and express hopes that the baby will acquire the virtuous qualities of the person after whom it has been named. (By the 1970s, parents who were practicing Catholics or Seventh-Day Adventists had given up this ceremony in favor of baptism according to their respective liturgical traditions.)

Gusii children are usually named after recently deceased local elders of the same sex, often but not necessarily those in the immediate lineage. When an old, well-known and respected man dies, a number of boys in the locality will be named after him in the next year or so; if no dignitaries have died that recently, the child may be named after a dead (patrilineal) grandparent or great-grandparent or even a deceased sibling. For a firstborn, the names are chosen by the paternal grandparents; the parents choose the names of subsequent children.

Traditional Gusii names fall into several groups based on their source of imagery: (1) female names of historical significance, referring to plants or geographical features seen by the Gusii people in their migration, probably during the 18th century, from the lake shore region to the north, where the Luo people live: *Moraa* (from *omoraa*, a plant), *Kerubo* (a swampy meadow), *Kemunto* (from *ekemunto*, the gulf), *Kwamboka* (from *okwamboka*, "to cross" referring to crossing the Kano Plain near the lake); (2) Luo names such as *Onyango, Ogembo, Ondieki*, and *Openda;* (3) names referring to circumstances of one's birth: for example, *Gesimba*, from *egesimba*, wildcat, a name given to a child whose mother accidentally gave birth in the forest, *Kerema*, from the word for cripple, a name given to a child born with disabling deformities of limbs; (4) names referring to the mother's reproductive history, that is, of losing children or being unable to conceive.[8] This last category is of particular interest here.

When a woman has lost a number of children in succession, she will call the next one born *Makori* (after *rikori*, a wide footpath where cattle are driven), *Nyabara* (after *ebara*, the Swahili loan word for road), or *Gesure* (after *egesure*, a top-knot left after shaving the head), and she will put the newborn in a basket (*ekeari*), go to a cowpath or road, and sit at a junction with some old women who ask those who pass to look at the baby and give it a (token) present, such as a penny. This is done from dawn to noon the day after birth; when the baby is ready to be named, a top-knot is left in the shaving, and one of the three names is used. This ritual is said to mobilize in a publicly visible symbolic action the community's support for the survival of this child, in order to counteract the ill will that killed the previous children.[9] As with the births of twins or a breech delivery, the exceptionally high infant mortality of a mother occasions a ritual form of protection, in this case marked by a special name.

An infant is also given a name by its mother's family; this is known as *erieta ria okogombia*, "praise name," or *erieta ri'ororera*, "name of the umbilical cord"; it is usually given by the maternal grandmother when she comes to "greet the child." This is the name that a person will be called when visiting the mother's kin, in adulthood as well as childhood, and its use, particularly by the maternal grandmother, is said to arouse unique feelings of emotional warmth.[10]

*Part III*

# Infant care and development in a
# Gusii community

# 6

## Infant care: Cultural norms and interpersonal environment

This chapter concerns how Gusii mothers define infant care – their shared assumptions about the tasks and standards involved – and examines the infant's interpersonal environment over the first 30 months of life. Age trends in the infant's social ecology are analyzed in relation to family characteristics and to developmental patterns measured by the Bayley Infant Scales.

### THE CULTURAL MODEL OF INFANT CARE

Despite their socioeconomic and religious differences, our sample families in Morongo varied little in how they defined the maternal role and its primary responsibilities. Their model of infant care largely replicated that of the preceding generation, whose norms and practices were recorded in the 1950s.[1] The *practices* of mothers had been affected by new scarcities as well as new resources. The new resources included blankets, which made it unnecessary to keep the cooking fire going all night, thus reducing the risks of burns; more clothing, keeping children warmer during the rainy season; bottles with nipples, making it unnecessary for child caregivers to force-feed babies from a calabash when the mother was absent; and the use of water from wells instead of streams. In other words, greater access to cash, imported consumer goods, and household improvements had brought a higher level of material welfare that reduced some of the risks to infants observable in the earlier study. Novel scarcities included firewood, still used for cooking but more difficult to obtain in densely inhabited settlements, and children to look after babies, now attending school during the years they formerly spent at home. Thus the material and social context of infant care in the 1970s differed from that of the 1950s.

In spite of these changes, the culture-specific shape of infant care was basically unmodified: Not a single sample mother failed to breast-feed her infant for at least a year, to sleep with the nursing baby every night, or to use children for daytime care-taking if and when they were available. Some mothers were better informed about infant nutrition and better able to improve their children's diet, as indicated in the next chapter, but there was no debate or evident diversity of opinion about the standards of infant care. The consensus of earlier generations remained intact.

In this section we attempt to explicate the assumptions underlying Gusii practices of the 1950s and 1970s as the commonsense model of infant care with which Gusii mothers operated at both periods but which were only partly formulated in verbal discourse or accessible to exegesis. Cultural models are, as Geertz[2] has proposed, simultaneously descriptive and normative: They are "models of" reality, beliefs about the way things are, and "models for" action, guides to appropriate behavior. Thus the Gusii model of infant care can be seen as a folk system of pediatric and educational thought – embodying premises about the determinants of infant survival and early learning – or as a folk system of ethics in the parent–child relationship. It is most appropriately seen as both knowledge and morality combined in a single customary formula – moralized knowledge.[3]

The assumptions that follow reconstruct the Gusii model of infant care from ethnographic evidence. The extent to which they guide maternal behavior is explored subsequently in the observational data.

First, a lactating mother and her breast-feeding child are interdependent and exclusive in their relations, to a degree that is unique in postnatal life and exceeded only by the relations between a pregnant woman and her unborn child. This resemblance is implied in the Gusii lexicon: The Gusii verb *okogonka* means "to give birth," and the closely related word *okogonkia* means "to suckle." In Gusii belief, the mother's presumed mutuality with her infant is evident from the fact that if the infant dies, the mother's future reproductive career is considered to be jeopardized, and ritual measures are required lest she lose future children (see Chapter 5). The infant's side of the interdependence is represented in the concept of the infant as a suckling with a unique place next to the mother in sleeping arrangements and a unique claim to be carried on her back. The exclusiveness of this arrangement is emphasized in Gusii thought: Once a child has a younger sibling, the child may not return to the breast or be carried on the mother's back. The possibility of breast-feeding two successive children simultaneously, even as a temporary expedient, is vehemently rejected by Gusii women. The uniqueness of the nursing infant's access to the mother's body has its counterpart in the position of the biological mother as the sole person responsible for the infant's welfare. It is assumed that no one could or would give the infant what his mother does in terms of physical nurturance and total concern for his survival. A well-known Gusii proverb grounds this in a visceral preference for one's own offspring: "Someone else's child is like cold mucous."[4] This means, according to Gusii informants, that wiping the mucous from the nose of a baby other than one's own would arouse disgust in a mother, although she does it for her own baby as part of routine care without experiencing that affect. The proverb seems to imply that a mother experiences her own infant as part of her body, and it legitimizes an aversion to caring for the infants of others.

Women will not suckle each other's children, and babies whose mothers die[5] or abandon them are in considerable jeopardy, as shown in the next chapter. It is not simply the prior fact of birth that is represented as motivating the mother's unique commitment to her biological child, but her sense that only children she has borne herself will enter into the long-term reciprocities that mothers are entitled to expect from their children. Orphans generously reared by others are believed to be ungrateful in adulthood, seeking affiliation with the kin of their biological mother and jural father in preference to those who sustained them when they were most in need. A Gusii proverb, endorsed as valid by a number of sample mothers, states: "Adopt an orphan calf rather than a human orphan,"[6] meaning that cows return milk to the owners who nurtured them as calves, but that human orphans become concerned with their socially defined parentage and will fail to reciprocate nurturance provided by nonparents in childhood.[7]

This concept of motherhood as an exclusive relationship between a woman and her offspring seems to be deeply felt by Gusii mothers as well as formulated in their culture. In the daytime, others may provide temporary care but they are not considered a substitute for the real mother. At the level of public norms, those who take responsibility for rearing a child from birth should be those who are entitled according to custom to expect reciprocation later in life, which means the biological mother and the man who has paid bridewealth for her. Others are reluctant to get involved, even when the mother dies, becomes ill, is called away for an emergency, or wants to seek her fortune in another consensual union. Thus, there is little flexibility in the social arrangements for Gusii infant care. This has the advantage of assuring most infants stable care by their mothers when they most need it, but its vulnerability lies in placing sole responsibility on a single person without providing socially or personally acceptable alternatives.

Second, the primary goal of infant care is survival, more specifically, the health and protection from harm required for the child's growth and development. In Gusii thought, infants are more vulnerable than adults because their skin is light in color and soft in texture, making it easily penetrated by particles that can lodge in the internal organs and kill the child. This lethal penetration can be caused by the malevolence of witches or by a form of involuntary "evil eye" called *ebibiriria*. To keep the skin free of particles, babies are washed and oiled daily (the protective cleansing is called *okongura*), and they are kept off the ground and carried as much as possible. Their growth occurs through the consumption of food, which makes "blood," and the body grows. The assumption is that if parents provide a protective and facilitating environment, including physical nurturance (i.e., adequate food, warmth, and protection against physical injury) in the context of the exclusive mother–infant relationship, then the infant will grow and develop normally without extensive parental intervention except for acute illness. Physical growth and motor development are seen primarily as health indicators, and receive more attention when they are abnormal or slow (providing negative feedback diagnostic of possible abnormalities) than when they are normal. When babies are ill, they are taken to indigenous healers or medical clinics. Encouragement for standing and walking, a traditional practice observed occasionally in the 1950s[8] and the 1970s, is not inconsistent with this noninterventive pattern, in the sense that it shows the concern with reaching those milestones but is not regarded as necessary for normal motor development.

This generally noninterventive stance and its concomitant sensitivity to signs of infant illness are not explicit in Gusii thought (e.g., in proverbs); they seem too obvious, too commonsensical to warrant formulation. It is our framework as outsiders that makes them noteworthy. We have termed this stance the "squeaky wheel" strategy of infant care, after the American proverb, "The squeaky wheel gets the grease." It is a naturalistic view of infant growth and development that mandates parental intervention primarily when something goes wrong.

Third, a mother is expected to be available to her infant (in ways specified in this chapter), to protect the baby from harm, respond to signs of distress, and alter her behavior selectively as the infant becomes more able to walk and communicate. This could be called the Gusii code of maternal conduct, but its precepts cannot be understood in the abstract but only as interpreted in specific Gusii contexts.

### Availability

A mother is expected to be near enough to her infant to attend to his needs whenever she is not working in the field or market. In the 1950s, women would weed eleusine with babies on their backs, carry babies on trading expeditions to markets 10 miles away, and have child caretakers bring infants to the fields they were hoeing for late morning periods of breast-feeding. By the 1970s, they were less likely to carry babies away from home at such times, because their fields were much smaller, the nearby market had expanded greatly, and there was usually someone at home who could take care of the baby for short periods of time (see the following discussion of child caretakers). Furthermore, the use of baby bottles by many mothers in the 1970s made it possible for them to leave babies at home for longer periods with something to drink and suck on without breast-feeding. On the whole, however, a mother was still expected to be near her baby – at home or away – whenever she was not engaged in activity that would make holding or carrying it impossible.

When the mother is not engaged in essential tasks, she should make herself available to the infant by holding, breast-feeding, co-sleeping, and comforting. She should also bathe, feed supplementary foods, permit the baby to play on her lap, and fall asleep on her body. Any mother who did not behave this way regularly and in an organized fashion would be considered remiss. Availability, however, does not include verbal and visual interaction. Gusii mothers are not *expected* to talk to or gaze at their infants or play with them, and mothers who are available in the aforementioned ways while keeping their visual and verbal attention focused elsewhere are not out of line with normative expectations. The extent to which Gusii mothers sing to and interact socially with their babies varies from one individual to another, but they are not under normative pressure to do so. Thus "availability" must be understood in terms of Gusii standards, not those of Western parents.

From the Gusii point of view, maternal availability has two most important components: breast-feeding and co-sleeping. The mother's duty to breast-feed her infant frequently each day is paramount, and she must organize her daily life so that this is always possible no matter what her workload. In a sense, co-sleeping is part of this mandate, for at night there is nothing to prevent the mother from making her breasts constantly available to the baby, and mothers sleep next to their infants with their breasts exposed, except when they are trying to wean. There is an explicit rule that a mother must never stay away from her infant overnight during the period of breast-feeding. Another basic assumption is that the baby is not put to bed separately at night but is free to fall asleep on the mother's body during the evening regardless of when she goes to sleep. Gusii do not emphasize the comfort infants get from these breast-feeding and sleeping arrangements, but they take it for granted. As they see it, nothing is so sure to comfort an infant as maternal holding and breast-feeding.

When an infant is ill, for example, with a fever, the mother is expected to depart from her work routine to hold the baby in her arms at home, all day if necessary, monitoring his condition until she decides a trip to the clinic is required. Thus she makes herself more available when she believes the baby needs it. Gusii women are devoted cultivators, but infant survival and comfort come first.

### Protection

The Gusii mother is fully responsible for the care of her infant, and protection from possible injuries is a major goal. The decline in physical hazards to infants and toddlers between the 1950s and 1970s is described in the following chapter, but the domestic setting is not free of risk. Thus Gusii mothers prefer to have babies carried on the back, sitting in the lap of the mother or a child caretaker, or kept on a small mat for sleeping and sitting. This restriction of the infant's movements, exploratory or otherwise, is regarded as an essential aspect of good care, to be enforced by the mother even when she has delegated daytime care to a child.

Constant physical protection of the infant is taken for granted. When it does not occur, however, the mother is blamed. One of our sample babies was dropped by her child nurse and suffered a dislocated shoulder. The young mother was not successful in getting the baby properly treated at the Kisii General Hospital, whereupon her husband came home from his place of work (100 miles away), saw to the baby's treatment, and furiously accused his wife of neglect. His indignation was based on the Gusii norm that a mother should constantly safeguard the physical well-being of her infant.

### Response to distress signals

The Gusii mother is expected to respond rapidly to the crying of her infant, by feeding and other soothing techniques, namely, holding and shaking. When she is not present, the child caretaker is expected to do that in her place. No virtue is seen in letting a baby cry; on the contrary, it is regarded as a disgrace. Gusii women have little tolerance for crying in a baby, particularly a very young one; they feel something must be done immediately to calm it.[9]

When we showed a group of our sample mothers a videotape of an American mother changing the diaper of her baby of a few weeks old, they became upset at the point where the baby was screaming on the changing table as the mother reached for and folded a clean diaper. From the Gusii point of view, a mother should know enough to clean her baby without that amount of unattended crying; they saw the American mother as incompetent. They were also startled by the sight of the same baby's grandmother holding the squalling infant for a while without being able to quiet it. One Gusii woman thought the grandmother was strangling the baby, but the others were simply amazed that a woman would not or could not soothe an infant immediately. This illustrates the Gusii assumption that the infant's cry demands a response intended to alleviate it and that a mother should be capable of doing so.

### Alteration of care with infant development

The Gusii mother is expected to be sensitive to certain aspects of her infant's development and to modify her care accordingly. These aspects are primarily physical growth (i.e., size and weight), the attainment of motor milestones (sitting, standing, walking), and disease symptoms (e.g., fever, cough, diarrhea), and they are monitored closely as indicators of health status. The squeaky wheel strategy is particularly relevant here, for the mother is sensitive to warning signals that would warrant giving more intense nurturance to her infant than she would ordinarily give to others of that age.

Thus an infant seen as very small should be fed more. An unusually small 1-year-old is considered not ready to do without a special child caregiver assigned to him, though a larger 1-year-old is considered ready. A child who reaches 16 or 17 months but is smaller than others should be kept on the breast a month or so longer, whereas those deemed to be of normal size would be weaned at that time. Delays in attaining motor milestones and recurrent bouts of respiratory disease have the same conclusion: more holding and other physical care, more feeding, delayed weaning. The feeding and protection of the exclusive mother–infant relationship constitute the solution Gusii mothers have at hand and believe in for the survival risks they are monitoring in infancy.

Extreme cases support this rule: A hydrocephalic child observed in the 1950s and a child with a serious metabolic deficiency observed in the 1970s, both of whom never became capable of standing or walking, were constantly held and fed (when they would take food) long after the normal age of weaning.

If all goes well with the health and the growth of the child, according to Gusii standards of size and motor competence, then the mother is free to diminish the intensity of maternal nurturance, letting the toddler join the older children of the household without an assigned caregiver – an expected transition from what Margaret Mead called being a "lap" child to being a "yard" child – or weaning him from the breast, signaling the end of the exclusive relationship with the mother. When these steps are taken, the mother can feel she has done her best for this child and is ready to bear another – with whom she may already be pregnant.

The development of the infant's cognitive, communicative, and emotional capacities – apart from their role in normal health and growth – is not high on the Gusii developmental agenda for the infancy period. There is the assumption that if the mother provides continual responsive care, based on the principles outlined above and modified by the emerging growth and motor skills of the infant – with particular attention to any perceived health risks – then the child's behavioral responses will fit in accordingly and pose no special problem. In any event, serious attempts to train and talk to the child are largely postponed until after weaning, when the child is believed to be capable of conversing, and mothers are not expected to concern themselves with infant behavior *as such* until then.

This code of maternal conduct – covering availability, protection, responsiveness to distress, and age-graded care – reflects Gusii concern with infant survival and the mother's workload in the context of the exclusive mother–infant relationship. It presumes a natural fertility schedule in which that relationship will end, in its exclusiveness, with the birth of the next child.

Fourth and finally, the child is expected to adapt compliantly to the predictable transitions of the second year of life, namely, weaning from the breast, the birth of a sibling, and reduced access to maternal attention. There is the expectation that infants after 12 months will be relatively quiet and easily soothed, not only by the mother but also by older children. It is assumed that weaning may occasion temporary distress and increased crying but that toddlers will find consolation with the other children of the home and reduce their expectancies for maternal attention well in advance of the birth of a sibling when they are 21 to 23 months old (in our 1970s sample; the birth interval was longer in the past). This assumption is explicitly revealed in its most typical (though infrequent) breach, that is, when a toddler has spent the postweaning period (between 18 and 24 months) with its maternal grandmother, returning after the mother has a new baby to care for. Should the 2-year-old act in a clingy, demanding way, for example, running after the mother when she is taking the baby to the clinic, the mother will become angry, not only with the child but with her own mother, whom she views as having encouraged excessive expectations for attention.

The impact of the birth succession on compliance expectations during the second year is similarly revealed by the concept of *omokogooti,* the lastborn, who is expected to be weaned later and "spoiled" by extra maternal attention, because the risks of a less compliant child are minimized by the fact that there is no successor.

The burden for the Morongo mother in caring for infants for at least two decades while cultivating the soil and managing the household is a great one, particularly by the 1970s, when reduced birth intervals meant that a woman had more small children at one time. With little cooperation among adult women, her only source of relief is the *omoreri,* the child nurse who cares for a baby in the daytime.

## SUBSTITUTE CARE: THE *OMORERI*

*Omoreri* (plural: *abareri*), from the verb *okorera,* "to take care of," simply means "caregiver" in the Gusii language. It is understood as referring to a child, usually a closely related girl, who cares for the baby for periods during the daytime when the mother is busy with other tasks. The mother is not an *omoreri,* though she cares for the baby; her role is presumed as uniquely important, with the child nurse as only a partial substitute. In this sense *omoreri* is roughly equivalent to the American term *baby-sitter.* The *omoreri,* however, is most often younger and has a longer relationship with the infant.

Though Gusii mothers used *abareri* as much in the 1970s as in the 1950s, there were many differences in how this system of substitute care worked. At both periods young children available for this purpose were in short supply. In the 1950s it was largely a matter of who was available to the mother through her immediate kin network: Her own daughters were her first choice, followed by her young sisters, who could be sent from her natal home, then her younger sons, and finally anyone else in the homestead – other young children and occasionally an infirm elder. Young mothers, with one or two children, would not have any of their own children who were old enough to act as *omoreri* and would have to get someone else. Even if they had daughters, those who had been initiated (circumcised) at 8 or 9 years of age were thereby promoted to cultivation and food-processing and were exempted from further infant care. Boys herded cows, sheep, and goats. Thus 4 of the 24 mothers in the 1956 sample had had no *omoreri* at all, taking care of the sample child as an infant without help.[10]

The *omoreri* role in the 1950s was defined as a full-time responsibility, to be carried out every day, whenever the mother was away from the house, at least until the baby could walk and in some cases until the baby was 2 years of age. This stabilized the infant's substitute caregiver, but it also made the job so onerous that, for the most part, no one did it who did not have to, and girls looked forward eagerly to initiation so that they could stop being *abareri*. This created a scarcity of help with infant care, and meant that most *abareri* were young children, aged 5 to 9 years old, who had no claim to more elevated forms of work.

By the 1970s mothers faced a changed situation. On the one hand, children were supposed to attend school beginning at 6 years of age, and a great many of them did, thus depriving their parents of their labor during the school hours. On the other hand, their labor was less needed in cultivation (because plots were smaller), in fetching water (because some families had wells), and in herding animals (because there were no sizable herds, only a few high-yield cows). It was still needed in infant care, but that task combined least well with school attendance.

Mothers adapted to the new situation in a variety of ways: keeping girls out of school until age 8 so they could serve as *abareri,* getting an *omoreri* from their parents' home (if they happened to come from a place where schoolgoing was less prevalent than in Morongo), insisting that girls act as *abareri* after school and postponing certain tasks until that time, and – in the case of wealthier families – hiring children of the poor to serve as child nurses. Dispensing with a strict definition of the *omoreri,* mothers took what help they could get from their children in the way of infant care: using them part-time and on holidays, sharing the task among several daughters (including those much older than the former *omoreri* role permitted), and abbreviating the period during which the infant had an assigned substitute caregiver. In the 1950s a baby either had an *omoreri* or did not, and that person cared for the baby for a long time, but in the 1970s this clarity no longer existed.

Table 6.1. *Substitute caregivers in the 1950s and 1970s*

|  | 1955–1957 Nyansongo sample ($n = 24$) | 1974–1976 Longitudinal sample ($n = 28$) |
|---|---|---|
| Sister | 12 | 12 |
| Brother | 2 | 3 |
| Father's sister | 2 | 2 |
| Other kin (15 or under) | 3 | 1 |
| Other kin (adult) | 1 | 0 |
| Hired caregiver | 0 | 2 |
| No stable *omoreri* | 4 | 8 |

Table 6.1 compares *omoreri* arrangements for the two samples of children studied 20 years apart.

These distributions look quite similar, except that a greater variety of kin were recruited in the 1950s, and the idea of hiring and paying an unrelated *omoreri* was new in the 1970s. The bigger differences are not shown on the table: All of the 1950s *abareri* were full-time, whereas only 20% (4 of 20) in the 1970s were. The others went to school from 8 a.m. to 1 p.m. and did their infant care afterward. Furthermore, in the 1950s all the *abareri* were under 10 years of age – the exception being an infirm man in his 70s who took care of a grandchild – whereas those of 20 years later included two 15-year-old girls; otherwise they were all between 6 and 11, with a median age of 8.

The other eight sample infants, those without stable *abareri*, were either cared for exclusively by their mothers or by an unstable variety of older siblings and other kin. Some of the mothers having no assistance were heavy drinkers, whose households were among the least well organized in Morongo.

Gusii child nurses, whether or not they are stable *abareri*, operate under a maternal mandate to protect the baby from harm, largely by holding, and to respond rapidly to distress with soothing and feeding. Their duty, in effect, is to follow the maternal code of conduct as much as they can, given the fact that they are not mothers and cannot breast-feed. They are not, for the most part, instructed to play with the baby, although they are free to do so according to Gusii kinship norms, and mothers *expect* that the *omoreri* will play with the baby. This freedom and expectation notwithstanding, our observations indicate that Gusii children are often remarkably quiet as infant caregivers and that they go for long periods of time without talking to, playing with, or otherwise stimulating their charges. Thus the Gusii infant's social contacts are too variable – across individuals, situations, and age – to predict simply from ethnographically derived norms; it is necessary to determine their actual distributions through systematic observation.

## SPOT OBSERVATIONS: A LONGITUDINAL INVENTORY OF CARE

The spot observation technique originated in a study of infant care conducted by Munroe and Munroe[11] among the Logoli (Maragoli) people, who live about 100 miles north of the Gusii in western Kenya. Its purpose was to collect frequency data, unbiased by reactions to the observer's visit, on the situations of infant care in the home. To collect a spot observation, the observer approaches the homestead and takes a "mental photograph" of what was going on before his or her presence was noticed, recording information on: the location of the infant; whether and by whom the infant was held; the location and activity of people within 10 feet of the infant; the location, identity, and activity of the mother and caretaker; and the personal cleanliness of the infant. The technique is particularly well suited to the dispersed settlement pattern in East Africa, with much family activity occurring out of doors, visible to an approaching visitor before greetings take place.

In our study the spot observation technique was selected as the means of monitoring the environments of our 28 sample infants over the period of longitudinal data collection. The following information was collected on the infants: their physical location; their position (e.g., sitting, standing, being held); who was holding them; their level of activity (asleep, awake) and type of activity (e.g., feeding, playing, locomoting, crying), state (unhappy, neutral, happy), and focus (e.g., a person or object). For the infants' mothers, the *omoreri,* and others present, information was recorded concerning actual distance from the infant, activity, state, and focus. A list of the categories for coding these records appears in Appendix A.

The spot observations were done by Joseph Obongo, a Gusii high school graduate and resident of the Morongo area, who knew most members of the sample families by name. A randomized schedule for observation was devised by Constance Keefer and Suzanne Dixon. Observations were done at all times of the day from dawn until dark, although not all times were observed equally. For each observation, the observer wrote a narrative description that included information about the categories presented in Appendix A. If either the infant or the mother was not present at the homestead, every effort was made to locate them according to the observation schedule. This produced some observations collected away from the homestead. In some cases data on the mother's location and activity are missing. The sample children were monitored in this way over time periods ranging from 11 to 15 months, the shorter periods representing those infants who were added to the sample last.

An average of 80.8 spot observations was collected per infant; the range was from 50 to 102. Data from the observational records were subsequently coded and prepared for computer analyses by six coders who had not been involved in the data collection.[12] In order to generate age profiles of the parameters of the infants' environments from 0–3 months until 27–30 months, data from the three cohorts of infants are combined.

### THE INFANT SOCIAL ENVIRONMENT: DENSITY AND COMPOSITION

The Gusii infant is never left alone, day or night, in the sense that there is always someone in charge who is close enough to see her or hear her cries. Figure 6.1 shows how many people are close enough to the child (within 5 feet) to be easily available for social contact or caregiving in the daytime, over the first 2 1/2 years of life. It presents the mean percentage of spot observations in which zero, one to two, and three to four people were within 5 feet, for all sample infants at each age level.

The proportion of observations in which no one is within 5 feet of the child never rises above 22.5% during the entire period. In other words, in at least three-quarters of the observations over the first 30 months of life, the child is within 5 feet of another person. The age trends are informative: The proportion of obser-

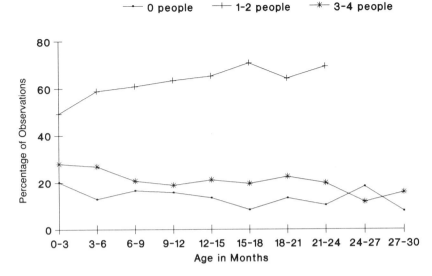

6.1 Social density: Number of people within 5 feet of infant, by age.

vations with one or two people within 5 feet of the child shows a linear increase with age ($r = .31, p < .01$), while being near 3 or four people decreases with age ($r = -.38, p < .01$). Being near no one shows two peaks – one in the first 3 months, when the baby sleeps a great deal and is put down on a mat, the other during 18–21 months, when the child has been weaned but the mother has not given birth again.

Much of the time (i.e., between 50% and 70%) the number of persons within 5 feet is one or two; only during the first 9 months do more than 20% of the observations show three or four persons that near. The latter curve declines steadily from 28.0% in the 0–3-month period.

That the youngest infants have the largest number of people near them reflects two factors. One is the Gusii custom of "greeting" a newborn (*ogokwania omwana*): The women of the vicinity, and kinswomen from farther away, come to share in the enjoyment of birth by visiting the mother and holding the baby during the first few months. This is perhaps the only time in a Gusii infant's life when the baby is at the center of attention of adults other than his mother and *omoreri*. The other factor is that the infant is being held so much in these early months (see Figure 6.4)

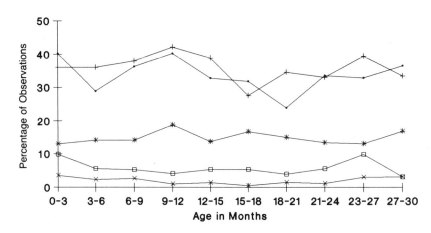

6.2 Categories of people within 5 feet of infant, by age of infant.

and is thus in proximity to those people with whom the person holding him is conversing. Most of the time after 6 months, however, Gusii infants have one or two persons in their immediate surround.

Figure 6.2 shows who the persons within 5 feet are, by five categories: mothers, female children, male children, fathers, and female adults. Male adults other than the father were so rarely near the babies that they have been omitted from the graph; fathers were also rarely seen in proximity to their offspring. In general, female children are the ones most frequently close to the babies, and mothers are second, with male children and female adults substantially lower in frequency. The drop in proximate female children between 12 and 15 months might reflect a decline in *omoreri* attention. Maternal proximity drops substantially between 9 and 18 months, as the mother judges that the growing baby can do without her more. It rises at around 2 years, when the mother's new pregnancy and childbirth force her to spend more time at home again – making her available to be approached by the sample child, though not nurtured as before.

The visitors greeting the newborn and his replacement (as a newborn) are shown in the two peaks of female adult proximity:

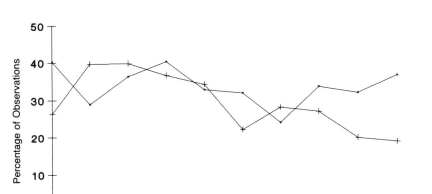

6.3 Proximity of mother and *omoreri* to infant (within 5 feet), by age of infant.

one at 0 to 3 months, the other at 24 to 27 months – roughly defining the birth interval.

Thus this crude inventory of persons near the baby in the daytime indicates some major events and transitions during infancy and early childhood. The Gusii infant is rarely farther than 5 feet from another person when awake, but is usually with only one or two others – most frequently female children and the mother. The high frequencies for these two categories during the first year (Figure 6.2) and their decline afterward suggest that caregiving is concentrated in the first year.

## CAREGIVERS AND TYPES OF CARE

Figure 6.3 shows for mother and *omoreri* the proportion of time each was within 5 feet of the infant, divided by the total observations for each. Unlike the female children shown on the previous graph, the *omoreri*'s frequency within 5 feet remains lower than that of the mother after the 21- to 24-month period. The baby has been weaned between 15 and 18 months and the daughter who had served as *omoreri* is no longer responsible for him (though

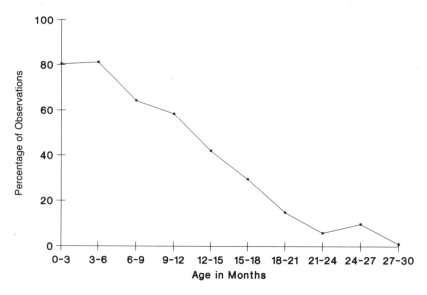

6.4 Holding of Gusii infants: frequency by age.

she is present), and he now spends time close to other girls as well. Thus the proximity pattern of the *omoreri* is distinct from, and more time-limited than, that of other female children.

The proximity data shown in this figure suggest that the *omoreri*'s duties begin seriously during the 3- to 6-month period, when the mother is recovered from the delivery and feels confident enough in the *omoreri* to leave the baby with her for longer periods of time. This is an age at which infants sleep much and are easily managed, and the mother is trying to catch up on tasks postponed when she was at home with the newborn. Thus she takes advantage of the opportunity to get some work done while the *omoreri* stays at home with the baby on her back. Although the mother's time spent near the baby increases after that, the *omoreri*'s proximity remains fairly constant from the 3–6- to the 12–15-month periods – that is, during most of the breast-feeding period. The *omoreri*'s care after that decreases significantly ($r = -.26, p < .01$). Maternal proximity rises, beginning at 21 to 24 months, reflecting the birth of the next child and the immediate postpartum period at home, where the toddler is. Taken as a whole, Figure 6.3 shows a generally complementary distribution between care by mother and *omoreri* during most of the first 2 years.

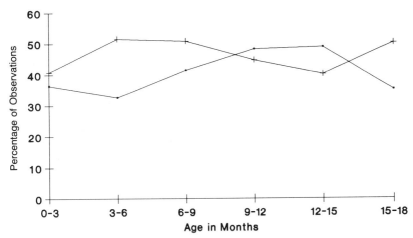

6.5 Holding of Gusii infants: by caregivers.

Holding (including carrying) is a major aspect of infant care among the Gusii. Figure 6.4 shows its age distribution in the sample. In the first 6 months Gusii babies are held all the time they are awake (80% of the observations), and the proportion of daytime they are held decreases sharply and consistently thereafter until 2 years of age ($r = -.86, p < .01$). From a cross-cultural perspective, however, it is remarkable how much they are held after they can walk. At 12 to 15 months, for example, when all the sample children could walk, they were being held in 42% of the observations, and at 15 to 18 months in about 30%. This shows that – in the absence of cribs, carriages, and playpens – holding children on the back or in the arms is the protective device of choice for the Gusii, and it is used for toddlers because they are mobile and are considered to be at risk for injuries. It also reflects the comfort Gusii children have learned to experience when they are being carried.

Most holding (80%–90% at all ages) is done by the mother and *omoreri*; their proportions of all holding at each age are shown in Figure 6.5. After the 3- to 6-month period, the proportion of maternal holding increases slowly until the 15- to 18-month period, when weaning is begun. The proportion of *omoreri* holding

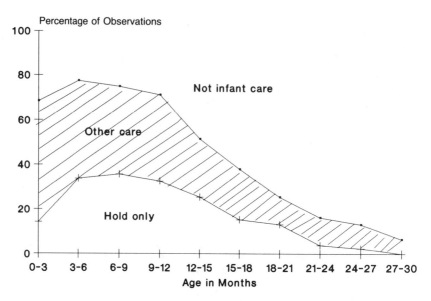

6.6 Mother's infant care as a percentage of all of her activities, by age of infant.

declines between the 6- to 9- and 12- to 15-month periods, presumably because the baby is being held less when not being breast-fed once he can walk, but it rises at 15 to 18 months, in apparent compensation for the mother's sharp drop at that time. (There is very little holding after 18 months.)

In order to understand better what is happening during the second year of life, particularly around the time of weaning, it is necessary to analyze the mother's activity in more detail. Figure 6.6 shows the distribution of maternal activities, that is, the proportion of observations on mothers in which they were engaging in physical care of all types (breast-feeding, cleaning, dressing), and holding without physical care. (In the other observations they were engaged in noninfant-related activities, e.g., agricultural and household work, but this is not shown.) A mother's infant-related activities as a proportion of her total activities decline steadily and significantly from about 70% at 3 to 6 months to 5.6% at 27 to 30 months; this decrease is seen both in Holding Only ($r$ with infant age $= -.42$, $p < .01$) and in Physical Care ($r$ with infant age $= -.58$, $p < .01$). In the early peak of these activities (3 to 9 months), the mother has returned to cultivation

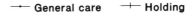

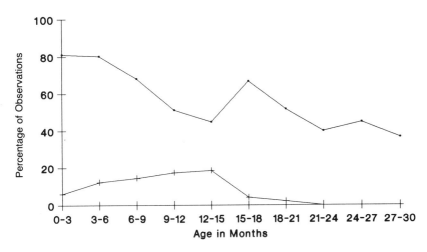

6.7 *Omoreri*'s infant care as a percentage of all of her activities, by age of infant.

(outside the immediate vicinity of the house) and is more dependent on the *omoreri*; that is, the mother is near the infant less, as shown on Figure 6.3, but when there, she is more likely to attend to him (Figure 6.5).

Physical Care and Holding Only, however, decline steeply after the 9- to 12-month period, that is, the period at which walking has been accomplished and can be taken for granted. In the 6 months prior to weaning (i.e., from 9 to 12 months to 15 to 18 months), the proportions of Physical Care and Holding Only by the mother are reduced by half, Holding Only goes from 25.5% of maternal activity at 9 to 12 months to 13.1% at 15 to 18 months, and Physical Care from 23.2% to 12.5% over the same period. We believe this reflects both the mother's belief that her child's motor skills show the baby is healthy enough to need less attentive care and her conviction that he should be prepared for the birth of the next child by maintaining greater distance from the mother.

In Figure 6.7 the *omoreri*'s activities are shown in a similar way, that is, as proportions of total activity spent in Holding and General Care. The latter means both physical care and social interaction, because engaging the baby socially is regarded as an acceptable and useful part of the *omoreri*'s role. Holding shows an expectable drop after the 12- to 15-month period, but General Care, while declining with age over infancy as a whole, rises at 15 to 18 months and then declines afterward. Though the *omoreri* does a larger proportion of all the holding done at this age, as seen in Figure 6.5, Figure 6.7 shows that holding as a proportion of all *omoreri* activities decreases sharply – in accordance with the drop in *omoreri* proximity seen in Figure 6.3. In other words, the *omoreri* seems to switch from proximal to distal contact at this point, suggesting an acceleration in social interaction as opposed to physical care during weaning. This may help the young child over the social and emotional transition precipitated by weaning and preceded by the mother's distancing (shown in Figure 6.6).

### VARIATIONS IN CARE:
### SOCIOECONOMIC CONDITIONS

In order to determine what might account for individual differences in the care patterns of the sample infants, we conducted a statistical analysis of possible relationships between spot observation variables and parental socioeconomic and attitudinal variables. Very few relationships emerged. (There were no differences by sex of child.) The only consistent set is shown in Table 6.2. There it can be seen that the frequency of nonmaternal care after 9 months, as indicated by proximity and holding, correlates strongly with the amount of land cultivated by the mother and the number of daughters she has. Both proximity and holding frequencies are highly correlated with land and daughters at 15 to 18 months, the weaning period. This means that at that period those mothers who have more land are leaving their babies at home more, depending on how many daughters they have to share the infant care.

We interpret this as signifying that the mother is doubly motivated to be away from home during the 15- to 18-month period: She thinks it will facilitate the baby's weaning process and she wants to work on her land now that the baby needs her less. The more land she has, the more likely some of it is at a distance, which means she *must* be away from home. The more daughters she has, the easier it is to delegate care and stay away longer cultivating the land.

Table 6.2. *Relationships of nonmaternal day care to socioeconomic factors*

| Age of child (in months) | Nonmaternal care (frequency of) | Amount of land cultivated | Number of daughters |
|---|---|---|---|
| 9–12 | Proximity | | .58* |
| ($n = 20$) | Holding | | |
| 15–18 | Proximity | .70* | .63* |
| ($n = 17$) | Holding | .90* | .86* |
| 21–24 | Proximity | .52* | .48* |
| ($n = 13$) | Holding | – | – |

*Note:* There were too few observed instances of holding at 21–24 months to calculate correlations.
*Spearman's rho:* * $p < .01$

The same factors operate at other ages once the mother believes her baby has surmounted the worst risks of infancy and is progressing normally. Thus mothers with more daughters leave their infants with others more at 9 to 12 and 21 to 24 months too, and the amount of land cultivated is correlated with nonmaternal care at the latter age point.

Nothing could better illustrate the predicament of the Gusii mother in balancing agricultural work with infant care than this finding. Her commitment to infant survival keeps the mother heavily involved during the first year, a partial exception being those women with many daughters to share the care. Once weaning is under way, she spends more time in cultivation, depending on how much land there is and how much help she can count on at home. Women with more land are fortunate, but they work harder. Women with more daughters have to feed them, but they free her to work more.

### THE CARE AND DEVELOPMENT OF GUSII INFANTS

This chapter has shown that Gusii mothers operate with indigenous standards of infant care attuned to infant survival and to their own family situations. It is particularly their workload as food producers, their lack of assistance from anyone but their own children, and their expectation of the next birth that stand out as constraints on their behavior as mothers. At the same time, their concept of infant care as a strategy for survival dictates that they concentrate their own time and energy and that of their older children on the first year of life and progressively diminish the infant's dependence during the second year if physical growth and motor development are normal. This way, a healthy child can be raised during the birth interval.

We have interpreted the diminution of maternal proximity, holding and physical care between 9 and 15 months, as shown in Figures 6.3 and 6.6, as a deliberate distancing by the mother to prepare the child psychologically for weaning and later, replacement. Is this hypothesis necessary? Is not the diminution adequately explained by the mother's judgment, based on her observation of physical growth and motor development, that the child's future is no longer in jeopardy and warrants less time that she could allocate to other tasks? Although Gusii mothers are not explicit about psychologically preparing their own children, there is evidence that they have this in mind and in fact see it as part of their strategy for minimizing time devoted to infant care and gaining time for cultivation. They believe that toddlers who receive "too much" attention, for example, those who have spent time with their maternal grandmothers, come to expect it and interfere with their mother's work routines. Grandmothers "spoil" by staying home with the child too much, giving him what he wants when he asks for it. The child returns home unwilling to let the mother go away without him and demanding food and other things instead of waiting for them. In talking about these well-known errors of grandmothers, Gusii mothers show that they operate with a great deal of insight about how attention affects the expectations of children in the second year of life. As they are determined to avoid the troubles of grandmother-reared children, they tend to anticipate the problem and keep the expectations of their children within bounds.

A system of child care that is successful in its own terms may nevertheless exact a price that goes unrecognized by those who pay it. In the Gusii case, the question is whether a price is not paid for concentrating care more on early than later infancy. We have shown the diminution of caregiving in the second year. Figure 6.8

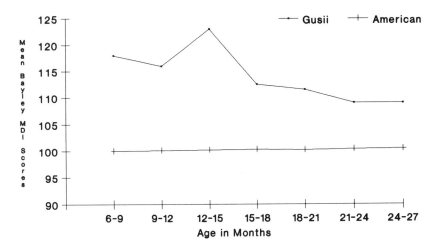

6.8 Mean Bayley MDI scores for Gusii and American infants at 3-month intervals.

Table 6.3. *Relationships between caregiving and Bayley Infant Test performance*

|  | 0–12 months (n = 12) | | 12–24 months (n = 14) | |
|---|---|---|---|---|
|  | MDI | PDI | MDI | PDI |
| *Mother* |  |  |  |  |
| Holding | NS | NS | .46[a] | NS |
| Physical care | NS | NS | .56[a] | NS |
| Combined | NS | NS | .39 | NS |
| *Omoreri* |  |  |  |  |
| Holding | −.56[a] | NS | .44 | NS |
| Physical care | NS | NS | NS | NS |
| Combined | NS | NS | .38 | NS |
| *Mother, omoreri and all others* |  |  |  |  |
| Holding | NS | NS | .39 | NS |
| Physical care | NS | NS | .65[b] | NS |
| Combined | NS | NS | .37 | NS |

Spearman rank-order correlations: [a]$p < .05$; [b]$p < .01$

is a graph based on the Bayley Mental Development Index (MDI) scores for the sample children. The Gusii sample scores above U.S. norms at every age level, but there is a sharp and steady decline after the 12- to 15-month age period. Is maternal behavior implicated in the decline of the MDI?

Table 6.3 shows higher MDI scores in the second year associated with more holding and physical care by the mother. In other words, during the period when maternal attention is scarce, those children who receive more of it perform at a higher level on the Bayley test. This does not answer the question, because the Bayley test cannot be interpreted as a universal measure of stable competence in young children, but it is interesting. To pursue the matter, we need to examine in greater detail the patterns of physical growth and social interaction.

# 7

## Survival and health:
## Priorities for early development

The first priority of Gusii parents is to provide an infant with the nurturance and protection to survive in the face of risks presented by physical hazards, infectious diseases, and seasonal food shortages. Gusii customs of infant care, as interpreted in the previous chapter, reflect an adaptive strategy for minimizing the survival risks and promoting physical growth in the first years of life, within a context of high marital fertility. The extent to which they actually achieve these goals is examined in this chapter. In considering whether folk practices of reproduction and infant care operate as an adaptive system, we pose three questions: (1) Do these practices normally result in adaptive outcomes, namely, increased probabilities of infant survival, as indicated by body size, physical growth, and motoric/behavioral maturation? (2) Are they responsive to variations in the age and health status of infants? (3) Are they responsive to environmental changes, for example, in the availability of food or medical care? We also consider the vulnerability of these practices, that is, the conditions under which they permit infant health and survival to be jeopardized.

In the mid-1970s, when the evidence presented here was collected, environmental risks to child survival in Gusiiland had changed from their values of 20 years earlier; this change must be taken into account in any assessment of the adaptiveness of infant care customs. During the 1974–1976 period, in general, food shortages posed more of a risk to infant health and survival than in earlier times. Infectious diseases and physical hazards constituted less risk than they had before. In the 1950s, more Morongo families owned cattle and therefore had cow's milk available for supplemental feeding to infants and children. Families had more land to cultivate, and devoted more of it to nutritious food crops such as millet, green vegetables, and beans. Though there was a "hungry season" before the harvest, the food supply was less endangered than it was to become. Indeed, by the 1970s, hospitality customs had changed so that it was tolerable in Morongo for someone to offer a visitor the excuse of having no food as an apology for not feeding him, whereas in the 1950s, this would have been considered disgraceful. Furthermore, at the earlier time, more eleusine – the African "finger millet" rich in calcium – was cultivated and fed to infants as their gruel. By 1974, the use of plastic bottles with rubber nipples had made the supplementary feeding of babies easier than before, but the gruel was most frequently based on less nutritious maize. Proprietary formulas and tea mixed with cow's milk were used by a minority of mothers.

Infectious diseases were less of a threat than they had been earlier, though this must be qualified by the apparently greater prevalence of malnutrition, which makes children less resistant to infection. Typhoid epidemics, frequent during the rainy seasons of the 1950s before latrines were widely used, did not occur in the 1970s when most homesteads had pit latrines. (A cholera epidemic in western Kenya during November 1974 was stopped by mass immunization before it reached Morongo, indicating the effectiveness of disease control at that time.) Many children in Morongo had been immunized against measles, diphtheria, whooping cough, and tetanus at a local clinic or in a rural immunization campaign. Respiratory disorders – always widespread in the cold highland climate – and measles remained threats to child health, but less so since the advent of warmer clothing for small children and the greater availability of clinics with antibiotics for primary and secondary infections. Mosquitoes had made their way into the Morongo area – apparently due to the collapse of colonial restrictions controlling their spread – and malaria posed a new threat to children there. On the whole, however, the threat of infectious disease to infant and child survival had been lessened.

Physical hazards to infants and toddlers had also been reduced. In the 1950s, indoor cooking fires presented a danger to small children because during the colder times of the year, they were kept going all night for the warmth of the family, which slept near the hearth. Toddlers sometimes fell into the fire when the family was rising in the morning; this was an all-too-familiar phenomenon. By the 1970s, however, the scarcity of firewood had made all-night fires impractical, and warmer blankets had been purchased by Morongo families, some of whom had also built kitchens separate from their sleeping quarters. Thus the probability of accidental burning had been reduced. Similarly, with fewer cattle around, there was less danger that children would be trampled. But families still lived on hillsides in houses with earthen floors and did not consider the physical environs safe enough to permit free exploration by infants.

The diets and diseases of children in Morongo are described later in this chapter. At this point, however, it is most important to bear in mind that although many of the most obvious threats to survival, particularly from epidemics of infectious disease, had been substantially lessened in the two decades preceding our study, the more insidious factor of an inadequate food supply presented an increasing – though often invisible – challenge to Gusii parents in caring for their children.

Gusii infant and child mortality was declining between 1974 and 1976. The deaths of children 2 years or less to mothers aged 20 to 24 in Kisii District declined almost 25% during the decade 1969–1979.[1] As Moseley[2] has suggested for Kenya as a whole, however, in Morongo this improvement was not evenly distributed among families within the population. Mass immunization campaigns and other preventive public health measures may affect all equally, but other critical factors – economic resources, health information and motivation, the stability of caretaking arrangements – vary from one family to another: Mothers with more cash are better able to buy milk and other foods for their babies, provide them with warm clothing, and pay the bus fares to take them to clinics. Mothers with more schooling or sophistication may use medical services, as well as dietary and sanitary measures promoting child health, more frequently and effectively. Infants whose mothers die, leave home without them, or neglect them due to personal disorganization may not be well cared for by those who take the mother's place. As families become increasingly differentiated by socioeconomic and social stress variables, then, so are the probabilities of child survival.

## NEONATAL PHYSICAL AND BEHAVIORAL CHARACTERISTICS

Examining the Gusii reproductive system from the viewpoint of the child, our first question must be: What is the health status of the

Table 7.1. *Infant anthropometrics at times of neonatal examination*

Infant characteristics

| Parameter (reliability) | No. of Ss | Mean | S.D. | Range |
|---|---|---|---|---|
| Age:  Exam 1 (early) | 15 | 2.2 days | – | 1–3 |
|       Exam 2 (middle) | 24 | 5.5 days | – | 4–7 |
|       Exam 3 (late) | 24 | 10.0 days | – | 9–12 |
| Weight (± .2Kg) | | | | |
|       "Birth" exam | 15 | 3.49 | ±0.42 | 3.0–4.4 |
|       Exam 2 | 24 | 3.68 | ±0.58 | 2.9–4.4 |
|       Exam 3 | 24 | 3.79 | ±0.41 | 3.1–4.9 |
| Length (± 1.5cm) | 22 | 50.0 | ±2.17 | 46.9–54.6 |
| Head circumference (± .5 cm) | 23 | 35.1 | ±1.56 | 33.0–39.4 |
| Gestational age (wks)[a] | 24 | 40.9 | ±0.85 | 39.5–42.5 |
| Percent weight for age[b] | 24 | 37% | ±24% | 3–90% |
| Ponderal Index[c] | 24 | 2.84 | ±0.24 | 2.53–3.49 |

[a]Calculated by the method of Dubowitz and Dubowitz
Validity established at ± 0.5 wks.
[b]Relative to standard intrauterine growth established by Lubchenco.
[c] $\dfrac{\text{wt (gms)}}{\text{length (cm)}^3} \times 100$
*Source:* Dixon, Keefer, Tronick, and Brazelton (1982).

Gusii infant at birth? The 24 Morongo infants born to the pregnant mothers described in Chapter 4 were examined several times during the first 10 days after birth. Table 7.1 shows their measurable physical characteristics. With an average "birth" weight of 3.49 kilograms (about 7.7 lbs.) and a mean length of 50 centimeters (22.7 inches), they were, by Western pediatric standards, good-sized neonates who lost very little weight during the first days of life, remained well hydrated, and showed no stigmata of the infant who is small for gestational age. Their impressive size and healthy appearance at birth are particularly remarkable in light of their mothers' health and diet problems noted in Chapter 5.

There were individual differences in these characteristics, and Table 7.2 shows how they correlate with maternal factors. Pregnancy weight change (i.e., maternal weight gain during the third

Table 7.2. *Correlations of maternal factors with infant physical characteristics*

| | Infant Factors | | | | | | |
|---|---|---|---|---|---|---|---|
| Maternal factors | Birth weight | Length | Head circumference | Gestational Age | % wt./G.A. | Ponderal index | Postnatal weight gain |
| Age | | | $-.59^a$ | | | | $-.65^a$ |
| Parity | | | $-.46$ | | | | |
| No. children | | | $-.45$ | | | | |
| Prior birth interval | $-.36$ | | | | | | $-.48$ |
| Weight | | | | | | | |
| Pregnancy weight change | $+.95^a$ | $+.92$ | | | $+.98^b$ | | |
| Height | | | | | | | $(+.46)$ |
| Head circumference | | | $-.48$ | | | | |

*Significance:* Unmarked = $p < .05$
$^a = p < .01$
$^b = p < .001$

*Source:* Dixon, Keefer, Tronick, and Brazelton (1982).

trimester) is strongly correlated with birth weight, infant length at birth, and percentage of weight for gestational age. (Earlier weight gains were also positively correlated with the infant outcomes, but not to a statistically significant degree.) Maternal age, parity, and number of living children, all highly interrelated ($r \geq .80$, $p < .001$), are negatively correlated with the infant's head circumference, and maternal age is also inversely related to its postnatal weight gain. This means that older mothers who had borne more children gave birth to smaller infants who gained less weight in the first 10 days of life than infants of younger mothers with fewer children.

The negative correlations of prior birth interval with birth weight and postnatal weight gain help explain this finding. The smaller infants with slower postnatal weight gains were born to older mothers after a longer interval since the last birth. As the mothers in this sample get older, they have longer birth intervals – indicating reproductive difficulties, including miscarriages – and they bear babies who are smaller and therefore at greater risk for survival. Another way of putting this is that it is the younger mothers who bear the largest and healthiest infants. By prolonging their reproductive careers well beyond five living children, Morongo mothers are putting themselves and their offspring at greater risk for reproductive casualty. Yet the healthiness of these newborns by global, particularly Third World, standards is undeniable.

The infants were examined during the first 10 days using the Brazelton Neonatal Behavioral Assessment Scale (BNBAS), which is designed to measure behavioral signs of neuromuscular regulation at birth (e.g., the infant's vigor, attention, and ability to regulate states of consciousness smoothly) and its physiological stability and the quality and maturity of motor performance over the postnatal period.[3] A series of assessments during the recovery period of the first 10 days allows a more accurate description of each infant's behavior and provides the opportunity to plot the neonate's acquisition of adaptive strategies for coping with its new environment.[4]

The results of the Gusii neonatal assessments are presented in Table 7.3. All of the item scores fall within the broadest normal range for the American standardizing sample, though there were significant differences in the central tendencies of the two groups and in their changes over time. The Gusii infants performed well

Table 7.3. *Neonatal behavioral assessment item scores*

| | | Assessment period | | | | | |
|---|---|---|---|---|---|---|---|
| | | Early | | Middle | | Late | |
| | | Mean | S.D. | Mean | S.D. | Mean | S.D. |
| Habituation: | Light | [a]6.39 ↑ | 1.64 | 6.26 | 1.25 | 6.20 | 1.42 |
| | Rattle | [a]6.92 ↑ | 1.82 | 6.83 | 1.26 | 6.69 | 1.53 |
| | Bell | [a]6.92 ↑ | 1.16 | 6.67 | 1.53 | 7.25 | 1.60 |
| | Pinprick | 8.00 | 1.55 | 4.73 | 0.77 | 5.23 | 1.37 |
| Orientation: | Ball | 5.93 | 1.91 | 5.96 | 2.12 | 5.91 | 1.91 |
| | Rattle | 5.73 | 1.77 | 6.42 | 1.11 | 6.04 | 1.79 |
| | Face | 5.71 | 1.83 | 6.09 | 1.64 | 5.78 | 1.74 |
| | Voice | 6.00 | 1.77 | 6.17 | 1.55 | 6.30 | 1.52 |
| | Face & voice | 6.14 | 1.96 | 6.08 | 1.82 | 6.30 | 1.68 |
| Alertness | | 5.00 | 2.10 | 5.17 | 1.93 | 5.83 | 2.01 |
| General Tone | | 5.80 | 2.01 | 5.83 | 0.69 | 5.92 | 0.91 |
| Motor maturity | | [a]6.67 ↑ | 1.30 | [a]6.82 ↑ | 1.32 | [a]6.79 ↑ | 1.38 |
| Pull-to-sit | | [a]6.21 ↑ | 1.61 | 5.29 | 1.43 | [a]5.21 ↑ | 1.04 |
| Cuddliness | | 4.87 | 1.59 | [a]6.17 ↑ | 1.34 | 5.96 | 1.40 |
| Defensive movements | | 5.80 | 1.87 | [a]6.71 ↑ | 1.86 | [a]6.33 ↑ | 2.49 |
| Consolability | | 6.21 | 2.48 | 5.96 | 1.87 | 6.00 | 1.82 |
| Peak of excitement | | [a]5.93 | 1.44 | 5.83 | 1.14 | 5.79 | 1.41 |
| Rapidity of buildup | | [a]3.39 ↓ | 1.82 | 4.45 | 2.02 | 4.19 | 2.04 |
| Irritability | | [a]5.29 ↓ | 1.58 | [a]5.43 ↓ | 1.61 | [a]4.38 ↓ | 2.00 |
| Activity | | 5.00 | 1.03 | 4.88 | 1.13 | 4.75 | 1.33 |
| Tremulousness | | 3.07 | 1.98 | 3.04 | 2.20 | 2.83 | 1.95 |
| Startle | | 3.00 | 1.36 | 3.29 | 1.37 | 2.92 | 1.26 |
| Lability of states | | 3.54 | 1.39 | 3.27 | 1.21 | 3.14 | 1.67 |
| Self-quieting | | 5.47 | 2.19 | 4.96 | 1.54 | 5.22 | 1.61 |
| Hand-to-mouth facility | | [a]6.80 ↑ | 1.60 | 6.33 | 1.62 | [a]6.04 | 1.74 |
| Smiles | | 2.60 | 1.63 | 2.1 | 1.04 | 2.39 | 1.27 |
| N | | 15 | | 24 | | 24 | |

[a]Significant ($p < .05$) differences when compared to a low risk American population. Direction of significant difference in comparison with reference to the American population (Keefer et al., 1976)

*Source:* Dixon, Keefer, Tronick, and Brazelton (1982).

on the BNBAS exams in comparison with a group of 15 healthy full-term white American infants who had been chosen for study because of low-risk pregnancy, labor, and delivery characteristics.

Differences between the Gusii and American samples were analyzed by grouping the items into seven clusters; this analysis is presented in Appendix H, Table H.3. Its major finding is that the motor maturity of the Gusii infants was superior to that of the Americans at each age point ($F = 18.75$, $p < .001$). There were a few other significant differences. The Gusii infants had better hand-to-mouth behavior, were less irritable, and had fewer startles and were less tremulous. With the exception of cuddliness, the Gusii infants' performance was strikingly stable over the examination period. The American infants showed better habituation to light and had fewer state changes; their startles decreased with time. In general, Gusii infants' performances were better than would have been predicted from the potential prenatal risks, and they compared very well to the low-risk American sample in all areas, surpassing them in motor performance.

Individual differences in BNBAS scores within the Gusii sample and their correlations with infant physical characteristics and maternal factors are presented in Appendix H. The smaller neonates who gained less weight – children of older mothers with more children – tended to be more irritable, more active, and less easily consoled. They did not perform as well as the others in the social orientation situation with auditory cues. The quality of their alert states was not as good as that of infants born of younger mothers. They were, however, more competent in shutting out noxious stimuli during sleep states.

Similar observations have been made on physiologically stressed Guatemalan infants, that is, larger infants with evidence of better intrauterine growth performed better on the social interaction items of the BNBAS.[5] In the United States, slightly undergrown full-term infants have been characterized as more irritable, hyperresponsive to stimulation, slightly more tremulous in the execution of movements, and moving more erratically from state to state.[6] Although they do not fit the criteria for intrauterine runting, the smaller and leaner Gusii infants did share some of these behavioral characteristics, perhaps as the result of less than optimal intrauterine nutrition.[7] Their behavioral profiles on the BNBAS were nevertheless within the normal range.

The pattern of behavioral recovery over the neonatal period is instructive from a cross-cultural point of view. The Gusii and the low-risk American infants showed relatively flat behavioral recovery curves, because most of their behaviors were already well organized at birth and remained so. This was in striking contrast with the steep recovery curves of the depleted Zambian newborns described in Chapter 2, who showed poor tone, motor maturity, and motor responses at birth but improved rapidly as the result of maternal care. The Gusii mothers, rather than having to compensate for the effects of intrauterine depletion, could count on large, vigorous, and well-organized babies to care for from the start.

## PHYSICAL GROWTH, DIET, AND THE FOOD SUPPLY

Surveys of diet and physical growth among Morongo children 36 months old or younger were conducted three times between 1974 and 1976, following the methods of Blankhart[8] that had been used elsewhere in Kenya and in other countries. Anthropometric measurements were taken on each child by trained Gusii fieldworkers, who also administered an interview questionnaire on diet, health care, and family socioeconomic characteristics.[9]

The first survey, conducted in December 1974 before the establishment of our pediatric clinic, covered 149 children under 3, about half of the population of Morongo children in that age range. A cluster sampling strategy was used. This survey, our first data collection effort in the infant project, occurred just after the major harvest, when food was abundant. The second survey, in August–September 1975, was conducted before the harvest of that year. Parents were complaining of low food stocks and a delayed harvest with poor yields. At that time our clinic had been in operation for 6 months; more children were showing overt signs of poor nutrition and compromised health. The change had been rapid; suddenly there seemed to be a subsistence crisis in Morongo.

To investigate the matter further, we decided to conduct a third survey, which was completed in April 1976 at the beginning of the long rains following a period of recovery from the previous year's scarcity. The food supply was intermediate – less than during the postharvest time of 1974, but greater than in the "hungry season" of 1975. These three surveys provide some basic data on the diet and growth of Morongo children at that time.

The longitudinal study provided additional material, because the 28 children in it were weighed and measured at virtually every encounter with the staff. The pediatric clinic kept records on all the Morongo children who were brought there, and added infor-

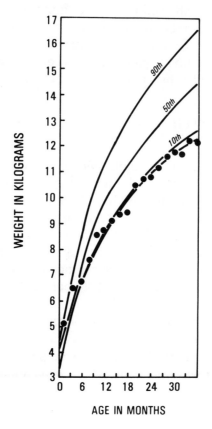

7.1 Mean weight gain pattern of Gusii male infants in comparison with Harvard standards.

mation on diseases of the first years of life, and their treatment by mothers. Finally, Suzanne Dixon carried out a special study of children classified in the second (1975) survey as severely malnourished in order to identify factors leading to this condition in the Morongo context.

The growth of Morongo infants, shown on Figures 7.1 to 7.4, followed a pattern observed in many Third World populations: Good growth is maintained for the first 3 to 6 months, after which the infants lose velocity in weight and height gain, then level off at or below the 5th percentile for reference populations in the West.[10] Tables presenting the means by age are in Appendix H. We believe this pattern represents risks for child survival, in that

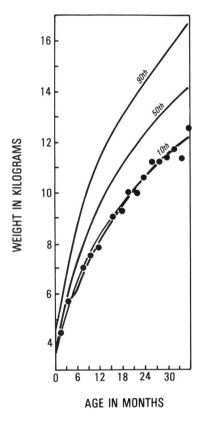

7.2 Mean weight gain pattern of Gusii female infants in comparison with Harvard standards.

the fall-off after 6 months indicates a period of precarious dietary transition, with an increased vulnerability to disease, concurrent with or preceding a diminution in the intensity of infant care.

The Morongo children surveyed were virtually all breast-fed throughout the first year of life; their mean age at weaning was 17.2 months. In the longitudinal sample, all 28 of the children had been weaned by 16 months. Mothers nurse in response to the infant's cry, as described in the previous chapter, but actual frequencies of daytime nursing at the breast declined after the infant was 3 to 4 months of age, probably because the mother had begun spending more time in the fields by that time. This is another example of the mother's greater intensity of attention in the earliest months, when the child is deemed most in need of it.

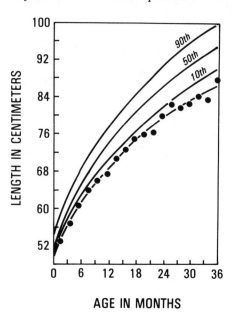

7.3 Linear growth of Gusii female infants in comparison with Harvard standards.

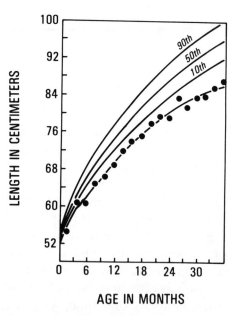

7.4 Linear growth of Gusii male infants in comparison with Harvard standards.

The relationship of breast-feeding to physical growth of the Morongo children was different in the first and second years of life. During the first year, the frequency of breast-feeding was positively correlated with a higher percentage of expected weight for age ($r = .39$, $p < .01$, for 0- to 6-month-olds; $r = .53$, $p < .001$, for 7- to 12-month-olds). In the second year, however, these relationships reversed, so that the percentage of weight and height were negatively correlated with the frequency of nursing ($r = -.36$, $p < .01$; $r = -.32$, $p < .05$, respectively). This is because frequent nursing in the second year indicates the mother's lack of supplemental foods, particularly cow's milk, to feed the child.

Table 7.4 shows the proportion of children in each age group who were reported by their mothers to have eaten various supplementary foods within the last 24 hours. The high proportion of maize as the primary constituent of infant gruel (*erongoori*) in place of the calcium-rich eleusine that was its customary base, is striking and represents a real decline in the nutritional content of the infant diet over the decades. The mean number of maize servings for 7- to 12-month-olds was 2.32, close to the mean of 2.39 for the sample of children as a whole. For all age groups the percentage of expected weight is correlated negatively with the frequency of maize feedings ($r = -.25$, $p < .05$) and positively with milk in the diet ($r = .26$, $p < .05$); expected height shows somewhat stronger correlations in the same directions, namely, $-.43$ ($p < .05$) with frequency of maize feedings and $.45$ ($p < .05$) with the presence of milk in the diet. The relationships between milk consumption and physical growth were particularly consistent between 13 and 24 months of age. This suggests that children get more maize when mothers have less of other more nutritious foods such as cow's milk and beans, and with a distinctly negative effect on their growth, particularly during the second year of life.

Using weights and heights as indicators, the nutritional situation of young children in Morongo must be classed as marginal by comparative standards. With expected weight for age as the criterion of acute malnutrition (Figure 7.5), a majority of the children are mildly or moderately malnourished in all 3 survey years. With expected height for age as the criterion of chronic malnutrition (Figure 7.6), close to one-third of the children fall into the mildly malnourished category (81%–90% of standard). Both measures show a decline in 1975 (i.e., more children were malnourished),

Table 7.4. *Proportion of children having certain foods in a one-day diet history with serving frequency*

| Age group | Maize | Meat | Eggs | Green veg. | Beans | Cow's milk |
|---|---|---|---|---|---|---|
| 0–6 mos. | .53 | 0 | .01 | .07 | 0 | .18 |
| 7–12 mos. | .84 | .08 | .02 | .22 | .02 | .36 |
| 13–18 mos. | .95 | .13 | .02 | .45 | .25 | .49 |
| 19–24 mos. | .98 | .17 | .06 | .53 | .23 | .73 |
| 25–36 mos. | .99 | .15 | .04 | .66 | .25 | .69 |
| All | .86 | .11 | .04 | .41 | .16 | .52 |
| Number of servings/ | 2.39 ± 1.28 | .13 ± .43 | .05 ± .25 | .61 ± .85 | .21 ± .53 | 1.16 ± 1.38 |

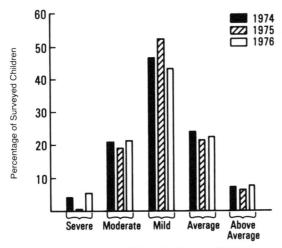

7.5 Distribution of Gusii children, 0 to 36 months, in categories of acute malnutrition in each of three survey years, 1974–1976.

when the children were surveyed during a preharvest food shortage of exceptional intensity. By the following year recovery is evident, though the postharvest levels of 1974 have not been reached. There are few severely malnourished children: Most are just above or not far below average.[11] The overall picture is not one of massive nutritional deficit but of a surprisingly precarious adaptation, given the agricultural resources of the region and robustness of Morongo infants at birth. The vulnerability of infant growth in Morongo to fluctuations in the domestic food supply indicates risks that could seriously endanger child health with relatively slight disruptions in the balance of resources to population.

The risks are unevenly distributed in Morongo. In the neighborhood populated largely by Seventh-Day Adventists, the children had a better diet, particularly after weaning, and showed better relative growth at all three survey periods. For example, *all* children aged 13 to 24 months in that neighborhood were fed cow's milk, whereas the proportions receiving cow's milk in the other neighborhoods were 90% and 76%. (Because many of the Adventists owned high-yield cows, milk was also available to the lactating mothers.) In the first two surveys, 16% of the children in the same neighborhood were fed meat but only 9% of those in the

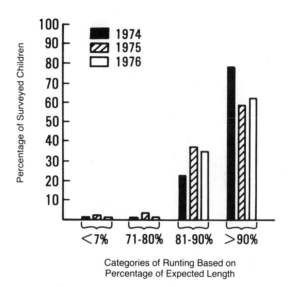

7.6 Distribution of Gusii children, 0 to 36 months, in categories of chronic malnutrition in each of three survey years, 1974–1976.

rest of the area were (chi-square $= 19.88$, $p < .001$). In the 1975 survey, the average meat consumption in the predominantly SDA neighborhood was .357 servings per child, whereas in the other neighborhoods it was .052 and .078 ($F = 6.57$, $p < .05$). Significant differences in expected weight and height during infancy, shown in Appendix H, Table 6, also favored the largely Adventist neighborhood. Getting a more nutritious diet, the children in that neighborhood grew larger and faster.

Why should the parents' Seventh-Day Adventist affiliation make a difference to the nutrition and physical growth of these Gusii children? There are both direct and indirect effects of religious affiliation. The indirect effects, which might seem more obvious, are mediated through church-inspired frugality and investment strategies of the previous generation, who directed their efforts toward optimizing agricultural production on their own land – adopting new crops and marketing techniques while preventing the fragmentation of landholdings, thus leaving larger and more rationalized farms to their children, the parents of the 1970s. From this perspective, the effect of the church on infant nutrition would be through the inherited economic advantages of the domestic group. But the Seventh-Day Adventist church, in addition to the ethic it shares with other Calvinistic denominations, also includes an ideology of health through good nutrition in the teachings of Ellen G. White, which are well known among the Adventists of Morongo. The keeping of recently introduced cows that require attentive care but which supply enough milk for home and market is strongly advocated by the SDA church, as is the importance of feeding milk to babies. Thus it is no surprise that children raised in SDA families are more likely to be fed milk than their Catholic and unaffiliated neighbors.

The distribution of serious malnutrition in Morongo, however, is the result of a breakdown in infant care without respect to religious affiliation or neighborhood. After the nutrition survey of 1975, Suzanne Dixon investigated a subsample of the worst cases, that is, 25 children whose weights were less than 80% of the standard for age or who were recorded as having edema, a swelling symptomatic of severe malnutrition. Five children were excluded because they could not be found again or were afflicted by a congenital disability (e.g., severe cerebral palsy, microcephaly). Each member of the final group of 20 children – 4 in the first year of life, 10 in the second – was visited at home, the primary caregiver interviewed, and the child examined. A developmental examination was attempted.

These children were spread across the neighborhoods, socioeconomic levels, and religious affiliations of Morongo; they had parents who varied widely in age and education. Tending to be first-borns or the youngest from large sibships of older mothers, the malnourished children were not distinguishable from the larger population in most other background characteristics. In almost every case, however, there had been at least one of the following events: (1) a breach in the relationships that normally support infant care in a Gusii family; (2) a physical or mental disorder affecting the mother's capacity to care for her own child; (3) premature birth, perinatal health problems, or other disorders affecting the infant's growth and behavior, usually from birth onward.

Seven of the children (35%) were born to unmarried mothers, a situation that is still strongly stigmatized among the Gusii and which, according to our census, accounts for only 3% of the children born in Morongo. Two of these malnourished children were being cared for by their natural mothers at the home of their maternal grandparents. Four of the other five were being taken care of by their maternal grandmothers, who had assumed responsibility reluctantly when the children were abandoned or neglected by their natural mothers, three of whom were said to have become prostitutes.

Altogether, 9 of the 20 children were being reared primarily by someone other than the mother – a rare arrangement in the larger Morongo population. This includes two cases in which the natural mother was employed outside the area for long periods and no specific substitute caregiver was designated; the child's older siblings were probably in charge. In the other seven cases of nonmaternal care, the designated caregiver was the mother's mother or sister. Because there is no established practice in which anyone permanently assumes responsibility for another woman's child, and because the mothers seem to have left their babies with kin after disgracing the family through premarital pregnancy or becoming a prostitute, the malnutrition appears symptomatic of grudging care given to abandoned children by covertly angry disgruntled family members.

Maternal illness was involved in seven cases. Three mothers were chronically ill and could not care for their fields or their children. Two mothers were chronic alcoholics, and two others suffered postpartum depression. In these cases, impairment of the mother's ability to produce food or cash for long or short periods of time resulted in a diminution of household resources available for infant nutrition in addition to its direct effects on maternal behavior.

Eleven of the children were reported to have been born prematurely and to be very small at birth. Three suffered from health problems during the perinatal period, including pneumonia diagnosed at the hospital and a gastrointestinal disorder. This picture stands in contrast to the robust children in the neonatal assessment sample described earlier, and suggests the possibility that their failure to meet maternal expectations for a newborn baby was involved in the failure to grow normally later on.

All in all, 18 of the 20 children in the malnourished sample showed at least one of three risk factors: lack of normal social support for infant care (through maternal abandonment or premarital birth), maternal illness, or abnormal perinatal history. Six children had two of these risk factors, and two had all three. (The two with no risk factors had overtly anxious or hostile mothers living in relatively affluent homesteads.) In most cases, these adverse conditions had been present at birth, suggesting early interference with the normal course of attachment to the primary caregiver. Thus the malnutrition is interpretable as a symptom of "bonding failure," in which the infant–caregiver relationship was compromised from the start by absent, unwilling, sick, or depressed caregivers on the environmental side, or a fragile, unhealthy, perhaps weakly responsive infant – or both, in a negative cycle precluding the reciprocal interaction that supports normal feeding and physical growth.

Recent events were identified that might also have contributed to the faltering of growth in these children. For example, of the 13 who were no longer breast-feeding when they were assessed, 5 had been weaned before 1 year of age, which was very rare in the population as a whole. Four children had experienced a sibling birth in the 3 months prior to the survey and showed signs of depression: persistent crying, lack of activity, and food refusal. Our clinic records revealed that 13 of these children had been brought in for "thinness." Six had persistent ascariasis and two had a prolonged recovery from viral illnesses. Our inquiries into the nutritional status of these children came as no surprise to their families, who were aware of their health problems. Physical examinations verified the presence of nutritional compromise and revealed a variety of skin diseases, both nutritional and infectious. Two children had minor burns and one was found to have unrecognized pneumonia. In general, they showed many signs of ill health and inadequate care.

The fact that virtually all the *severe* cases of acute malnutrition we could find in Morongo in 1975 turned out to be cases of social deviance, maternal illness, or perinatal deficit – with multiple symptoms of family stress and ill health – instead of poor families who simply ran out of food, is an indication that the overall food supply for young children at that time was not as bad as might have been thought. Reduced foodstocks in 1975 had a marked negative influence on weight and height, but not beyond *moderate* malnutrition except for children who were already ill or who had a disturbed caregiving relationship before the local food shortage occurred. On the other hand, these cases revealed dramatically the vulnerability of a child care system that puts so much responsibility for producing food and providing care on one person – the mother – with so few alternatives and so little emergency backup or support when that person proves unable to function normally. Widespread malnutrition of the more serious kind was averted in 1975, but it may not be avoidable in a future of greater population density, land scarcity, and social stress.

## CAREGIVER RESPONSIVENESS TO INFANTS

Turning to the environmental side of infancy, we ask whether our sample mothers and their child nurses differentiated their behavior according to the individual differences in their infants we have already noted and to developmental changes in infant capacities during the first year. We are particularly interested in whether such caregiver responsiveness to specific infant characteristics, if found, might plausibly be interpreted as representing maternal implementation of the Gusii model of infant care described in the foregoing chapter.

Our hypothesis was that Morongo caregivers would respond consistently to infant characteristics signaling failure to achieve age-appropriate goals specified in Gusii models of infant development. During the early months, when survival of the infant is the major goal, maternal responsiveness would be elicited by cues indicating fragile health. Later in the first year, when survival seems assured, mothers would focus on the goal of producing a docile infant easily managed by child caregivers. At this age, the infant's irritability or above-average activity level would elicit attentive care. We hypothesized, then, that heightened responsiveness – in terms of the gross structure of caregiving as well as communicative responsiveness in interaction – would be received by infants with poor neonatal assessments (BNBAS scores) and small size during the early months, and irritable temperament ratings toward the end of the first year.

This hypothetical model was confirmed and further specified by an analysis of the data on the 12 children of Cohort I, who were examined at birth and observed naturalistically at home over the first year of their lives. Those who showed behavioral signs of vulnerability in their neonatal assessments did indeed receive more maternal attention and physical care during the first 3 months. Although infants at this age are held in 80% of spot observations when awake, the frequency of holding is elevated for those with poor habituation ($r = -.95$) and poor motor performance ($r = -.83$, $p < .05$) on the BNBAS. Increased maternal proximity during this period is related to poor orientation ($r = -.76$) and poor motor performance ($r = -.76$, $p < .05$) and to a large number of abnormal reflexes ($r = .78$ and .74 for first and second BNBAS examinations respectively, $p < .05$).

In contrast, child caregivers do a higher proportion of the holding of ($r = -.78$, $p < .01$) and maintain a closer proximity to ($r = -.73$, $p < .05$), infants with fewer abnormal reflexes. Children also do more of the holding of infants who showed better orientation ($r = .62$, $p < .05$) on the BNBAS. Thus mothers permit infants who showed better organization in neonatal assessment to be held more frequently by children during the first 3 months, while giving more of their own attention to infants whose BNBAS performances indicated vulnerability.

When the infants are between 3 and 6 months of age the pattern of caregiving shifts dramatically, with greater involvement of the *omoreri* in the care of infants who were more poorly organized at birth. Child holding is related to a poorer range of state on the BNBAS ($r = -.66$, $p < .05$). Child proximity (child within 5 feet, and mother not in the area) is strongly related to poor orientation ($r = -.77$, $p < .01$), poor motor performance ($r = -.87$, $p < .01$), and poor regulation of state on both the first and second neonatal assessments ($r = -.64$, $p < .05$; $r = -.76$, $p < .01$). Other findings as well support the conclusion that infants with worse performance on the BNBAS are provided with the closer company of more children in the 3- to 6-month age period.[12]

At this same time, when mothers have returned to a full load of work, they more frequently hold their babies with *more* optimal motor performance ($r = .80$, $p < .01$) on the BNBAS. This suggests that after the early period of maximum infant vulnerability, mothers may depend more heavily on the *omoreri* and other children for taking care of those infants who appear less robust, while carrying with them the infants whose better motor performance and orientation permit the mother to combine infant care with other domestic tasks.

The mother's response to infant cries, as assessed through naturalistic home observations at 3 months, is strongly related to indications of vulnerability at birth. Maternal responses to infant distress were analyzed into two factors, one of "physical" behaviors involving touching but also looking, the other "distal" behaviors like talking, gesturing, and offering objects.[13] The physical strategy is more frequently used in response to the cries of infants who habituated poorly on the first BNBAS exam ($r = -.78, p < .05$) and oriented poorly on the second exam ($r = -.77, p < .05$). Thus more poorly organized newborns elicit an intense pattern of maternal response to crying at 3 months, characterized by physical contact and care and heightened visual attentiveness. The distal strategy is reserved by mothers for better-organized infants, for whom physical soothing may be unnecessary.

Mothers' responses to nondistress vocalizations display a markedly different pattern, characterized by increased responsiveness to the vocalizations of the better organized infants. Mothers respond more frequently, for example, to vocalizations of infants with better state regulation on the third BNBAS exam ($r = .87, p < .01$). By the 6-month observations, mothers are still more frequently responding with distal behaviors to the crying of infants who were better organized at birth, but they show no heightened tendency to respond generally or in any specific way to those who had had poorer neonatal performance. This pattern supports the view that the selective responsiveness to the crying of the worse-organized neonates in the earlier period represents a perception of vulnerability specific to the first months after birth.

Gusii mothers use size as an indicator of how much care and protection an infant needs, leading us to predict that small babies would receive more intensive care. The frequency of holding by any caregiver in the spot observations is consistently related to smaller weight at 3, 6, and 9 months ($r = -.78, -.82, -.79$, respectively, $p < .05$ for each). During the first 3 months, child caregivers are more likely to be in close proximity to infants with lower birth weights ($r = -.81, p < .01$) and smaller head circumferences at 3 months ($r = -.72, p < .05$). In the naturalistic home observations at 3 months, mothers respond more frequently to the cries of babies who are shorter in stature ($r = -.85, p < 05$).

In general, the relationships between responsiveness factors and physical growth measures exceed chance levels through the first year, considering all possible combinations between physical growth measurements at birth, 3, 6, and 9 months and responsiveness factors from the concurrent and subsequent observations. The strongest relationship occurs at 3 months: There are 12 possible correlations, of which 6 could be expected to be significant (3 positive and 3 negative) by chance; 12 significant correlations are obtained, of which 11 are in the negative direction and 1 is positive. At this age, then, small size is related to a variety of indicators of heightened responsiveness.

In order to measure infant behavioral characteristics that might elicit caregiver behavior in the second half of the first year, we made two assessments of temperament when the Cohort I babies were between 8 and 11 months of age. Ratings were made by staff pediatricians during videotaped sessions designed to investigate attachment behavior.[14]

During the 6- to 9-month period, infants rated high on "irritability" are more frequently in close proximity to a child caregiver ($r = .65, p < .05$) and those rated high on "negative mood" are more frequently held by an *omoreri* ($r = -.64, p < .05$). In contrast, docile infants are more often held by the mother rather than an *omoreri* and nursed by the mother than more active infants are ($r = .71, p < .05$).

From 9 to 12 months the pattern is similar: The *omoreri* gives increased attention to irritable infants, while the mother's involvement continues to be limited to those who are more docile. Mothers who are more frequently in the general vicinity (within 50 feet) of babies at this age scored lower on irritability on a summary measure than the first assessment ($r = -.62, p < .05$). This same measure is positively correlated with *omoreri* involvement in infant care ($r = .73, p < .05$). More irritable infants, then, are frequently in the care of an *omoreri* while the mother is engaged in nonchildcare activities; less irritable infants are more often nursed and have mothers involved in their care.

The naturalistic home observations at the same age show that responsiveness to crying (by all caregivers combined) is related to higher ratings of irritability/reactivity on the temperament measure ($r = .72, p < 01$). More irritable children receive more attention to their crying. But these observations confirm that mothers respond more to social behavior from less irritable children ($r = -.75, p < .05$). In other words, irritable infants tend to receive high levels of response to their cries, and the response is usually aimed at soothing distress through physical care. This care is usually, in the daytime, administered by child caregivers. Docile infants, on the other hand, receive more responses from mothers to nondistress signals, and these responses more frequently include behaviors other than direct physical care. During the second half of the first year, then, when *abareri* are doing a large share of the daytime infant care, they are also given the infants who need, according to Gusii standards, the greatest amount of attention because they are most likely to be crying or fretting.

## THE DISEASES OF CHILDREN AND THEIR HEALTH CARE

Our experience in the clinic and the community provided insight into disease prevalence and severity among Morongo children. Their marginal nutritional states were dramatically illustrated by their responses to illness. Even minor nongastrointestinal viral illnesses were accompanied by a dramatic loss of weight with slow recovery. Convalescence was prolonged, and it was not uncommon for illnesses to follow one another rapidly.

Parasitic infestation with ascaris and tapeworms was the most common complaint. All of the 28 sample children over 9 months had these complaints one or more times. Of those 272 children assessed during the nutrition survey who had used our clinic, 56% had presented with that complaint one or more times. Acute bacterial or viral gastrointestinal disease was relatively uncommon; about 1 in 12 to 15 children had complaints of diarrhea, and its course was similar to cases seen in the United States. Bloody diarrhea or diarrhea with high fever was unusual, though one 2-year-old died of acute bloody diarrhea during our time in the field. No cases of cholera were seen, and the incidence of amebiasis could not be ascertained without access to a laboratory. Scabies and impetigo were extremely common and severe. Gusii mothers were well aware of the perniciousness of skin diseases, brought their children to the clinic early and repeatedly, and applied their own salves and criticized mothers who did not attend to the skin eruptions of their children.

Falciparum malaria had only recently found its way into Morongo through migration from areas of lower elevation; many children had high fevers that we could not diagnose accurately but treated as malaria. There were no central nervous system presentations of that disease.

Respiratory illnesses in this cool, wet climate were severe and prolonged. Lobar and generalized pneumonias, many part of a rubeola (red measles) or other viral exanthems, were very significant, and recovery was slow. Only one child demonstrated chronic wheezing or other evidence of allergy. This sample infant had asymptomatic wheezing during the first year of life while continuing to grow and do well, but he died suddenly during a pneumonia episode in the second year of life.

Accurate estimates of infant and child mortality rates prevailing in the Morongo population under normal circumstances are not possible because we saved a number of children who would probably have died without our clinic or emergency transportation to the Kisii General Hospital. The cases of actual mortality during the period of our fieldwork included two other deaths from pneumonia in the first year of life and a neonatal death from noncyanotic congenital heart disease. One 8-year-old was murdered by poisoning and another infant probably died of an overwhelming infection. There were also malformed children: five had the deformities of polio, one child had a multiple malformation syndrome and was retarded, and another was microcephalic and severely retarded with prenatal onset. Other vulnerable children included premature infants (two singleton and one set of twins). One of those twins died of failure to thrive in the second half of the first year, and a singleton preterm infant died of pneumonia at about the same age. One infant was born with tracheomalacia and had severe feeding difficulties until 4 months of age. He was treated attentively and patiently by his mother and maternal great-grandmother, using short periods of nursing and spoons of maize porridge. In general, Gusii families made heroic efforts to save deformed, disabled, and vulnerable infants, often successfully.

The Morongo mothers, like all Gusii mothers we observed, were eager to obtain modern medical care for their infants and young children and willing to go to great expense and inconvenience to do so. Until the establishment of our clinic, they had a choice of three fairly distant facilities: the district hospital 8 miles away but accessible by a 20-minute *matatu* (bus made from a small pick-up truck) trip on the main road, a government health center about 14 miles in the opposite direction on the main road, and a small church-affiliated clinic (with beds but no resident physician) only 6 miles away but hard to reach by *matatu*. The district hospital was overcrowded and oriented primarily to trauma and operative medicine, but one sample mother gave birth there and many took their children to its pediatric outpatient clinic.

Our own weekly clinic for children under 5 at Morongo, which was limited to families in the area covered by our census, served 30 to 50 children per session and another 10 to 18 for immunizations. We were impressed with the level of maternal vigilance for disease in the community and the willingness of Gusii mothers to take time off from agricultural work to seek treatment for sick children and to nurse sick infants on their own bodies for many hours on end.

## GUSII INFANT CARE AS ADAPTATION

In this chapter we have examined the health and physical growth of Gusii children, from birth to 4 years of age, as outcomes of the caregiving environments in Morongo during the 1970s. The overall picture compares favorably with many populations in tropical Africa: Infant mortality is moderate and declining, malaria and diarrhea are not widespread, neonates are large and well organized, severe growth failure and clinical symptoms of malnutrition are rare. Comparison with optimal medical standards developed in the West, however, reveals serious problems: Growth faltering begins at 6 months of age and continues into the third year; many children are infested with worms; variations in diet, height, and weight across the families and neighborhoods of Morongo, and over the seasons of the year, show vulnerabilities in the food supply – particularly during the postweaning period – that could lead to more widespread and severe malnutrition. Both pictures are correct but represent only part of the truth: The conditions for child survival, health, and nutrition are worse elsewhere in Africa than they are among the Gusii, but even the Gusii of Morongo looked precarious in the growth and health of children after the first year.

This can be understood in terms of the priorities of Gusii parents and their strategy for investing resources, including maternal attention, in their children. They are most concerned with infant survival, allocating maternal attention to the early months of life when survival is most at risk – and to infants who look vulnerable – and subsequently diminishing their attention if physical growth and motor development are progressing at what appears to be a normal pace. In these terms, Gusii parents are getting what they most want from their child care system, namely, the largest number of surviving offspring, at a cost that is not yet disturbing them: slower growth and nonlethal morbidity during the postweaning period.

We began this chapter by asking whether Gusii practices of reproduction and infant care have adaptive outcomes and respond effectively to change in the short and long term. We can now provide a preliminary answer in terms of the data we have just presented. The size, healthiness, and low mortality of the average infant at birth and in the first months of life show that the Gusii system of birth-spacing and perinatal care is working effectively, and the growth of infants over the first year, though not optimal, is consistent with a high rate of survival and with normal development. Gusii mothers respond to perceived vulnerability in newborns with extra physical care, supported by both ritual and routine arrangements, as they do when an infant becomes ill, and they tend to reduce their attention to a child's care as they perceive the child to be growing and developing normally. In this sense, maternal care is adaptive – that is, flexible, responsive to the infant's individual characteristics, and sensitive to the child's need for physical care, as interpreted through the Gusii model. Finally, Gusii mothers have altered their model of protection and care over the decades in response to new constraints and opportunities, eliminating birth rituals for normal newborns and the practice of force-feeding, adopting plastic bottles and rubber nipples, seeking modern medical treatment, and – in some cases – obtaining cow's milk as the duration of breast-feeding has decreased. This is, as a whole, efficacious infant care, given the Gusii assumptions that every woman must continue childbearing until menopause and that child survival and health – rather than some form of optimal development – are the primary goals of parental care during infancy.

That this efficacy has its limits cannot be doubted. The high fertility of the Gusii means that each woman has more children than are likely to be born at good weight or more children than she can afford to provide with enough supplementary food. The system as we observed it is remarkable in fulfilling the immediate goals of Gusii parents while generating longer term problems of child health and ecological decline.

# 8

## Communication and social learning during infancy

Gusii parents tend to view infant care primarily in terms of protection and nurturance, and to postpone deliberate instruction until the child is able to talk and understand commands, but the experience and learning of Gusii infants, as for all humans, begins at birth and is culturally organized. Infant psychosocial and behavioral development, though not prominent in Gusii formulations of parental priorities, is culturally shaped even in the early months, anticipating later developmental goals that are salient for Gusii parents. This chapter presents and interprets evidence from naturalistic observations and videotaped samples of elicited caretaker–infant interaction, to provide a portrait of communication and social learning over the first years of life.

### A PROFILE OF GUSII MOTHER–INFANT INTERACTION

Describing mother–infant interaction in any human population means, at least implicitly, comparing it with the pattern best known to the child development field, namely, that of the American white middle class, so we shall present Gusii evidence in comparison with observations of middle-class Americans from the suburbs of Boston, Massachusetts, before exploring its meaning and functions from a Gusii perspective.

The overview with which we begin is based on naturalistic observations of Sarah LeVine, who visited each child in the Gusii longitudinal sample at home every 3 months, thus covering children at each 3-month age point between 3 and 30 months, for a 1-hour observation that was subsequently coded. Comparable home observations were later conducted in suburban Boston; Appendix A and Appendix B describe the recording methods and coding catego-

Table 8.1a. *Mean proportions of maternal behaviors in the Gusii sample (n = 12)*

| Behavior | 3–4 months | | 6–7 months | | 9–10 months | |
|---|---|---|---|---|---|---|
| | x̄ | S.D. | x̄ | S.D. | x̄ | S.D. |
| Talk | .11 | .08 | .12 | .06 | .11 | .08 |
| Look | .12 | .06 | .09 | .07 | .01 | .07 |
| Physical | .26 | .13 | .19 | .05 | .32 | .17 |
| Hold | 1.00 | .17 | 1.00 | .23 | .93 | .51 |
| Nurse | .08 | .05 | .04 | .04 | .06 | .07 |

Table 8.1b. *Mean proportions of maternal behaviors in the Boston sample (n = 9)*

| Behavior | 3–4 months | | 6–7 months | | 9–10 months | |
|---|---|---|---|---|---|---|
| | x̄ | S.D. | x̄ | S.D. | x̄ | S.D. |
| Talk | .25 | .08 | .26 | .14 | .29 | .07 |
| Look | .40 | .17 | .45 | .18 | .43 | .19 |
| Touch | .09 | .04 | .05 | .02 | .04 | .03 |
| Hold | .54 | .16 | .30 | .14 | .25 | .09 |
| Feed | .04 | .06 | .07 | .06 | .05 | .06 |

ries. Classifying maternal behavior into five crude categories, we compared the Gusii and Boston samples in the frequency of the five behaviors.

Tables 8.1a and b show the average proportions of maternal behavior falling into each of the five categories for 12 Gusii and 9 Boston mother–infant pairs, each of whom was observed at home three times during the first 9 months, at roughly 3, 6, and 9 months of age. The distribution of maternal behavior across the categories is extremely different for the Gusii and Boston mothers: For the Gusii, holding and physical contact are most frequent at all age periods, whereas for the Bostonians, looking and talking are relatively frequent at first and become the most frequent behaviors by 9 months. The Gusii-Boston differences in *overall* holding ($t = 5.96$), looking ($t = 4.67$), and talking ($t = 4.24$) are statistically significant ($p < .01$) at 3 months and stay the same or become

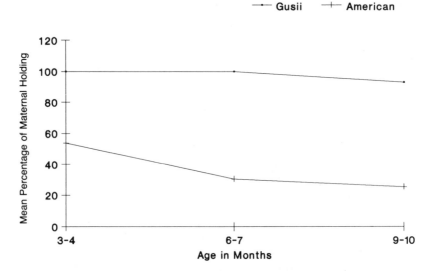

8.1 Mean percentage of maternal holding over the first 10 months: Gusii (*n* = 12) and American (*n* = 9) samples.

slightly larger at the later age points, as Figures 8.1, 8.2, and 8.3 portray graphically.

Comparing the rank orderings of maternal response to specific infant behaviors (vocalizations, cries, and looks) across the two samples at the three age points, in Table 8.2, leads to the conclusion that maternal responsiveness to infants in the first year is organized differently among Gusii and Bostonians. Gusii mothers seek to soothe their babies rather than engaging in interaction that involves looking and talking (e.g., mock conversation or play). Virtually all of their interaction with the babies includes holding or carrying, and they often respond to infant vocal or visual signals with physical contact rather than reciprocal talking or looking. By contrast, the Boston mothers, who hold their babies in less than a third of their interactions from 6 months onward, seek to engage their infants in visual and verbal communication at a distance.

The Gusii pattern of mother–infant interaction becomes clearer in a closer examination of infant crying and looking. The question of whether holding actually operates to soothe and comfort cannot be answered easily from sequential analysis of the Gusii data, be-

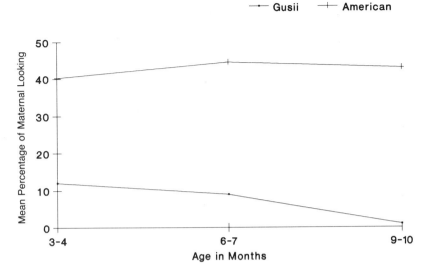

8.2 Mean percentage of maternal looking over the first 10 months: Gusii ($n$ = 12) and American ($n$ = 9) samples.

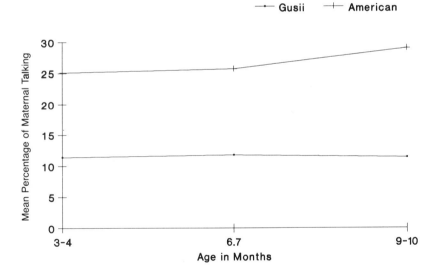

8.3 Mean percentage of maternal talking over the first 10 months: Gusii ($n$ = 12) and American ($n$ = 9) samples.

Table 8.2. *Comparisons of rank orderings of maternal responses to infant vocalizations, cries, and looks*

|  |  | Vocalization | | Cry | | Look | |
|---|---|---|---|---|---|---|---|
|  |  | Gusii | American | Gusii | American | Gusii | American |
| *4 mos.* | | | | | | | |
|  | 1 | Hold | Look | Hold | Hold | Hold | Look |
|  | 2 | Talk | Hold | Phys | {Look | Phys | Talk |
| Rank | 3 | Phys | Talk | {Talk | {Talk | {Talk | Hold |
|  | 4 | {Look | Touch | {Nurse | Touch | {Look | Touch |
|  | 5 | {Nurse | Feed | Look | Feed | Nurse | Feed |
| $r_s$ | | | .23 | | .30 | | .18 |
| *7 mos.* | | | | | | | |
|  | 1 | Hold | Look | Hold | Look | Hold | Look |
|  | 2 | {Talk | Talk | {Talk | Talk | Phys | Talk |
| Rank | 3 | {Phys | Hold | {Phys | Hold | Talk | Hold |
|  | 4 | Look | Feed | Nurse | {Touch | {Look | Feed |
|  | 5 | Nurse | Touch | Look | {Feed | {Nurse | Touch |
| $r_s$ | | | .10 | | −.13 | | −.20 |
| *10 mos.* | | | | | | | |
|  | 1 | Hold | Look | Hold | {Look | Hold | {Look |
|  | 2 | Phys | Talk | Phys | {Talk | Phys | {Talk |
| Rank | 3 | Talk | Hold | Talk | Hold | Talk | Hold |
|  | 4 | {Look | {Touch | Nurse | Touch | Look | Feed |
|  | 5 | {Nurse | {Feed | Look | Feed | Nurse | Touch |
| $r_s$ | | | .10 | | −.28 | | −.13 |

*Note:* Frequencies within 2.0 of each other are bracketed as tied ranks.

cause the Gusii babies are being held so much of the time. In the Boston sample, however, where holding occurred in about one-third of the total observations, it was possible to examine the relationship between the occurrence of holding and subsequent infant behaviors. Using lag sequential analysis,[1] we calculated the conditional probability of occurrence of infant crying following maternal holding and compared it to the baseline or unconditional probability of crying. Crying was significantly less frequent following maternal holding than it was at its baseline level ($p < .05$).

That maternal holding in the American sample seems to "dampen" crying may explain why in the Gusii sample, where 3- to 4-month-old infants are held most of their waking hours, the mean frequency of crying during 4 hours of observation is 81, whereas it is 190 in the Boston sample. This evidence that the Gusii pattern of physical responsiveness to infant crying serves to reduce its frequency is consistent with a number of studies conducted in North America.[2] It suggests that the soothing of Gusii mothers is successful in achieving their goal.

A complementary finding concerns visual and verbal interaction. In the Boston sample mothers were looking at their 9- to 10-month-old babies in 28% of the intervals of observation, whereas the infants were looking at their mothers in only 8% of the intervals, an imbalance that is typical of the Western European samples in which we have conducted comparable observations.[3] Among the Gusii mother–infant pairs at the same age, however, the mothers gaze at their infants no more than the infants gaze at them – 9% of the intervals in both cases – suggesting that Gusii mothers are seeking (or permitting) eye contact much less than their Euroamerican counterparts. And although Boston mothers responded to 20% of their infants' vocalizations with speech at 9 to 10 months, Gusii mothers responded with speech to 5% of their infants' vocalizations at that age.[4] This is consistent with the hypothesis of soothing, as Gusii mothers try to prevent their infants from becoming positively aroused in emotionally exciting social interaction as well as negatively aroused in crying.

In comparison with American white middle-class mothers, then, Gusii mothers try to keep their babies calm, avoiding positive or negative arousal states by preventing or dampening excitement. They hold and lull their babies more, respond rapidly to cries and frets with physical care or breast-feeding, rarely engage them in long bouts of play or vocal excitement – all consistent with the goal of maintaining the baby in a quiet state free of distress or unmanageable activity – a kind of postpartum incubation attributable to the survival concerns discussed in the foregoing chapter. Gusii mothers are no more homogeneous in their behavior than Americans, but there can be no doubt that the goals of maternal care among the Gusii, and their style of mothering during infancy, differ in these observable ways from their American counterparts.

The incubation pattern does not mean that the Gusii infant is excluded from the social life of the family, particularly by comparison with his American counterpart. Although American infants are put into isolation for sleep periods during the day and the entire night, the Gusii infant is rarely alone in the daytime and never at night. Sleeping at the mother's breast throughout the night, with the next older sibling or two nearby, and in bodily contact with mother or a child caregiver throughout the day, a Gusii baby is present during most of the family's social interaction *without* becoming the center of its attention. In contrast, the American infant's day is sharply divided into periods of total isolation and periods of infant-directed social excitement.

## INTERACTION WITH OTHERS

The Gusii infants are in contact with nonmaternal caregivers, mostly older sisters, during much of the daytime, as indicated in Chapter 6, and this is a major contrast with our American sample. Most observational studies have been of American or European mothers and their firstborns living in nuclear family arrangements in which infants interact rarely with anyone except their mothers. To reduce the bias of birth order, we selected American mothers with second- or later-born infants for our sample, but most of their other children were much younger than the siblings available to interact with a Gusii infant. This reflects the differences in sibship size between the United States, where children typically have one or two siblings, usually quite close in age, and Gusii-land, where an infant typically has seven or eight siblings, some of whom are adults, with as many as five still living in the mother's house. So the Gusii infants observed have a larger share of their total interaction with their child caregivers and other older siblings, and a correspondingly smaller share with their mothers, than the American infants do.

Figure 8.4 compares the proportions of all behaviors directed toward the Gusii infant by girls between 6 and 12 years old with those by mothers, at six age points over the first 2 years. We chose 6- to 12-year-old girls because they are most often daytime caretakers for infants when mother is away (see Chapter 6). The mother and girls in this age range together account for at least 75% and as much as 95% of the observed behavior directed to the infants at all of the age points. The higher figure applies to the 3- to 4-month period, when the mother is returning to agricultural work and uses an *omoreri* most heavily, whereas the lowest figure

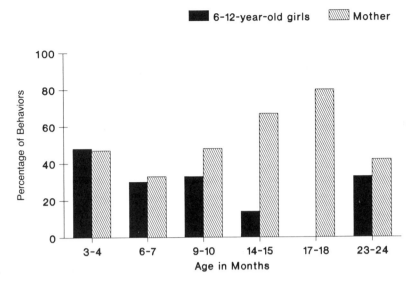

8.4 The interactions of Gusii mothers and children with infants: percentages and frequencies.

applies to 23 to 24 months, when the child is acquiring a more varied social life in the sibling group. It is only at 3 to 4 months that girls exceed mothers (slightly) in their proportion of the infant's total interactions; after that, mothers exceed all others and only at 23 to 24 months constitute less than 50% of all observed interactions with the infant. The relative importance of the mother in quantitative terms is particularly noteworthy in light of the fact that observations were conducted on a daytime schedule regardless of maternal absence, and numerous observations were carried out when mothers were absent.

Figure 8.4 also shows the greater proportion of infant interaction with 6- to 12-year-old girls during the first year of life than during the second year. Once the infant has survived the first year and can walk, the mother considers her need for an *omoreri* to have diminished and is less likely to press her daughters into service. Thereafter there is a steep decline in the percentage of interaction with girls until 2 years of age, when maternal interaction with the toddler has declined (in many cases after the birth of a new sibling) and he becomes a fuller participant in the group of older siblings. The total *number* of infant-directed behaviors by

Table 8.3. *Mean frequencies of caregiver behaviors*

| Age in months | Hold | Physical | Vocalization | Look |
|---|---|---|---|---|
| 3–4 | 135.75 | 33.72 | 12.00 | 10.06 |
| 6–7 | 145.75 | 35.76 | 14.48 | 11.23 |
| 9–10 | 90.37 | 30.63 | 16.34 | 12.62 |
| 14–15 | 65.21 | 19.47 | 25.61 | 10.50 |
| 17–18 | 47.84 | 12.97 | 12.21 | 7.11 |
| 23–24 | 21.67 | 9.67 | 29.65 | 11.17 |

mothers and girls combined (not shown on Figure 8.4) drops continuously, from 3 to 4 months (more than 170) to 17 to 18 months (about 50). The overall picture is one of diminishing infant-directed behavior after the initial period of postpartum incubation and particularly after the first year, with 6- to 12-year-old girls important as caregivers during the first 9 months.

Table 8.3 shows the mean frequencies of four categories of caregiver behavior directed toward the infants at the six age points. Holding and physical care decline more or less continuously over the first 2 years, while vocalization rises and looking stays about the same. Thus as interaction as a whole declines over this period, it shifts in content from holding and physical care to speech. By 23 to 24 months, this new pattern is firmly in place, suggesting that infancy is over and childhood has begun.

The profiles of mothers and child caregivers as interactors with the infants are shown on Figures 8.5a and 8.5b. These specify how the behaviors of mother and children are distributed over the several categories of behavior at each age point. The profiles are quite similar in terms of most and least frequent behaviors – holding and physical care rank higher than vocalization during the first year – and in terms of the trends toward less holding and physical care and more vocalization, especially during the second year. Apart from the fact that mothers breast-feed and children do not, and that children do less holding after the first year when they are no longer assigned to do so, there are few differences that stand out.

Table 8.4 confirms this conclusion in a different analysis of the data, namely, by the proportion of each behavior attributable to

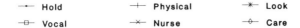

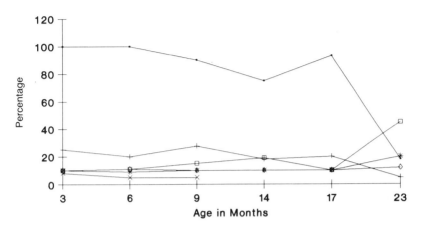

8.5a Percentage of Gusii caregiver behavior: mother.

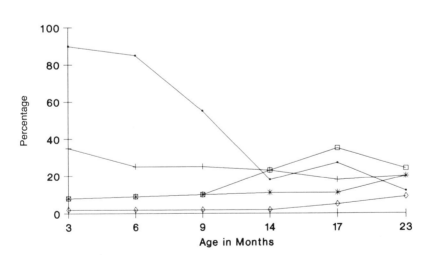

8.5b Percentage of Gusii caregiver behavior: child.

Table 8.4. *Relative frequencies of caregiver behaviors by mothers and children*

|  | Hold | | Physical | | Vocaliza-tion | | Look | |
|---|---|---|---|---|---|---|---|---|
|  | M | C | M | C | M | C | M | C |
| *Age in months* | | | | | | | | |
| 3–4 | .51 | .55 | .43 | .62 | .48 | .61 | .59 | .60 |
| 6–7 | .54 | .39 | .49 | .43 | .57 | .33 | .51 | .40 |
| 9–10 | .59 | .39 | .51 | .46 | .47 | .47 | .48 | .41 |
| 14–15 | .76 | .19 | .62 | .33 | .68 | .26 | .67 | .26 |
| 17–18 | .89 | .19 | .80 | .32 | .74 | .35 | .86 | .35 |
| 23–24 | .32 | .18 | .31 | .44 | .48 | .28 | .48 | .33 |

*Note:* The mean proportions of each behavior for mother and children often add up to more than 100.

mother or children. The means for mother and child on each category of behavior are quite similar during the first year, and at no point do they suggest that children have a more active and engaging style in interacting with their baby siblings. In other words, there are no striking complementarities in child–infant and mother–infant interaction, indicating that child caregivers and other siblings act under maternal mandate to treat the baby as she says and does – at least in terms of major categories of behavior. This finding is counter to our expectation, based on the Kikuyu study by Leiderman and Leiderman,[5] that child caregivers would provide infants with more social interaction than their mothers.

## GUSII INFANT BEHAVIOR TO MOTHERS AND OTHERS

Here we consider the interactive behavior of the Gusii infants, its distribution over the first 2 years and its differentiation by mother and children. Table 8.5 shows the relative frequencies of five categories of behavior: cry, vocalization, look, physical contact, and explore. Although these figures do not capture the rapid maturation of the child during this critical period of development,

Table 8.5. *Relative frequencies of infant behaviors*

| Age in mos. | Cry | Vocalization | Look | Physical contact | Explore |
|---|---|---|---|---|---|
| 3–4 | .31 | .25 | .24 | .12 | .17 |
| 6–7 | .23 | .28 | .22 | .14 | .29 |
| 9–10 | .18 | .24 | .22 | .18 | .23 |
| 13–14 | .21 | .18 | .18 | .18 | .22 |
| 16–17 | .12 | .14 | .24 | .12 | .36 |
| 22–23 | .13 | .17 | .22 | .08 | .29 |

they do show the decline of crying from its place as the most frequent interactive behavior and the relatively narrow range within which most of the other behaviors vary. Given the amount of time a baby is held even when able to move by himself, and the tendency of caregivers to soothe crying and avoid vocal interaction, it should not be surprising that there are no strong, consistent upward trends in vocal and exploratory behavior. Looking at others is maintained throughout the 2 years at roughly a fifth to a quarter of the intervals; this is probably a more important source of learning for the Gusii infant than for his American counterpart, given his visual access to the social interaction of the Gusii family while being restricted motorically much of the time. Nevertheless, the decline in physical contact after 14 months and the concurrent rise in exploratory behavior show a child who is moving around the house and yard on his own (and with less vocalization) rather than being intensively cared for by others.

Examining the proportions of infant behaviors to mother and children in Table 8.6 shows the same sharp drop in looking and physical contact after the first year that we have already seen in terms of the child caregiver's behavior. The mother, as opposed to older children, is the person an infant looks at most often after the first year, makes physical contact with most after 4 months, and approaches most once walking is achieved at 9 to 10 months. By 23 months, however, the child has begun approaching other children more than the mother. Were we to interpret the approach figures as proximity-seeking and thus an indicator of infant attachment, we would have to conclude that by the time attachment is

Table 8.6. *Comparison of relative frequencies of infant behaviors directed at mothers and children*

|  | Look | | Physical contact | | Approach | |
|---|---|---|---|---|---|---|
|  | M | C | M | C | M | C |
| *Age in months* | | | | | | |
| 3–4 | .48 | .62 | .37 | .49 | 0 | 0 |
| 6–7 | .34 | .56 | .64 | .19 | 0 | 0 |
| 9–10 | .31 | .51 | .61 | .33 | .48 | .39 |
| 13–14 | .49 | .39 | .74 | .16 | .59 | .30 |
| 16–17 | .62 | .42 | .72 | .20 | .57 | .43 |
| 22–23 | .43 | .39 | .49 | .02 | .38 | .40 |

established at 9 to 10 months, mother is the primary attachment figure. This does not mean that the Gusii infants are not attached to the children who take care of them but that their attachment behaviors are not as frequent to children as to their mothers and these behaviors wane when the children are no longer assigned to carry them.

Another measure of the differential responsiveness of Gusii infants to mother and children concerns how much crying they do when held. Figure 8.6 shows the mean proportions of crying at different ages, when anyone is holding the baby and when the mother or a child is holding the baby. In the first year, the rate of crying is consistently lower when the infant is held by the mother than the base rate of crying or the rate when the infant is held by a child. In the second year of life, there is no difference between the rate of crying when the child is held by mother and the rate of crying overall, but being held by a child is associated with increased crying. This pattern is not found for nondistress vocalization (not shown); holding by mother and child produce minor decreases in the rate of infant vocalization compared with the base rate. The Gusii mother's selective response to infant vocalization, that is, responding specifically to crying (rather than nondistress vocalization) with rapid physical care intended to soothe, seems to result in more effective soothing during the first year than is possible for the child caregiver. The mother emerges

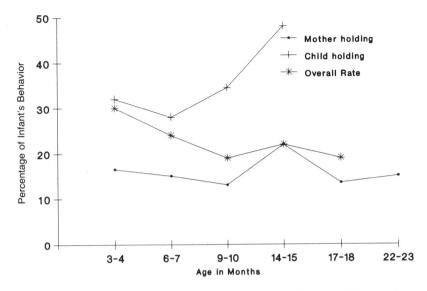

8.6 Mean proportions of crying by age, according to which caregiver is holding infant.

in these data as a unique source of comfort for her infant. This may not be surprising in the light of co-sleeping and intensive breast-feeding, perhaps, but it is nevertheless noteworthy because these infants spend so much of the daytime in the care of children.

The relatively weak indications of the infants' attachment to their caregivers compared with their mothers are consistent with the caregivers' style of interaction, which follows the maternal goal of soothing and maintaining calm rather than stimulating the baby through visual and verbal attention. In other words, if the children behaved toward their infant charges in a way that comple-mented the mother's way by engaging the babies in visual and verbal interaction, one would expect the infants to become strongly attached to them. Because the child caregivers do not behave this way but act like the mother (i.e., attempting primarily to provide comfort rather than excitement), though with some inherent disadvantages from the perspective of a nursing baby, it is no wonder that the infants appear much less attached to them. Thus as far as these observations show, daytime care of infants by children does not interfere with the attachment to the mother and does not in itself create strong relationships between infants and their child caregivers. The latter relationships seem to emerge around 2 years of age when the child has less interaction with the mother and is beginning to participate more fully in the group of older siblings.

## FACE-TO-FACE INTERACTION BETWEEN MOTHER AND INFANT

A more detailed examination of "postpartum incubation," that is, Gusii infant care during the first 6 months, is provided by the structured observations of nine mother–infant pairs who were videotaped at home by Suzanne Dixon twice a week when they were 2 to 12 weeks old, then monthly until they reached 6 months. The procedure of data collection and analysis followed the laboratory methods used by Tronick, Als, and Brazelton[6] with American mothers, and we shall make some comparisons of the Gusii and American interactions.

Mothers in Cohort I of the longitudinal study agreed to video-taping with their infants in the yards outside their homes. The infant was seated in an American infant seat and the mother was sitting or kneeling on the ground in front of him. An assistant held a tarpaulin curtain behind the baby to eliminate distracting stimuli. Another assistant held up a mirror at the side, facing the mother and the camera, which was aimed at the baby. This arrangement made it possible for one camera to record the baby and the mother (in the mirror) in interaction at the same time. The taped sessions lasted an average of 2 minutes, 22 seconds.

The Gusii mothers were instructed in this situation, as in the American laboratory situation, to "talk to your baby," "play with your baby," "get your baby's attention." It was a novel situation for them, and although they saw the tapes after each session, became accustomed to the situation, and enjoyed their participation in it, they said it was of course silly to talk to a baby. The videotapes were analyzed by dividing the interaction into segments characterized in terms of behavioral phases displayed by each interactant.[7] Individual clusters of behavior were classified into seven monadic phases: (1) Avoid/Protest, (2) Avert, (3) Monitor, (4) Elicit (mother only), (5) Set, (6) Play, and (7) Talk. Each monadic phase encompasses mutually exclusive behavioral descriptors identified in micro-analysis of videotaped interaction. The composite cluster of behaviors can be reliably (> .85) scored directly from the videotapes. Examples of the descriptors for several of these phases for mother and infant are shown in Appendix A. The phases consitute a 7-point scale of attention and affect, from negative to positive (1 to 7). In analyzing the Gusii tapes, a monadic phase was identified for mother and infant in each 1/4 of a second of interaction.

The Gusii mothers appeared relaxed and comfortable in the situation but were restrained in terms of facial expression, body movement, and tone of voice compared with American mothers. Their speech to the infants consisted largely of repeated verbal formulas familiar in routine interaction, for example, "seka, seka, seka" (smile); "kira, kira, kira" (hush), or the making of attention-getting sounds. Though the situation of interacting with mother face-to-face without being held by her may have been unique in the experience of these babies (in the first session), they responded with evident pleasure vocally or motorically and sometimes moved their arms in a way that seemed to indicate the expectation of being picked up.

Some of the infants laughed, with much movement and vocalization. These peaks in affective display produced a mixed response in mothers: Some giggled nervously; others turned away, their faces suddenly devoid of expression. The infants usually responded with milder but still positive displays. The sessions seemed flat and monotonous to the observer in the field (Suzanne Dixon), but microanalysis of the videotapes[8] showed that the mothers' sudden gaze aversions were closely linked to the infants' peaks of affective display and as such were important junctures in the interactions. There were many individual variations in the proportions of time and duration of each phase, which are probably attributable to infant temperament and maternal personality, but there was also a distinctive profile of interaction of the Gusii as compared with the Americans.

Complete data on the proportion of time that Gusii and American infants and mothers spent in each of the seven phases, and the mean durations in seconds, are shown in Appendix H, Tables 7a and 7b. Here we present some of the most illuminating differences that emerged in this comparison.

Figure 8.7 shows the mean duration of each monadic phase for the Gusii and American mothers. Although the proportion of time the two samples of mothers engage in Play and Talk with their

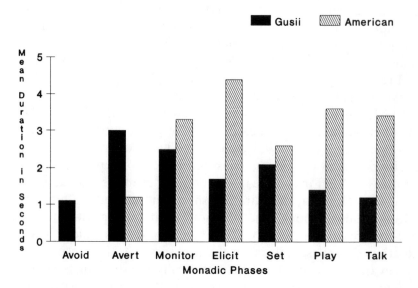

8.7 Maternal behavior during videotaped face-to-face interaction: mean duration of monadic phases.

infants is almost exactly the same, the duration of these two phases is shorter on average among the Gusii (1.4 and 1.2 seconds) than among the Americans (3.6 and 3.4 seconds). Gusii mothers look away from the infant a greater proportion of the time than do American mothers (7% vs. 4.8% in Avoid and Avert combined). Both of these contrasts suggest a different level of interest in sustaining affectively charged episodes, because "avert" behaviors serve to dampen and diffuse an affect display and to limit its duration. Play sequences of short duration, such as those that characterize the Gusii mothers, do not allow time for affective arousal. In further support of this interpretation, Figure 8.7 shows that Elicit has the highest mean duration for the American mothers, but is relatively low for the Gusii.

The Gusii mothers want to keep interaction smooth and even. Their interactions are in balance with those of their infants – matching each other in specific phase 40% of the time, as contrasted with 19.8% for the Americans. As a result, there is a certain monotony to the Gusii interaction, which lacks the peaks of affective excitement seen in the American sample. Only 8.1% of the time are the Gusii interactions in joint *positive* states (Talk or Play), compared with 17% of the Americans. Their synchrony is achieved most frequently, 20.6% of the time, in the *neutrally engaged* states, compared with 12% for the Americans.

These differences in interaction are not attributable to the Gusii infants but to their mothers. The Gusii infants are in Play or Talk 32% of the time, compared with 19% for the American infants. But 39% of the time when the infant goes to Play or Talk, the Gusii mother goes to Set or Monitor, and 5% of the time she goes to Avert/Avoid. The mother's response to these displays of positive affect is thus to dampen, diffuse, or diminish the affective level of the interaction. Among American mothers, by contrast, the goal is usually to build upon, amplify, or extend these infant behaviors; every effort is made to sustain Play and Talk episodes up to the limits of the infant's capacities. Thus the American mothers change among phases in two-step units – which serve to heighten and intensify the interaction – 51% of the time, and in one-step units, 38%. Gusii mothers change 71% of the time in one-step units and only 17% of the time in two-step units; they want to minimize affective intensity in interaction, as well as re-spond sensitively to their infants. Finally, Gusii mothers stay in a phase longer and change less drastically across categories than their American counterparts.

The Gusii profile of maternal interaction in these videotaped samples reflects a number of factors, to be explicated in the next section, in the microsocial and macrosocial environments of Gusii mothers. At this point, however, it is most important to bear in mind that this videotaping was done during the first 6 months postpartum, that incubation period in which mothers see them-selves as nurturing a vulnerable infant over risks to survival, largely through protective and responsive physical care that seeks to soothe rather than stimulate.

## MOTHER–CHILD TEACHING: FROM 6 MONTHS TO 2 YEARS

To assess the Gusii mothers' interaction with their children after the period of early infancy, we videotaped them in a situation structured around a teaching task and compared the results with those of a sample of American mothers who had been given the same instructions.[9] This situation was chosen not as a simulation of what normally goes on in a Gusii family but because it had been used in previous infant research in the United States[10] and offered a means of comparing culturally organized responses to a universally comprehensible task. There were 18 children in each culturally defined sample, divided into three cohorts by their ages at the time of observation: Cohort I, 6 to 8 months; Cohort II, 12 to 14 months; Cohort III, 19 to 25 months.

Mothers were instructed to teach their children age-appropriate tasks borrowed from the Bayley Scales of Infant Development (Bayley, 1969) and modified in their range of difficulty. For the Cohort I children, the tasks were picking up blocks and reaching around a glass barrier to obtain a toy; for Cohort II, stacking blocks to make a tower and putting pegs in pegboard; for Cohort III, the same block and pegboard tasks plus the placement of forms in a formboard. The Gusii children, drawn from our longitudinal sample, were familiar with the objects because they had taken the Bayley test and other cognitive tests. The exact conditions of videotaped assessment, and the categories for second-by-second scoring of the videotapes, are described in Appendix A.

The Gusii mothers tended to instruct the infant verbally, to repeat the instructions and to demonstrate the entire task in advance; they more rarely used praise or demonstrated part of the task for the child to imitate. Among the 12- to 14-month-olds, for example, the mean frequency of "model the whole task" was 4.81% for the American sample and 16.09% for the Gusii ($Z = 2.21, p < .05$). The mean frequency of "model part of the task only" was 13.22% for the American sample and 4.58% for the Gusii ($Z = 2.88, p < .02$).

Maternal response to the infant's successful completion of the task also showed group differences. The most frequent response of the Gusii mothers was no response in the following 2 seconds, which hardly ever occurred in the American sample ($X^2 (1) = 3.87, p < .05$). The most frequent response of the American mothers was praise or encouragement, which hardly ever occurred among the Gusii (Fischer exact $= 10.30, df = 1, p < .01$). This is consistent with the Gusii style of teaching and communicating with children at all ages, namely, the avoidance of praise as leading to conceit or dangerous social visibility, but it raises questions about how learning occurs, which are discussed in the next chapter.

There were some marked differences in how the Gusii and American infants responded to the situation. Signals of distress – that is, fussy vocalization, crying and/or moving away from the setting – occurred 24 times among the 6- to 8-month-old American infants and only once in the Gusii group. American children showed distress 11 and 17 times among the 12- to 14-month-olds and 19- to 25-month-olds, respectively; Gusii children did so 8 and 11 times. For the total sample, distress was significantly more frequent among the American infants ($X^2 = 16.32, p < .01$).

At a more general level, the Gusii mothers offered clear, unambiguous instruction frequently and modeled the expected tasks in their entirety. They appeared to expect the task to be completed exactly as specified if the child attended to it. Their goals include getting the job done, even if it were done accidentally by the child rather than by staging a process of discovery for the child, or exploration of the limits of play. The Gusii mothers responded to inattention by the infant with reinstruction and modeling; motivation to conform to expectations was taken for granted. The almost monotonous verbal and manual focusing maneuvers served to contain the child's attention rather than tempt or arouse him. These resembled the containment of attention and affective display of the young infant in the face-to-face situation described in the previous section. To the outside observer, the interaction appeared slow, as the Gusii mother rarely guides the learning sequence except at its inception (i.e., modeling and instruction) or at times of distraction (i.e., focusing or resetting). Periods of modeling, rather than of successful completion or social interchange, occasioned the most intense interaction.

The American mothers interpreted their tasks differently. They tempted, teased, and encouraged the children's own exploration of the toys, providing motivation and direction by shaping the child's behavior. Their use of questions to instruct, and of reflections on the child's mood or behavior to provide encouragement, were distinctive components of this approach. Periods of inattention in the infant were countered by a prompt increase in the tempting, refocusing behaviors. Breaking down the task into its parts (*modularization*) was a major strategy in their teaching style. Gusii mothers, in contrast, depended on the presentation of *advance organizers* – the whole task laid out for visual assimilation and direct imitation by the child.

The Gusii child's orientation to the task was often maintained by the mother's use of physical control measures such as tugging and restraining – rarely used by American mothers. The Gusii children did not resist being pulled and pushed, but the American infants did in almost every instance. Thus the divergent effects of culturally organized social experience are in evidence as these children and their mothers respond to the common situation.

The Gusii mothers clearly experienced this situation as being less familiar than their American counterparts did. In the Gusii context, the child is expected to learn skills by watching and imitating older children (*legitimate peripheral participation*)[11] rather than being taught by the mother. The assumption is that important skills are locally, indeed immediately, available for observation by the infant and that the infant will naturally acquire them without special training or encouragement. It is also assumed that a child's motivation for learning comes from wanting to be able to do what the older children do; the mother need not provide motivation. If asked to participate in an experiment, the Gusii mother will comply and get her child to do so, too, but the process and product look very different from the American mother's play orientation and motivation-building strategies of teaching.

## SPEECH DIRECTED TO THE INFANT

The young child's everyday language environment can provide important clues to the contexts in which early social and emotional development take place. Indeed, in some societies there is so much talk going on around infants and toddlers (or directed to them), that speech would be the most obvious place to seek the meanings of child care for young children and their caregivers. Gusii is not such a society: Normal social interaction in domestic settings is verbally restrained, with a slow conversational pace, a strong reliance on conventional routines and indirect speech, and a tendency to put responsibility for comprehension on the hearer rather than the speaker (as in the conventions of talking about pregnancy described in Chapter 5).

This restraint has a powerful effect on the early language environment of the child. Observation showed that Gusii mothers talk to their babies during the first 9 to 10 months after birth only about half as frequently as their American counterparts

(Figure 8.3). They are verbally responsive to infant vocalization less often than the American mothers are, and we rarely found Gusii mothers attempting to elicit a vocal response or carrying on a sustained verbal exchange with a baby or even a toddler. Mothers do not eagerly await or promote the toddler's speech skills, and calling a young child *omokwani* (a talker) is closer to criticism than to praise. Nevertheless, mothers and other caregivers do talk to babies, and what they say is revealing.

For an assessment of speech directed at the Gusii infants, we turn to a third body of naturalistic observations carried out on the sample of 28 children over a period of 8 months by two Gusii observers, Truphena Onyango and Mary Kepha Ayonga, who had recently graduated from high school. Unlike the spot observations of Joseph Obongo (Chapter 6) and the narrative records of Sarah LeVine (presented in the first part of this chapter), this set of observations did not cover the entire period of the study (17 months), because of the educational obligations of the observers, and it used a precoded system that was less effective than the narratives were in capturing interactive sequences. But the observers carefully recorded separately, in Ekegusii, everything said to the sample child during a period of up to 2 hours of observation at home (mean = 105 minutes, s.d. = 24) and these records permit an analysis of speech.[12]

Infant-directed utterances from all caregivers combined, occurring in 18.5% of the minutes of observation across all ages from 3 to 27 months, were rare, as shown on Figure 8.8. But the range of variation across individuals was very wide, from 1% to 83%, indicating that some children were talked to a great deal and some hardly at all.

The utterances from all caregivers, classified into crude grammatical categories, were predominantly imperatives (mean = 61.4%) at all ages (Figure 8.9a); there was a slight rise in the proportion of interrogatives, and a drop in declaratives, around 2 years of age. (But many of the interrogatives were rhetorical questions that have the force of imperatives – "Why do you cry?" "When will you ever sit down?" – or even threats – "Do you want me to beat you?" – uttered by a mother we thought of as especially benign, to her 6-month-old son, who was fussing at the breast.) Utterances were also coded by the speaker's intent, for example, as Soothing if they were intended to reduce crying with-

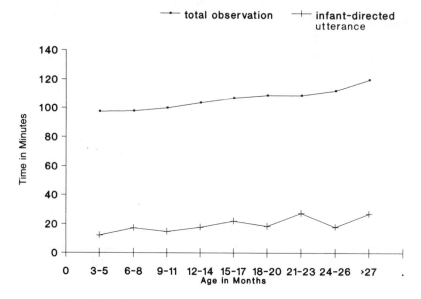

8.8 Average number of minutes of observations (total) and minutes in which infant-directed utterances from all caregivers occurred, by infant age (*n* = 28).

out also expressing anger or impatience. An example is *kira,* which translates as "hush" and is often accompanied by holding and rocking. Averaged across all age points, Soothing occurred in 9.6% of observational minutes, but was strongly age-related. Figure 8.9b shows that Soothing from all caregivers declined sharply over the first 15 months, particularly between 9 and 12 months.

The same general contour holds for all positive utterances, which includes not only Soothing but also Praise (appearing in less than 1% of all minutes of observation) and Endearment (5.8%), that is, calling the baby *baba* ("mother"), *tata* ("father"), or *monene* ("big boy"). Figure 8.9c shows a major drop in positive utterances after the first few months, followed by a lower level during the second year.

Negative utterances directed to the infant rise after 1 year of age and remain a larger proportion of all utterances through the second year. This category consists of Negative Commands like *Tiga!* ("Stop"), and *Karwo!* ("Get away!"), which are most frequent; warnings such as "You'll fall," or "You'll get burned"; and threats such as "I'll beat you!" One kind of warning intended to

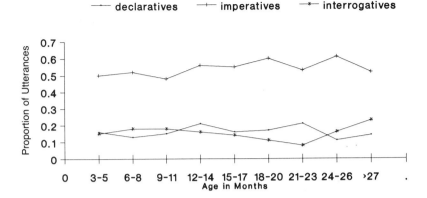

8.9a Infant-directed declarative, imperative, and interrogative utterances from all caregivers, by infant age ($n = 28$).

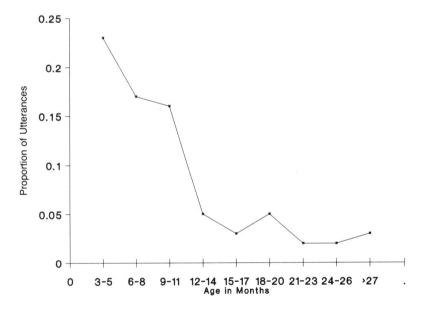

8.9b Proportion of infant-directed utterances that were soothing, from all caregivers by infant age ($n = 28$).

frighten the baby involves pretending to call a dog (*Aso, aso, esese!*) or an imaginary animal (*ekuku,* a rare baby-talk word meant to refer to an animal that might hurt one).[13] For example, when her 9-month-old daughter approached an axe, a mother

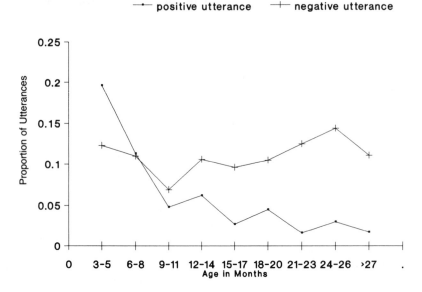

8.9c Overall proportions of negative and positive utterances directed to infants from all caretakers by infant age ($n = 28$).

shouted, "Kuku!" to stop her. Sometimes mothers seem to be joking in their threats, and as children get older, they appear not to take them seriously: In one observation, for example, a 30-month-old girl asks her mother for a banana. When the mother says, "Go and get one," the girl accuses her mother of having eaten her banana; the mother defends her authority by saying, "Today your uncle will beat you hard," whereupon the little girl says, "I'll run away." Though overt verbal defiance of this kind is rare, the understanding that maternal threats are not genuine may be widespread among Gusii children during their third year of life.

The *omoreri* accounts for a large share of the Soothing, especially at 3 to 6 months when it is most frequent, but the mother accounts for more of the negative commands, particularly during the second year when that category reaches its peak.

These data clarify a number of the trends that have emerged from other observations. Speech directed to infants is infrequent on average from 3 to 27 months, but there are large individual differences, probably depending on characteristics of the caregivers. The form and content of utterances directed to infants reflect Gusii assumptions about what infants need and the domestic hierarchy in which they are participants. The imperative mode dominates at all ages, emphasizing the age-based authority structure into which the child is growing. Questions – the staple of infant-directed speech in Western middle-class samples – are rare. Utterances with a positive emotional tone, including those we have called Soothing and Endearment, have their peaks in the first 6 months – the "postpartum incubation period" – and decline sharply afterward, whereas those with a negative emotional tone, particularly negative commands, rise continuously between 12 and 24 months, as the child is socialized into a place at the bottom of the domestic hierarchy. Vocal exchange is not a goal early or late: In the postpartum incubation period, caregiver speech is part of a package of behaviors, mostly physical, directed toward soothing the young and vulnerable infant; in the second year, the focus is on obedience to commands, particularly those issued by the mother. Praise has no place in this sequence.

## SOCIALIZATION OF THE INFANT

The Gusii mother's concept of infant care as nurturance and protection for a vulnerable newborn child, with survival rather than psychosocial development as its goal, provides a social environment for the infant in which learning inevitably takes place. To keep the baby calm and quiet, the mother tends to do more holding and less talking to and looking at the baby than her American counterpart, and she instructs the children who take care of the baby in the daytime to do the same. The effectiveness of Gusii mothers in comforting their infants is demonstrated by the fact that the latter cry much less than American infants at the same age. Gusii babies cry less with their mothers than with their child caretakers and seek proximity to their mothers in the second half of the first year, indicating infant–mother attachment. We interpret this observational evidence as meaning that the responsive physical care of what we have called the postpartum incubation period results on the average in a quiet baby, one who is relatively easily handled but primarily attached to the mother.

Gusii responses to the structured situations showed a distinctive maternal style of social interaction and teaching. In the face-to-face interaction with children under 6 months of age, the Gusii style was (in contrast with Americans) slow, neutral, and unchanging, involving play and talk episodes of brief duration and a tendency to dampen infant affective displays with gaze aversion, thereby cutting short interactions of increasing excitement. Here soothing – of positive emotional display rather than distress – emerged as something not simply dictated by circumstances but preferred by the Gusii mother. In the teaching situation at a later age, the Gusii mothers assumed a hierarchical position by showing the whole task to their infants, telling them to do it, shoving them somewhat to obtain results, never praising, and rarely acknowledging task completion. The infants resisted little, much less than their American equivalents, but completed the tasks less often. The situation was an unfamiliar one for both mothers and infants, because the acquisition of skills by the Gusii child normally occurs in a context defined by older children whom the child observes and imitates. The mother provides comfort and overall direction, but in her position at the apex of the domestic hierarchy of the household she does not engage in training tasks and motivational routines herself but delegates them to her older children.

These patterns of maternal behavior, and the preferences expressed through them, are influenced by the Gusii code of face-to-face communication and the cultural model of avoidance as moral order (Chapter 3). Proper social interaction among the Gusii entails the avoidance of eye contact, particularly between those of unequal status, including parents and their children. Adults rarely converse in the *en face* position but tend to speak side by side, back to back or at a 90-degree angle, in which one looks at the ground while the other speaks. Mutual gaze usually occurs at the moment of greeting and is avoided during the interaction that follows. Excessive eye contact is interpreted as disrespectful familiarity or improper intrusiveness with sexual or aggressive intent.

In this context, the Gusii mother's avoidance of eye contact with her child can be interpreted as first of all an interactive habit that she brings to all interaction, and second, one that reflects her authority and status in the household vis à vis the children, and third, a reflection of the specific kin-avoidance norms (*chinsoni*) that will later apply to her interaction with each child. In addition, the Gusii mother is aware that eye contact is exciting to a child and builds expectations that the mother knows will be frustrated when she bears the next child. Furthermore, looking fondly at her own child in front of others can invite jealousy and witchcraft. For all of these reasons, both normative and strategic, the mother adopts gaze aversion as part of her maternal style of interacting with her own children. The infants eventually become habituated to body contact and verbal interaction with the mother without the concomitant of eye contact. They are in effect being socialized into what might be described as a cool or subdued style of social interaction and affective expression.

Gusii mothers organize a learning environment for their children in which the acquisition of culturally valued skills and forms of competence will be acquired largely without deliberate training. They do teach infants to go on a caretaker's back when the mother or caregiver says *titi;* mothers were occasionally observed teaching 8- to 9-month-old babies to stand (*Tenena iga!* – "Stand here!" – which they say while they hold up the child's hands); they also taught babies to shake hands with visitors by holding out the baby's hand for a visitor to shake. The rest of the child's earliest learning, from the mother's point of view, consists largely of learning to accommodate to and respond appropriately to the situations she has organized – by not straying into dirty or dangerous places, by taking the breast when it is offered. A large proportion of maternal speech to infants consists of commands and warnings – what might be called verbal shoves – urging the child to do this or not do that. The observational records indicate that mothers do not teach children words, phrases, or sentences. In addition to physical comfort, they distract the baby by pointing out chickens and dogs (*ekuku, esese*) to instill fear, which they consider a valuable childhood basis for prudence and obedience. On the whole, the Gusii mothers, like the Kipsigis mothers studied by Harkness and Super,[14] seem most concerned that their young children learn to respond to maternal commands and other urgings rather than to speak themselves. This is consistent with the compliance required of the child as he grows up in the domestic hierarchy of the household.

# 9

## Variations in infant interaction: Illustrative cases

Gusii parents share a cultural model of child care, but their central tendencies in implementing it, as described and examined comparatively in the previous chapters, do not convey adequately the diversity of environmental conditions in which Gusii infants are raised. We found as much variation in personality, family background, and current situation among the 28 sets of parents in our longitudinal sample as one would find in any population, and more socioeconomic differentials than one would find in rural African communities less affected by recent change. All of this translated into varying environments for their babies, who also varied in their temperamental responsiveness and in their birth order among the children of one mother. Although we could not investigate these individual variations systematically in our small sample, we can illustrate them with cases of particular conditions that run counter to the statistical norm or represent extremes within it, thus showing the imperfect realization of a cultural model in actual practice.

To exemplify this diversity, we chose parents differing in age and infants differing in birth order. Older parents tended to be wealthier, less educated, and more experienced in child care – wealthier because men in their 40s and 50s during the mid-1970s had inherited land at a time when it was more abundant and had had more time to accumulate possessions, but less educated because they belonged to a cohort in which school attendance was relatively rare. By 1975, their wives had raised a number of children and were experienced in child care. With less land and more schooling, younger fathers had obtained higher-level jobs outside the district, were more exposed to urban influences, and were more likely to have adopted "modern" attitudes and practices. Their young wives were junior members of the local women's hierarchy; they were less secure in their connections and had fewer children to help them in their work. The most burdened were those women with three or four preschool children, none of whom were old enough to contribute effectively to home management. Thus parental age was associated with many factors accounting for family differences in the care of particular infants.

Birth order is one such factor, because a ninth child born in 1974 would, given Gusii reproductive practices, have older parents than a first or second child born the same year. But birth order in itself created a special situation for some infants, regardless of co-varying socioeconomic factors. A firstborn child (*omotangani*) was more likely to be cared for by the mother herself most of the time, since she had no older children. A lastborn child (*omokogooti*) would be favored for more leisurely care, because the mother was no longer under the pressure of the birth succession to wean and prepare the baby for her reduced attention. Thus the lastborn was stereotyped as "spoiled" but permanently closer to the parents, and the firstborn son as a potential future replacement for the father in the domestic hierarchy. Children of intermediate birth orders, the overwhelming majority, had their early lives defined more by relations with those before and after them in the birth succession than by a special relationship with the parents.

Given the importance of parents' age and its correlate, birth order of the infant, as a determinant of the child's experience, we selected Salome, a ninth (and last) child; Justin, a fifth child; and Evans, the secondborn of his mother.

## SALOME

Salome was the ninth child and the fifth daughter of Makori and Kwamboka. A member of Cohort II, she was first observed by Sarah LeVine at 7 months and followed until she was 19 months old. Her father Makori was nearly 50 years old; her mother, unsure of her age, guessed that she was over 40 at the time. Makori and Kwamboka already had two married daughters and three grandchildren. Kwamboka said she expected Salome to be her last child, *omokogooti,* though this did not turn out to be the case. Salome was cared for by her mother and her 9- and 11-year-old sisters, Agnes and Sarah, after school hours; all showed delight in their contact with her to a degree that was unusual in the sample. In the mornings she would be left with her brother, Osoro. We never saw her with Makori, her father, who spent virtually all his waking hours out of the homestead.

Makori, the youngest of three brothers, had attended school for 2 years, was neither baptized nor belonged to any church, and had always lived at home. He inherited 4.5 acres from his father, who had died when he was very young. In his youth Makori had worked as a mason for the government in Kisii Town, but for the last 15 years he had a meat business at Morongo market: Makori bought cattle and slaughtered them in his older brother's butcher shop, and they shared the proceeds from the sale of the meat. On his land Kwamboka raised pyrethrum and coffee for cash, as well as food crops and a few African milch cows for home food consumption.

Kwamboka had been the oldest of four children; her mother died at the time of her circumcision, and she had been sent to live with her maternal grandmother until she married. The marriage was arranged by her father, who received the bridewealth cattle; she had never seen Makori before. Although it seemed strange at first, she became attached to his place and his people, particularly her mother-in-law, who was kind to her from the start.

The well-kept homestead of Makori and Kwamboka was entered through a picket gate between high cypress hedges into manicured pastures. The houses, with mud walls and thatched roofs, were also exceptionally tidy. From the main house there was a view over meadows all the way down to the river, and the bachelor's hut was surrounded by a hedge enclosing a small flower garden. The homestead had a well for its own water.

Kwamboka worked hard in the fields, usually alone, though the unmarried children helped with fetching water, cooking, and babysitting. Apart from one of her married daughters, who visited occasionally, we never saw her with a visitor. Her social isolation seemed odd, because she appeared to be a warm and friendly woman, but eventually we learned what caused it. Her fourth son, Getonto, whom Salome followed in the birth order, was 3 years old when we first saw him and had been crippled by polio at the age of 2, shortly before Kwamboka became pregnant with Salome. Getonto had a withered leg and hopped about with the help of a stick. He was chronically unhappy, cried and whimpered a great deal, and was always afraid of the observers. Kwamboka appeared to pay little attention to him; and when she did look at or even speak to him, she was noticeably sad. We offered to take him to an orthopedic hospital 40 miles away to have him fitted for a brace, but Kwamboka was not interested. In the face of her continued lack of responsiveness, we eventually stopped raising the subject.

Then Kwamboka told us that in the past she and her sisters-in-law (husband's brothers' wives living in adjacent homesteads) had been close friends and had helped one another. When Getonto was stricken with polio, however, she had decided that her sisters-in-law, out of envy of her continued fertility and the health of her children, had bewitched her by disabling her son. This was why she had allowed the hedges to grow 6 feet high around her property and no longer visited her friends or allowed them to visit her. She was afraid for her other children and her cattle as well. As for Getonto, she said, nothing would help him now. Moreover, if she got a brace for his leg, her enemies might renew their efforts to harm him.

From the beginning of our observations, Kwamboka seemed rather depressed and cheered up only when she nursed and played with Salome. When her mother-in-law died at the end of our first year at Morongo, she was sadder still. Within a short period of time, her son had been crippled by polio, she had become estranged from her sisters-in-law, and she had lost the woman she considered her dearest friend.

Kwamboka had never lived out of Kisii District and had visited the town infrequently. She was not a baptized Christian and had never attended school, but she did not drink alcoholic beverages. She brewed millet-beer (*busaa*) for Makori, who was a heavy drinker and drank distilled spirits (*chang'aa*) as well. He admitted getting into fights when drunk and also beating his wife. Kwamboka never mentioned this, however, and rarely talked about him at all. Their lives seemed quite separate, with Kwamboka as the day-to-day manager of the home, and Makori as provider and disciplinarian to the children. As she neared the end of her child-bearing years, Kwamboka had virtually perfected the organization of her household. She had five "big" children to help her, and with them she ran things smoothly.

Salome's parents were among the most traditional in the sample. Their landholding was extensive by Morongo standards, and Kwamboka was able to produce enough food to feed her household. Makori's small-scale business was barely enough, together with the income from Kwamboka's cash crops, to cover their basic needs. Their primary school-aged children were all attending school, but the eldest son had been waiting at home for a couple of years because they could not afford secondary school fees, and given their alienation from closest patrilineal kin after Getonto's illness, they could not get help from the most expectable income source. Without launching their son into the level of education needed for employment, the family's long-run prospects were bleak, despite the parents' seniority within the structure of the traditional Gusii life course.

Salome was a robust, healthy infant, observed by Sarah LeVine at 7, 9, 11, 13, and 19 months. The only people observed in her immediate environment were her mother and her siblings: Agnes (11) and Sarah (9), who care for her in the afternoon, when their mother is away from home; Osoro, the 6-year-old brother, who cares for her sometimes in the morning while his sisters are in school; Getonto (the 3-year-old brother crippled by polio), and two older brothers, Gichaba (13) and James (16). Her eldest married sister Mary is also present on one occasion.

From the beginning we were struck by how much pleasure Salome and her mother seemed to derive from their relationship and, although they were less enmeshed physically as time went on, their mutual enjoyment remained evident. At 7 months, Salome (S) is sitting on her mother's (M) lap:

> S is playing with M's breast, which is covered. S pats it through the cloth, her eyes on her M's face. She pulls the breast out of the dress and lunges for it, pushing against it and taking the nipple forcefully into her mouth. From time to time, S stops sucking momentarily, then she lunges for it again. She is wearing only a shirt and a length of red string tied around her waist. M laughs and kneads S's bottom, taking the flesh of S's buttocks in her two hands. S rolls off M's lap, and M continues to caress her from head to toe.

At 9 months we have the following observation of Salome with her mother, who is just entering the homestead:

> 3:28: M calls to S, who is standing on sister Sarah's lap with her finger in Sarah's mouth. In response to M, S smiles and vocalizes. She laughs as M comes up to the house, and M and S make eye contact.

3:30: M sits down and takes S onto her lap. She helps S take out the breast. They have eye contact and both smile. M looks away but S's eyes remain on her face as she muses. Then S turns from the breast to watch Sarah running off.

3:32: S leaves the breast to look up at Agnes to whom M is talking, then she turns back to nursing. S has eye contact with M, who smiles and talks to her. S takes the breast in both hands and squeezes it. Sarah returns with a comb with which Agnes starts to fix M's hair. S watches them closely while she nurses.

3:35: S. vocalizes briefly to M, but M is talking to Agnes. S resumes nursing, her eyes on M's face.

3:36: S sits up, sputtering. Without looking down at her, M asks what she is saying. S has her hand on M's neck and is vocalizing softly.

3:38: S nurses again, playing with her mother's neck and leaning back luxuriously against her. Meanwhile, S fixes gaze on the hairdressing being done by sister Agnes.

3:40: S. finishes nursing, sits straight up, grabs another comb and examines it. She leans against M, vocalizing softly.

A little later Salome seems ready to play.

3:53: S catches M's eye. M turns her over and then lifts her up, holding her face-to-face. M caresses S's buttocks; they gaze at one another, smiling, for a full minute. M carries S to a grassy place and they sit down. Agnes resumes combing her mother's hair, and S stands and leans against M. S squeals with delight, has eye contact with M, and both are laughing. They play. M says, "See that chicken!" but S wants the other breast. They have a game getting it out, and while S is nursing she and M gaze at one another.

Much of the time in which Salome and Kwamboka are observed together is taken up with nursing, which is both a serious and playful activity. Kwamboka initiates a great deal of play, and sometimes Salome seems to have a hard time deciding which appeals more, nursing or playing. She is closely and intensely involved with her mother, and with her sisters Agnes and Sarah also. In one observation (11 months) she has been left with Sarah while her mother is at the coffee cooperative:

2:40: They play a greeting game. S hits Sarah, who pretends to cry. They give up that game and Sarah stands S alone on the ground, saying "I have gone away." S cries loudly. Sarah goes off a short way and brings back a skin for S to sit on. They begin a game of combing their hair.

2:42: S turns away, but Sarah continues the game. She re-engages S, who laughs, takes the comb, laughs again, and drops it. Throughout this sequence, she has eye contract with Sarah, who takes the comb, pretending to hide it. S "finds" the comb and laughs. Sarah hugs her from behind. S is laughing delightedly.

2:44: S looks away but Sarah soon reengages her in the combing game. S laughs.

2:45: "Follow me," Sarah tells her. Sarah stands waiting for S and their eyes meet. S smiles and goes back to sit on the skin with Sarah. The game continues. S laughs. Sarah tickles her feet and she snatches the comb away. S "hits" Sarah with it, and then sits down on her lap to be combed.

2:47: S smiles at Sarah who combs her hair. She is alert but serious. A goat comes onto the skin and Sarah chases it away; S smiles at this. Sarah goes back to combing S's hair.

They play with the comb intermittently for 40 minutes, and then Sarah lays aside the comb and begins a new game of "Making Salome a pair of shoes." This in turn leads to a game of "hiding" things for which S then searches.

In general her siblings, including her brothers, respond to Salome's demands for attention, but on one occasion, when she was 19 months old, she was observed with her brothers Osoro (6) and James (16). Their mother was out, Agnes and Sarah were at school, and Osoro was the designated *omoreri*.

9:49: S is standing in the doorway of the boys' house. She clasps her hand over her stomach.

9:50: In silence she stares at the chickens pecking in the grass. The brothers are standing listlessly in front of the house, also in silence.

9:51: S glances up at Osoro, who stands a foot away. He does not look down. A chicken squawks but S does not react.

9:52: S is looking up at the sky. Osoro moves away from the house and S follows him.

9:53: S looks at observer.

9:54: S retreats into the house, where she cowers back, poking at the door.

9:55: S continues jabbing at the door with her finger, her face immobile.

9:56: Osoro goes into the house and S follows him. He touches her arm and they look one another in the eye. S vocalizes.
9:57: In silence, S leans against the bed, examining a bottle.

This very slow pace, almost devoid of interaction, was typical of the time Salome spent with her brother. Indeed, when she was with Osoro, Salome almost seemed like a different child from the one we had seen before with her mother and sister. As Salome got older, however, Kwamboka left her more often and for longer periods with Osoro, who had been kept out of school for the very purpose of caring for his little sister and his disabled brother, Getonto. As time went on, the joyfulness of Salome's infancy became less and less evident.

Salome's early interactions deviated from those of the sample as a whole in having a mother and siblings who played with her during infancy, engaging her in joyful and exciting bouts of interaction. Her mother Kwamboka, enduring a self-imposed isolation in response to the fear of others aroused by her son's polio affliction, may have comforted herself by playing with the baby; the isolation itself kept her from being observed by those who would consider it unseemly according to the Gusii code of conduct. The play episodes involved face-to-face smiling and laughing coupled with touching but relatively few words and fewer still efforts at conversation. And despite Salome's status as a lastborn child expected to have longer access to her mother, Kwamboka appeared to have reduced her daytime involvement by 19 months as though she were pregnant again. In other words, Salome's observed environment was unusual in the amount of interactive excitement generated and tolerated during the first year, but its nonverbal format and temporal schedule for diminished maternal attention resembled that of other children in the sample.

### JUSTIN

Justin was the fifth child and fourth son of Marisera and her husband Charles, a clerk in the Indian Ocean port of Mombasa about 500 miles from Morongo, who was rarely at home and was remiss in his financial and ritual support for their household. In fact, between his leave in September 1974, when Justin was conceived, and the end of our field study almost 2 years later, Charles did not return to visit his wife and children; we never saw him. He did not send money for baby clothes at Justin's birth, as is customary among labor migrants. Charles invited Marisera to visit him when Justin was 6 to 8 months old, to "let the father see the child before the first tooth appears" – another custom among men working far away from home – but she refused to go, on the grounds that he was needed at home not only to see the baby but also to attend the festivities surrounding the circumcision of his only daughter and supervise the construction of a new house. He did not come, and his elder brother paid most of the costs of building the house. Once it was built, that is, after Marisera finished daubing on the mud walls (a customary Gusii woman's task), she could not move in, because her husband had not performed required rituals. Thus Justin's infancy coincided with the increasing estrangement of his father from his mother, who became markedly depressed as the months went on.

Marisera lived with her five children in a large homestead. It was headed by her elderly father-in-law, a respected Morongo elder, living with his third (and only surviving) wife. The other residents were his two youngest sons, still teenaged schoolboys; the first wife of Charles's elder brother (a highly placed government official in Mombasa) and her five children and a granddaughter; and one of Charles's half-brothers (son of one of the elder's deceased wives) with his two wives and 14 children – all of whom were frequent visitors at her house.

Marisera was a member in good standing of this extended family and was appreciated and supported there. She had never attended school, had been married before her first menses through the arrangement of one of Charles's half-sisters (who was married into her father's lineage), and had met Charles only once before 14 cows were paid for her and she moved in as his wife. She had been a hard-working daughter-in-law and had borne four sons, the eldest of whom had been circumcised several years before and was now 13; this gave her a strong and secure status in the family. Despite Charles's erratic performance as her husband, the reasons for which were unclear, his parents and brother were committed to her and provided the material and social support that should have come from him.

Marisera, who was 30 years old in 1975, was well liked in the neighborhood. Women who might have envied her membership in a prosperous homestead could pity her because of the difficulties she had with Charles, thus giving her security from the fear of envy. She had a bright social manner in adult company, but when alone or with her children, she sometimes appeared self-absorbed and depressed. Having grown up about 4 miles from Morongo, Marisera visited her mother and sisters frequently, and they also visited her. She attended every gathering in the neighborhood, including the Roman Catholic mass, and enjoyed socializing with other women on all these occasions. She went out drinking with her sister-in-law and mother-in-law every afternoon. Marisera's drinking habit was not criticized because she could afford to buy beer without depriving her children, and she had a 9-year-old daughter, Jane, who cared for Justin and cooked for all the children when she was out. Furthermore, Marisera was always home by nightfall and did not get involved with men, even when she had been drinking.

With five children, Marisera was in the middle of her childbearing years and had children big enough to help her. Jane and Jared, her second son, were the right ages to act as *abareri* for Justin, but Jane was in school all morning. When Jared also went to school, Marisera hired a 9-year-old boy, from a neighborhood family too poor to send him to school, to be *omoreri*. He seemed an intelligent, alert boy and was more visibly attentive to Justin than Jane or Jared had been. In the course of a day, Justin would be held, jiggled, and carried about by numerous people apart from his designated *omoreri*.

Meanwhile, however, Marisera was socially unresponsive to Justin's continued attempts to engage her. During the first months after his birth, she would offer her breast in response to any sign of his distress. Only occasionally did she engage him in social exchange, which was almost always initiated and terminated by him, and by 7 months, these episodes had become rare. When Justin was 12 months old, an all-day observation and videotaping was done at their home, and Marisera evaded all but a few seconds' eye contact with Justin, despite his repeated and vigorous attempts to get her attention. Although this kind of behavior is not so exceptional in a Gusii context as it would be in an American one (as indicated in the previous chapter), Marisera was less socially responsive to her baby during numerous observations than were other women of her age and stage in the life course.

This reflected in part her emotional state as a neglected wife, but she seemed to enjoy infant care less, and relations with older women more, than many others we observed.

Justin was one of the smallest children in Cohort I in terms of weight and height, though he was far from abnormally small. In each of his first four home observations – at 6 weeks and 3, 7, and 9 months – at least four persons were present, including siblings and cousins, grandmother, and various aunts. Each person held Justin at some point but few interactions were sustained for a long period; he tended to be fussy and was thus passed from one person to another. Frequently he tried to elicit attention from one of them, but they were too involved in other activities to respond to him. When Marisera was present, her interaction with Justin consisted primarily of nursing him, while keeping her attention on the visitors with whom she was talking.

When Justin was 3 months old, we see him in the fields where his mother has brought him while she harvests her maize. Several small children have followed into the maize field, but none is an *omoreri*. Marisera intends to leave Justin (J) to sleep on a mat in the shade between nursings. At this point, he has awakened, and she holds him on her lap:

> 10:34: J is watching M's face. He smiles and laughs. M looks down at him briefly, but she is talking to a visitor. M looks down at him intermittently but there is no eye contact.
> 10:35: J is fretting while M talks. M picks up a leaf and waves it in his face. She lays him over her knees. J quiets, staring at the leaf. Then J looks at the observer and frets again; he waves his arms. M shakes the leaf harder, staring beyond J while he looks around.
> 10:37: M continues with her conversation with the visitor; she shakes the leaf but J pays no attention to it; he stares at the observer.
> 10:39: J cries and stretches. M holds him face to face and says "Ero, ero" (an exclamation to catch the attention of a baby) very loudly to him. M initiates a playful interaction (not noted). J quiets for 20 seconds, but there is no eye contact and M stares away over his head.
> 10:40: J smiles at M and she smiles back. J vocalizes happily and M responds, imitating him; they copy one another, both with bright faces. J squeals and M sticks out her tongue at him. J's eyes are always on her, but M is constantly looking around.

At 9 months we see Justin and his mother at home. Marisera has been daubing mud on the walls of her new house, while her daughter Jane cares for Justin. But now Justin has awakened and Marisera is nursing him under the eaves.

> 1:45 p.m: M stares at the ground, her face still and silent.
>
> 1:46: M suddenly shouts at one of her other children, supporting J with one arm and looking over his head at his sibling.
>
> 1:47: For 2 seconds M looks down at J and then away. J holds her breast.
>
> 1:48: As M nurses, she cuts her fingernails with a razor blade. J watches this.
>
> 1:49: J is still nursing, now slipping off M's lap.
>
> 1:50: M doesn't readjust J or look at him; she is talking to her sister-in-law.
>
> 1:51: M calls to Jane to come and take J, but he complains and leans back against M, so she brings out the other breast.
>
> 1:52: As J nurses, he watches his aunt (the sister-in-law, father's elder brother's wife), who says to him, laughingly, "Drinking, are you? Leave some for me!"
>
> 1:53: As M talks to one of his siblings, J holds her finger.
>
> 1:54: J releases M's finger; she turns to chastise a sibling, and the nipple falls out of his mouth. J waits silently until M pops it back into his mouth.
>
> 1:55: J nurses briefly while M chats. When he stops nursing, M cleans his nostrils quickly and hands him to Jane. Then she resumes daubing mud on the house.

These passages show that Marisera now devotes little attention to the baby apart from feeding and cleaning, although occasionally engaging in a playful interchange. When she turns away from him to talk to someone else or to resume her activities, Justin usually frets, at which point she reengages him by offering the breast again; as soon as he seems to be pacified, she turns her attention elsewhere. Almost all the interaction between them, from the earliest observation at 6 weeks, is initiated by Justin, as is generally true for Justin's interactions with others as well.

Jane, Justin's 9-year-old designated *omoreri*, is present in almost every observation, although she is not always caring for him. She was never observed playing with him, although she jiggles him when he cries and sometimes tries to feed him gruel; she tends to hold him passively with only an occasional nuzzle. Jane was circumcised shortly before Justin's 7-month observation, in fact, that observation took place while the family was celebrating her *ekiarokio,* the emergence from seclusion. After her initiation ceremony, she no longer consistently cares for Justin, although she is still regarded as his *omoreri.*

Several others care for Justin but rarely play with him: Jared, his brother, carries him on his back during one observation; Agnes, an aunt, holds him, attempts to quiet him when he frets, and tries to feed him. Justin's grandmother interacts with him on several occasions and has more sustained and involved interactions with him than the others. At 6 weeks, for example, there is this observation:

> 9:35: J, who is crying, is handed to grandmother (G).
> 9:36: G holds J face-to-face and says, "What is it? I haven't got any milk. Why are you crying? You're a naughty boy!" G bounces him, sings, wipes his bottom quickly, and sits him sideways on her lap. G pats J and he soothes and is quiet.
> 9:38: J appears to doze.
> 9:40: J opens eyes briefly, makes eye contact with G; J eyes rest on G's face.
> 9:41: J is crying, in the full sun. G picks him up and holds him face-to-face, singing and talking to him. She bounces him on her shoulder, singing meanwhile. She lifts him up and down. G examines J's bottom, because he has defecated a little, and comments that he never sleeps. J cries harder; he is trembling and agitated. G tried hard to calm him, jiggling and talking to him rhythmically, in time with the jiggling. She then rocks him in her arms.
> 9:45: G says rhythmically, "Kira, kira" (hush, hush), holding J on her lap. She is feeling tired, so she lays him down on a sack. J cries louder, so G picks him up again and holds him face-to-face. She scolds him, jiggles him, and talks to him.

In most cases, however, caregivers' interactions with Justin are brief, as they turn away to converse with each other or carry on with their activities. At 7 months old, for example:

> 12:04: J is lying alone on a blanket, watching M 12 feet away. He moves his arms and vocalizes happily. M leaves.
> 12:05: J is waving his arms in the sunlight, vocalizing loudly and happily.
> 12:06: J is still waving his arms; no one is paying attention. J vocalizes. All the older children are some way off and the adults

are talking with each other around him. Suddenly J begins to cry, waving his arms, but in distress now. The sun is hot in his face. A brother, aged 4, is told to move him.

12:07: On his brother's lap, J cries harder still. No one else pays any attention.

12:09: J's 13-year-old brother takes J on his lap and he stops crying.

12:10: The brother takes him into the house to M, who is busy heating beer. He is left on his sister Jane's lap beside the fire.

12:11: Kemunto, a teenage girl, takes J and he quiets and has eye contact with her. Kemunto jiggles him while the other children run out of the house. J urinates.

12:12: J frets as M passes. M imitates his fretting, hands him a corn cob to pacify him, and disappears. J seems to be pleased; he beats the cob on the ground and examines it.

At 9 months, we see many different people taking a momentary interest in Justin:

2:01: J vomits on Elizabeth's (aunt) dress; she looks him in the eye briefly. J vocalizes.

2:02: Elizabeth looks away. J slaps his leg, vocalizes, and seems to be singing to himself.

2:03: J has eye contact with observer. J touches her leg. Another aunt comes up and talks to him, and J vocalizes in return. After 20 seconds, she leaves.

2:04: Agnes, his mother's younger sister, picks up J and holds him on her hip, while she continues to converse with another woman.

2:05: J touches Agnes's mouth, vocalizes, and pulls on her hand. J catches M's eye.

2:06: Agnes hands J back to Jane, the *omoreri*. Gladys, a 2-year-old cousin, puts her face close to J's.

2:07: A third aunt takes J, but she is talking to other people. J vocalizes in her direction.

The 2-year-old cousin was one of the few persons observed playing with Justin; usually he tried to interact with others who were near him without success. It was not clear why this was so among the many adults and children of this large extended family. It was clearer to all on our research team who observed her that Marisera avoided social engagement with Justin, reflecting – by comparison with other sample mothers – a general lack of interest in interacting with children as well as the depressed mood induced by her husband's abandonment. This behavioral style might be cause for concern in a Western middle-class context, but not in Morongo, where Marisera's behavior was seen as consistent with the requirements of the Gusii maternal role.

### EVANS

Evans was the second child (and second son) of Joshua and Elizabeth; he was observed by Sarah LeVine from 9 to 21 months of age. Joshua, a Catholic who had attended school for 8 years, was 27 years old in 1976 and worked as a surveyor for the Ministry of Lands and Settlement about 25 miles east of Morongo; he usually came home every other weekend. The eldest of eight children, Joshua had gained admission to secondary school but went to work instead because his parents were unable to pay the school fees. He was fluent in Swahili and English, attended Mass regularly, and owned a radio and other consumer goods indicating involvement with the mass media and the world outside Morongo. His wife, Elizabeth, who was 24, had also been the eldest of eight and was raised a Catholic; having attended school for 5 years, she could read the newspaper in Swahili, write a letter if necessary, and listened to the radio regularly. Her marriage to Joshua 6 years earlier had been a love match; they had "eloped," and the bridewealth was not paid until Evans, their second child, was 18 months old.

Elizabeth and Joshua's house was small, meticulously clean, and stocked with European-style furniture and newspaper photographs on the wall; the grass in the yard was kept short and the surrounding hedge was clipped by Joshua on his weekends at home. This little enclosure, a conspicuously Westernized setting for family life, was also an island of peace and order within the tumultuous homestead in which it was embedded.

Joshua's parents, the paternal grandparents of the baby Evans, both drank heavily (and in the case of the father, also took *enyasore,* marijuana) and were persistently engaged in quarrels with each other and other members of the homestead that Joshua, as their oldest son, and Elizabeth as his wife, were called upon to settle. Joshua was also the main source of school fees for his younger siblings. Joshua's father had inherited 7 acres of land but had four sons, who had to look to employment rather than agriculture for their livelihood. As the elder of his generation in the lineage, the father had taken two widows of kinsmen as his leviratic wives, creating tension with his wife and compounding long-standing disputes among his younger brothers' families. Thus, though Joshua and Elizabeth were surrounded by his kin, their relationships represented problems to be dealt with rather than sources of support for them as young parents.

Elizabeth was a quiet, cheerful, and energetic young woman who seemed to enjoy her work and her children, dealt effectively with her difficult parents-in-law (who were quite attached to her), and had achieved more stature within the homestead than would have been due her as a mother whose eldest son was still years away from circumcision. She was on speaking terms with everyone (she was possibly the only adult who was), worked for and soothed her mother-in-law, and managed to find a good friend among Joshua's middle-aged aunts – a woman from whom she could draw emotional sustenance. An important bond with this older woman was the latter's loss of a young son, her ninth child; at the same time, one of Elizabeth's brothers, whose *omoreri* she had been, had also died. Elizabeth remembered loving this child more than anyone else in her family, and at the time she talked about him to us 4 years later, she was still sad about his death.

In contrast to most of the mothers in the sample, Elizabeth was often seen playing with her children. She delighted in talking to and being entertained by her two young sons. In the privacy of her own yard, surrounded by high hedges so that nobody could see the fun she was having (inappropriately, by Gusii standards), she spent many lively hours with her children. Paul, the elder, was a remarkably articulate 4-year-old. So precocious was he that Elizabeth constantly worried he might provoke jealousy and consequently malevolence should he wander in the neighborhood, and she tried to keep him home. Whenever he escaped to another homestead, Elizabeth punished him severely.

Joshua was closer to his wife and children than most men in Morongo. He did not drink, and he spent more time at home and less with his male peers on the weekends when he returned to Morongo. Neighbors commented on how closely Elizabeth and Joshua "listened to each other" and how well they "went together." Joshua saw his role primarily as that of provider, as other fathers did, but he also said that a father should be involved in the routine daily care of small children, as well as teaching them respect, *ogosika*. He was seen at home talking to his children. Elizabeth and Joshua both wanted to have four children, which they thought was the number they could educate; then they would practice birth control. Elizabeth recalled that caring for her little brother had been the most pleasurable experience of her childhood. Her love of children made her popular with those nearby, and Joshua's younger sisters were always willing to care for her children, although they complained about other young mothers in the homestead.

Evans's height was close to the average for American children the same age, but his weight was considerably lower than children in the same cohort of the sample. He was observed by Sarah LeVine at 9, 13, 16, 19, and 21 months. In more than half of the observations only nuclear family members were present; in the others, there were two uncles, Elizabeth's younger sister Agnes, who acted as his *omoreri* for several months, and several child cousins from the homestead. In this world Evans seemed secure. During some observations, Elizabeth played with him *and* his brother Paul; few other mothers were ever observed playing in this way with both an infant and an older sibling at the same time. Elizabeth, in contrast with Marisera, was consistently attentive and congenial to her baby, but without being as relaxed or sensuous with him as Kwamboka was with Salome. One factor in this latter contrast was the older child: Paul, the 4-year-old, was extremely active and insistent on getting her attention, unlike Kwamboka's Getonto, who sat sadly by himself. Unless her husband was home, Elizabeth hardly got an uninterrupted moment with Evans. On one such occasion, when Joshua was home for the weekend and was distracting Paul, Elizabeth (M) was sitting with 9-month-old Evans (E) on her lap.

> E pounds on M's breast, but he has already nursed at length, so she ignores him and listens to the conversation her husband is having with Paul and a relative. E sucks one of the buttons on her dress. He trills. E looks down briefly at him, catching his eye. E begins to whine, so M stands him up on her lap and holds him face-to-face. They have eye contact. M smiles at him and tries to soothe him; she gives E the breast momentarily but he turns away. Meanwhile, Joshua and Paul are laughing together

and E turns briefly to see what is happening. E wriggles on M's lap. M fondles his head as he makes periodic lunges at her breast, playing his own game. M raises him to a standing position on her lap, and E mouths M's cheek. They play at mouthing each other's cheeks, smiling and laughing. Paul comes over, puts both arms around E, who quietly sinks down to his mother's lap again and resumes nursing. As soon as nursing is finished, Paul embraces E again.

Only rarely is Elizabeth alone with Evans; usually she has to deal with both children at once, which requires considerable patience and skill. When Evans is 13 months old, we record following sequence:

10:35: E trying to get on M's lap. "What are you doing?" she laughs. E swings round onto her lap. Paul is playing at M's feet.

10:37: Paul plunges forward, laughing. He shoves E, wherupon M tells him to lie down. He does so, pretending to sleep. E is sitting next to him, engaged in a game with M: They are playing with the lid of a can. M tosses and catches it as E laughs. The he tries to copy her, as she smiles encouragingly.

10:39: E stands, waving the lid. M watches him. He drops it.

10:40: M helps him pick it up. They go on with this game until E laughs and reaches for the zipper of M's dress. He remains where he is, sitting next to her on the skin, and reaching up to nurse.

10:41: Ten seconds later E stops and plays with the nipple. Paul laughs at E, distracting him. M tells Paul to go away and leave them alone, and E nurses again. Meanwhile, M examines his scalp for lice and Paul romps noisily around them.

10:43: As Paul flops down beside him, Evans stops nursing momentarily, then begins again.

10:44: E bumps rhythmically as he nurses. This annoys M, who tells him to stop. He fondles the nipple briefly and nurses again. Paul races toward them and M scolds him.

10:45: E finishes nursing. He stands up and climbs on M's lap to hug her. She laughs, "Are you full?" at which point E tries to pull down her zipper again. M hands him his can lid to distract him. "Go after this can," she says, so E turns and catches Paul's eye. E wants to be involved in the game Paul is playing with a corn cob.

At first, E is cared for by his young aunt, and later, after she returns home, by two cousins. Although he seems to be more attached to his brother than to any of his assigned caregivers, he is nevertheless content to stay with them. On one occasion when he is 16 months old, Elizabeth, who is in and out of the homestead, has put her sister Agnes in charge of Evans:

> 1:05: "Mama has gone," Agnes says, as M leaves. She and E play a game, tapping on the top of a wooden stool.
> 1:06: E is enjoying the game, but he whimpers. Agnes examines his hand and sees he has a splinter, which she removes.
> 1:07: E, his face interested and alert, turns to watch a visitor with Paul.
> 1:08: E turns back to Agnes and the stool, but does not resume playing; he stands quietly next to Agnes.
> 1:09: Agnes tells E, "Go to Paul." E vocalizes in response and trots over, bright-faced. He squats down to look inside the visitor's basket, smiling.
> 1:10: Agnes says, "Come back here, don't touch anything." E does as she says, and grasps her knee. She is eating sugarcane; E wants some, too. He reaches for it.
> 1:11: E frets and looks about for support. Agnes gives him some sugarcane.
> 1:12 M comes into the yard and Agnes disappears into the house. E vocalizes a greeting to M, but does not seek her attention. He is happy with his sugarcane.
> 1:13: M goes out of the yard into the field to pick vegetables. E toddles after her.
> 1:14: "Go away, go home," M tells him. E stops in the gateway, chewing his cane.
> 1:15: M comes toward E, so he retreats into the yard. He squats in the entrance, chewing.
> 1:19: "Mama, Mama," E murmurs, but makes no further move to follow his mother.

Evans was an alert child, clearly accustomed to a good deal of attention. His contacts with people involved much play, some initiated by himself, some by others. Rarely was there the abrupt and terminated interaction with others that was so typical of Justin. After he was weaned at 17 months, however, his mother reported that he cried for 3 days. At 19 months, he was noticeably more clingy than he had been shortly before weaning. Evans was the only one of the three children discussed in this chapter who was observed at home after weaning. His shift in mood was quite striking. Evans was distinctly less playful than before. The last observation was at 21 months. In his mother's absence he was solemn and passive. He rarely became involved in sustained interaction with any of the four persons in his immediate environment, even though these included his brother and his regular *omoreri*.

Elizabeth was a mother who broke some of the rules of Gusii mothering: She gave her young children a good deal of exciting interactive attention, playing with them and tolerating a certain amount of interference by the older one of her attention to the baby. A traditional Gusii mother would say it was no wonder that Evans was sad and disappointed by his weaning; his mother raised his expectations by her playfulness – like a maternal grandmother – rather than preparing him properly for diminished attention. Perhaps there was some truth in this. On the other hand, Paul's liveliness and playfulness long after his weaning suggested that Evans's shift in mood and activity level, though still evident 4 months after weaning, might have been a transient phase.

## THREE CASES IN PERSPECTIVE

By examining three sample infants in their particular family contexts, we have encountered themes of family and infant care that appeared in earlier chapters: The heavy, almost solitary responsibility of the married woman for the home; her frequently problematic relationship with her husband and/or his parents, brothers, and their wives; the importance of age-seniority to a woman's freedom and power within the family; the assumption that a woman will continue bearing children until menopause and will benefit from their help in the absence of her husband from the home – these themes of family life are present in each case. We see here the variation in infant care according to the affluence and seniority of the mother and the birth order of the child; the competing demands of work, maintenance of adult relationships, and child care on mothers; the reliance on older children to take care of babies; the attachment of babies to their mothers, even though they spend much of the daytime with child caregivers.

The quality of interaction between mother and child sampled from our observations deserves special notice. These three mothers differed considerably in the amount and type of attention they gave to their infants when they were together, and their infants differed in their physical growth and emotional responsiveness, too. Play occurs between Gusii mothers and their babies as the vignettes show, but it is relatively rare in the observational record, and like other interactive episodes, it tends to be brief and nonverbal – with child caregivers and other children as well as with the mother. The pace of social interaction between the infant and others tends to be extremely slow, rarely reaching high levels of excitement. Infants are often spectators of social interaction going on between their caregivers and older children and adults. They assert themselves with their mothers to get fed and to attract their attention for social interaction. Gusii mothers are uniformly responsive in feeding but variable in their social attention to the infant, depending on the mood, situation, and the personality of the mother and age of the child – in the context of a cultural code that does not encourage mothers to play with their children. The vignettes show that however dominated Gusii mothers may be by the normative code and the pressures of work, they develop individual relationships with their children in accordance with their personal inclinations and family situations. Two of the three mothers described – the first (Kwamboka) and the third (Elizabeth) – were exceptional in the amount they played with and took evident delight in their babies and in their relative lack of concern about the dangers of getting them excited. Yet in both cases they followed Gusii norms in the nonverbal quality of their play routines and in their diminishing attention to the child during the second year of life.

*Part IV*

# Interpretations

# 10

## Early child development in an African context: Comparative lessons

In this book we have focused on the *ordinary devoted mother* of Kisii District, Kenya, and her provision of a *facilitating environment* for the *maturational processes* of her infants during the years 1974–1976. Using these terms coined by the British pediatrician-psychoanalyst D. W. Winnicott[1] implies a general similarity between Gusii mothers and the English mothers Winnicott observed: Both are committed to help their infants grow and thrive. It does not mean, however, that the care they provide is the same. On the contrary, the evidence presented in the foregoing chapters indicates that Gusii mothers' understanding of what is best for their babies, the goals of care to which they are devoted, the specific processes they seek to facilitate, their methods of facilitation, and the kind of caregiving environment in which the methods are embedded, differ from those of London or the suburban United States.[2] In this chapter we analyze these similarities and differences comparatively as cultural models with developmental consequences, taking first the perspective of the parent and then that of the developing child. Moving beyond the cultural relativity of these divergent models, we assess the costs and benefits of their associated practices during infancy and in subsequent development. Finally, we explore the implications of this analysis for theories of child development and the acquisition of culture.

### INFANT CARE AMONG THE GUSII AND THE AMERICAN WHITE MIDDLE CLASS

In comparing these two populations, we cross the major socioeconomic and demographic divisions between a rural African people and the affluent, urbanized people of a Western industrial country. Gusii mothers bear many more children and have much less access to material resources than their American counterparts, and they participate in a community founded on patrilineal kinship, polygyny, and women's agricultural work. There are abundant reasons *why* the environments they provide for their infants might differ from those of the American white middle class, but a closer look at *how* their practices and assumptions differ can give us insight into the shaping of infant care by particular social and cultural conditions.

Gusii infant care as we observed it at Morongo in the 1970s was influenced by the precolonial models of domestic social and moral order described in Chapter 3. The hierarchical organization of the homestead, the necessity for a wife to live on and cultivate her husband's land – in her own house but under the supervision of his mother – and high fertility as a positively valued reality, were among the elements of Gusii culture that continued to make a visible impact on the environment of infant care. Moreover, the cultural models with which these elements were associated remained primary frames of reference for conceptualizing the life course (Tables 3.1 and 3.2). As ideals for personal development, the models diverge sharply from those of the American white middle class, particularly in their emphasis on domestic hierarchy and high fertility. Thus there is reason to expect, on cultural as well as socioeconomic and demographic grounds, differences in infant care between these two populations.

A cultural model of early child care, by which we mean an ethnographic reconstruction of the premises on which the child care practices of a people are based, can be seen as having three parts: *moral direction,* a *pragmatic design,* and a set of *conventional scripts for action.* This is the cultural software driving parental behavior, as we termed it in Chapter 1. The moral direction covers the normative assumptions about what is best for an infant and what the goals are to which mothers and other caregivers should be devoted. The pragmatic design refers to the general strategy for attaining these goals, specific behavioral devices used, and the schedule for their deployment over infancy and early childhood. The conventional scripts for action are socially expected sequences of caregiving behavior in specific situations, such as responding to the infant's states and communicative signals, that are considered not only normal but natural and necessary. These three parts comprise a "commonsense" folk model,[3]

Table 10.1. *Maternal attention in early child care:*
*Quantity and quality*

|  | Gusii: Pediatric model | American: Pedagogical model |
|---|---|---|
| Goal | Protection | Active engagement, social exchange |
| Means | Soothing | Stimulation, protoconversation |
| Temporal distribution over first 30 months | Decreasing | Increasing |
| Cultural script for selective responsiveness | Respond to distress | Respond to babble |
|  | Modulate excitement | Elicit excitement |
|  | Commands | Questions, praise |

which is often unformulated in local discourse and difficult to elicit from parents because it is taken for granted and seems too obvious to mention. It is the ethnographer's task as an empathic outsider to explicate the assumptions, based on lengthy observation and repeated interviews, and to formulate them as models that guide parental behavior. Although there is the danger that the ethnographer's formulations may overinterpret or misconstrue parental behavior, this can be counteracted by checking them against the observational evidence (as in the earlier chapters) and by presenting them to the parents to see if they recognize the connections between intentions and behavior that are being attributed to them.

The differences between Gusii and American white middle-class mothers in the kinds and amount of attention they give their infants over the first 30 months of life are summarized schematically as cultural models in Table 10.1. For each culture the goal of maternal activities (moral direction), the means of attaining the goal and a schedule for their distribution over infancy and early childhood (pragmatic design), and a script for responding to infant signals (conventional script for action) are listed. We call the Gusii model *pediatric,* because its primary concern is with the survival, health, and physical growth of the infant, and the American model *pedagogical,* because its primary concern is with the

behavioral development of the infant and its preparation for educational interactions. The titles exaggerate, but they serve to
mark the distinct moral directions represented by the two models,
as they influence maternal attention.

In keeping with its pediatric direction, the goal in the Gusii
model is *protection* of the baby from life-threatening illness and
environmental hazards. Gusii mothers do not overtly describe
their task as promoting the survival of their infants, and they do not
understand disease in terms of Western biomedicine, but their
concern with the dangers of infant illness and vulnerability is unmistakable (Chapter 7). Like mothers elsewhere in Africa, the Gusii
implicitly assume that infancy is a period of great danger to the
child's life, requiring virtually constant protection.[4] Furthermore,
no other goal commands their attention to the same degree.

The goals of the American Pedagogical model are active engagement and social exchange, that is, the infant's alertness, curiosity,
interest in surroundings (including physical objects), exploration,
and positive vocal and visual interaction with other persons.[5] Survival and health are background concerns, not commanding immediate attention (except when a child is ill), given reliance on modern medical experts and an infant mortality rate that is only a
fraction of the Gusii rate.[6] In the model we have constructed, the
American white middle-class mother sees herself as a teacher,
among other things, and the infant as a pupil whose readiness for
early education should be in the forefront of maternal attention.

The means shown on Table 10.1 include only the general strategies: soothing for the Gusii, stimulation and protoconversation
for the American. The other components of the Gusii pragmatic
design can be seen in the right-hand column of Table 3.2, that is,
feeding, holding, and physical care as the means of protecting the
baby from disease and injury. Holding on a caregiver's body (including back carrying) is, along with breast-feeding and co-
sleeping, the basic protective formula for infant care among the
Gusii (as for other African peoples).[7] Given that as the context,
maternal activity is to be focused primarily on soothing distress
and calming excitement, such as keeping the baby as satisfied,
calm, and quiet as possible, in other words, in a range of states the
Gusii mother defines as indicating that the baby is well and safe
from harm.

The American means of promoting the goals of active engagement and social exchange are also broader than those indicated on Table 10.1 and include providing long periods of sleep, away from others, so that the infant will be rested enough for the next bout of activity. The well-rested baby is seen as ready to be stimulated by toys and social interaction, specifically by the proto-conversations in which the mother talks to the infant, eliciting a (vocal and motor) response that she interprets as a conversational turn in a continuing "play dialogue."[8] Mothers stimulate verbally by using the simplified, high-pitched register known as "baby talk," and by "scaffolding," that is, taking the preverbal infant's part in the mock conversation, and, later, recasting and expanding the toddler's utterances in forms that better approximate adult speech.[9] These are deliberately educational interventions. As Heath concluded from a study of middle-class urban parents and children in the southeastern United States, "Before the age of 2, the child is socialized into the initiation-reply-evaluation sequences repeatedly described as the central structural feature of classroom lessons."[10]

The temporal distribution of maternal attention is also pragmatically related to the respective goals of the Gusii and American models. For the Gusii mother, her greatest attention to protection through soothing, feeding, and other activities is concentrated on the earliest months of the child's life, when survival is most at risk. We have called this time, ending between 3 and 6 months of age, the period of *postpartum incubation;* after that, she can more confidently reduce her infant-directed care and interaction, leaving the baby with elder siblings in the daytime, working harder in the fields, and anticipating a new pregnancy and the birth of the next child. Some specific features of this phenomenon have changed over time with the introduction of modern medical services and the contraction of the birth interval. But the Gusii strategy of investing more maternal attention in infant care during the early months makes pragmatic sense if (1) the primary goal is protection from risks to survival, (2) the mother has a heavy workload apart from infant care, (3) she is further constrained to ration her care to any one infant by a regular schedule of childbearing from marriage to menopause, and (4) the mother can depend on her older children to provide the toddler with opportunities for play and social interaction, particularly during the second and third years of the child's life.

In the American model the temporal distribution of maternal attention is quite the opposite; it increases over time, as the toddler becomes more capable not only of conversations with the mother but also of attracting and keeping maternal attention through solicitations, demands, long dialogues, displays of accomplishment, tantrums, and other maneuvers of the 2-year-old. Having fostered the infant's capacity for verbal communication and active engagement, the mother finds herself engaged in an expanding relationship with a toddler who sleeps less, talks more, and takes the initiative in interaction.

Each model includes a cultural script for selectively responding to the infant's signals, indicating specifically *which* signals to respond to, *how* to respond to infant excitement, and *what types of utterances* to use in verbal response (Table 10.1). The Gusii, as we have seen in Chapters 6 and 8, are primarily and rapidly responsive to distress signals (i.e., to the baby's cries and frets), much more than to its other vocalizations (i.e., babbles). This is consistent with their protective attitude: Crying indicates a need for immediate soothing, but babbling is unrelated to the Gusii mother's agenda for responsiveness, which does not include mock conversations. American mothers also respond to infant distress, although not as rapidly as their Gusii counterparts, but their responsiveness to babbling distinguishes the American mothers in this cross-cultural comparison. They seize on their babies' apparently random but positive vocalizations to build a pattern of reciprocal and contingent verbal-vocal exchange, approximating the turn-taking conventions of conversational speech.

The scripts also entail different responses to positive emotional excitement in the infant, as shown in the study of videotaped mother–infant interaction presented in Chapter 8. Having elicited the infant's positive excitement along with its vocalization, the American mother attempts to heighten that response in a sustained rhythmic exchange. The Gusii mother, on the other hand, faced with an excited baby following the investigator's instructions, tends to avert her gaze, thus dampening the excitement. This suggests that Gusii mothers tend to consider all forms of infant excitement, positive (joy) or negative (distress), as being equally distant from the calm state they seek.

Finally, the scripts for talking to infants, Command for the Gusii versus Questions and Praise for the Americans, are strikingly divergent. American mothers frequently use questions to promote the infant's excited participation in social exchange: They create a protoconversation with repeated questioning, lavishing praise on the infant for each vocal or motor response, which is taken as if it were an answer to the question. Praise continues to be an important part of maternal speech as the child grows older and the mother thinks of herself as building self-confidence by rewarding the toddler with her verbal approval for each new sign of mastery. In terms of the American Pedagogical model, both questions and praise are essential to the encouragement of learning and social engagement in the preschool child.

The Gusii script is antithetical in this respect to the American one, as indicated by the rarity of praise and questions in speech directed to Gusii infants, and the predominance of commands intended partly to prevent or stop them from getting into danger, particularly as they get older (Chapter 8). It is noteworthy in this connection that physical exploration by the toddler is seen as dangerous rather than promoting development: Satisfaction with the developmental accomplishment of walking is qualified by the concern that the child might stumble into the cooking fire or otherwise become injured.[11] Thus at 12 to 15 months of age the sample infants were still being held or carried in 42% of daytime observations (Figure 6.4), though most had been able to walk since 9 months. Nevertheless, verbal controls (i.e., negative commands) by the mother or older sibling gradually replace the safety of being carried on the back. Gusii mothers consider it useful in terms of control for a baby to acquire fear, not only of actual hazards such as fire but also of domestic animals, especially dogs, and imaginary creatures, which are used by the mother or a sibling to frighten the child.[12]

To understand the meanings of command as the dominant script for talking to young children, the avoidance of praise, and the positive value placed on inculcating fear, it is necessary to go beyond the Pediatric model to the model of training in respect and obedience (*ogosika* and *okoigweera*, respectively), which overlaps it in time, as indicated on Table 3.2. The Pediatric model, with protection as its goal, applies fully only to infants being breast-fed (up to 15 to 17 months in our samples). Weaning means that the child has survived the worst risks of infancy and is healthy enough to thrive without mother's milk and sleeping next to her; birth of the next child (at 21 to 23 months in our sample) means that the mother's attention must be shifted to the newborn. After that, the Respect-Obedience model prevails, with its goal of a compliant child who comprehends maternal commands, obeys and makes few demands (Table 3.2) – a child, in other words, who fits into the hierarchical organization of the home and does not undermine it. In the context of this model, praise is explicitly rejected by Gusii mothers as a verbal device that encourages conceit and would make even a good child rude and disobedient,[13] meaning disruptive of the hierarchy. Thus the avoidance of praise is part of the pragmatic design by which mothers hope to develop a child who will become a compliant subordinate in the domestic hierarchy.

Deliberate training in respect and obedience can be traced back into the first year of life, in the prevalence of maternal commands even at 3 months, or more firmly after 9 months, when positive utterances have declined and negative utterances (largely commands) are rising (Figure 8.9.c). But the command script becomes primary during the second and third years, especially after weaning, when the child is deemed old enough to learn how to function within the age hierarchy of the household headed by the mother, as the most subordinate person in the sibling group. On the assumption that the 2-year-old is fully integrated into the sibling hierarchy, a mother tends to intervene only when something goes wrong, issuing orders and sometimes reprimands.

Both the Pediatric and Respect-Obedience models set a low priority on mothers talking to infants and young children altogether, even after they are capable of understanding speech. Conversations between mother and child are not encouraged or expected, though they occur every day at low frequency and brief duration. More frequent is the kind of interaction in which a toddler asks the mother for something and the mother gives it, or the mother issues a command and the toddler obeys with action, not words.[14] The mother does some tutoring in obedience, but the expectation is that the rest of the child's socialization – including play, speech, and interaction – will occur within the sibling group, where the toddler is an apprentice, that is, an initially peripheral participant in an ongoing social order.[15] Having protected the infant during the period of greatest survival risk, the mother turns her attention to other work and then to the next baby, confident that the toddler will be cared for and participate in the sibling group with only occasional intervention by her – to support the hierarchical norms.

Cultural models like the ones reviewed here, imbued as they are with moral rectitude, pragmatic coherence, and the absolutism of conventional practice, provide mothers with a sense that they know good infant care, and perhaps even more certainly bad care, when they see it. For comparative purposes, it is interesting to consider how Gusii and American white middle-class mothers might criticize each other's customary practices if they saw them.[16] (We have fragmentary data on this, but we shall speculate beyond them.)

The Gusii would be shocked at the slow or casual responsiveness of American mothers to the crying of young infants (we know this from having shown them videotapes; see Chapter 6); this signals incompetent caregiving from their perspective. They would be similarly appalled by the practice of putting babies to sleep in separate beds or rooms, where they cannot be closely monitored at night, rather than with the mother. In general, the Gusii would find it strange that a mother would permit the baby so little access to her body even when they are in the house together. They would be baffled by the discovery that some of the American mothers (about half in our Boston sample)[17] did not breast-feed for more than a few weeks and that they talked so often and so intensely to young infants who can neither comprehend their words nor reply in kind. They would strongly disapprove of the unruly, disrespectful American toddlers, and might well attribute their disobedience to excessive praise bestowed on them as babies, and to maternal solicitation of their preferences as toddlers.

The Americans, on the other hand, would not only classify the Gusii practice of using an unsupervised child 5 or 6 years old for infant day care as a type of neglect, but they would consider the Gusii infants deprived of the stimulation and emotional support that comes from a mother's playing with her baby, using toys, speech, eye contact, and vocal tones coded by Americans as forms of warmth and affection. They would be appalled that Gusii mothers often do not look at their babies when breast-feeding them (or at most other times) and that praise is more or less prohibited in the Gusii script for maternal response. Despite the lengthy breast-feeding and co-sleeping, then, the Americans would probably see the Gusii mothers as emotionally unavailable to their babies, giving them a poor basis for the competence and self-confidence they will need as they grow up. They would also see the Gusii mothers as unacceptably authoritarian and punitive with their children. The American mothers might describe the quiet and easily comforted Gusii babies and toddlers as "vegetables." And they would probably feel that a child at 17 or even 24 months was not ready to be consigned by the mother to socialization in the sibling group.

Thus each culture's model of infant care constitutes a moral and pragmatic position from which the other's practices can be devastatingly criticized as misguided, ineffective, and even immoral. Our answer to these ethnocentric critiques is that the infant care practices of the Gusii and the American white middle class represent strategies and scripts aimed at different goals, each of which makes (or did make) moral and pragmatic sense in its own context. This does not mean, however, that our examination of them must rest there. On the contrary, it remains possible to ask what the benefits and costs of these practices are to the infants as well as their parents, and to use the data from our research to answer this question for the Gusii.

### ASSESSING THE BENEFITS AND COSTS OF GUSII INFANT CARE

To what extent does the application of the Pedagogical and Respect-Obedience models in Gusii practices of early child care operate to achieve their culture-specific goals or other beneficial or desirable outcomes, and does it lead to outcomes that might be considered costly or undesirable? What is the effectiveness of Gusii child care practices as a parental investment strategy in which resources are committed to maximize certain goals and minimize certain risks? In this section we consider these difficult questions in the light of the evidence presented in previous chapters and other findings from child development research. We begin by asking about Gusii practices: Are they effective in protecting against risks to child survival and in raising obedient and compliant children?

## Protection: The soothing strategy

The major risks to the survival of infants, namely, infectious diseases, were largely uncontrolled in Gusiiland until the middle of the 20th century, when Western medical care, public health measures, and rising material living standards began to have an effect on child mortality rates. Prior to that time, Gusii mothers could depend only on intensive and prolonged breast-feeding and physical protection day and night to safeguard children from ill health and injuries within a larger context of environmental danger. Here we consider whether their practices of continuous holding, co-sleeping, soothing distress rapidly, and feeding frequently, applied in a concentrated way during the first months of life, worked to promote survival and other positive outcomes.

One survival-relevant consequence of these practices is the ensurance of early weight gain: Body contact, frequent breast-feeding, and minimal crying contribute to metabolic efficiency, increased caloric intake, and reduced caloric expenditure, respectively, leading to an infant who gains weight more rapidly in the weeks and months after birth and is better able to survive infections. Recent studies of early infancy provide support for this claim.

Premature infants who are massaged during the first 10 days after birth, for example, gain more weight during that time than those who are not massaged, without a difference in caloric intake.[18] Insofar as the continuous holding and handling of the Gusii infant provides the tactile and kinesthetic stimulation of a massage (we believe it does), then it promotes metabolic efficiency during the postpartum period. Second, more frequent breast-feeding (briefer interfeeding intervals) is associated with greater infant weight gain in the early months.[19] The rapid responsiveness of Gusii mothers to the infant's cry with breast-feeding during the early months, means their interfeeding intervals are brief, thus enhancing caloric intake and contributing to weight gain. Third, being continuously carried on the body of the mother or another caregiver who responds rapidly to distress, as the Gusii infant is during the first months, reduces the duration of crying bouts and the total amount of crying, as shown in experimental studies in North America.[20] The Gusii babies at 3 to 4 months cried less than half of the time that their American counterparts did (Chapter 8), and informal observations at our clinic and at the Kisii General Hospital consistently indicated very little crying in a crowded pediatric waiting room, which was surprising from an American perspective. The prevention of crying diminishes caloric expenditure in the early months.

Hence Gusii infant care practices are likely to have a positive effect on postpartum weight gain by keeping the baby's caloric intake up (through frequent breast-feeding), its caloric expenditure down (through reduced crying), and its metabolic efficiency high (through tactile stimulation). These are among the few means that populations without immunization or antibiotics have to fight the risks of life-threatening infections at the most vulnerable period in the human life span. Following their Pediatric model of protection and its strategy of soothing, particularly in the months after birth, Gusii mothers are able to contribute to the survival of their infants.

There are other positive outcomes from Gusii infant care practices during the period of postpartum incubation. Co-sleeping of the infant with the mother may well protect the baby against breathing irregularities (e.g., acute hypoxia) that can lead to death in the early months.[21] By responding rapidly to infant distress, Gusii mothers produce quiet, easily calmed infants and thereby prevent the excessive crying that appears to precipitate disruptions of the mother–infant relationship ranging from early termination of breast-feeding to maternal violence, in Euroamerican populations.[22] Furthermore, because the infant's experience with distress-relief sequences shapes the formation of social expectations of the mother and others by 4 to 5 months of age,[23] maternal responsiveness to distress also helps establish a stable mother–infant relationship. Finally, there is evidence that carrying babies from birth onward, as Gusii mothers do, promotes more secure infant–mother attachment at the end of the first year.[24] As developmental studies explore the consequences of soothing, carrying, and body contact during the first months of life, they find advantages in practices that have long been institutionalized among the Gusii.

The quiescence of Gusii babies, that is, the ease with which they can be calmed, especially by their mothers, has another advantage from the perspective of the Gusii mother, namely, as the first step toward a docile toddler who will acquire respect and obedience easily and naturally, as discussed in the following section. This might not count as a positive outcome for the American white middle-class mother following the Pedagogical model, which calls for liveliness and activity during infancy, but it is a high priority for the Gusii. The Respect-Obedience model lends a strong moral flavor to what an overworked mother might want on purely pragmatic grounds: easily managed children. The infant, once its survival seems assured, is already a participant in the domestic hierarchy headed by the mother, but all that is required of the baby is that he or she fit into the household operation with a minimum of trouble.

However beneficial the Pediatric model and its soothing strategy might be in early infancy, it has some evident disadvantages, particularly in its schedule for the distribution of maternal attention. After the period perceived to be most critical for survival – the first 3 to 6 months – Gusii mothers typically return to work in the fields and depend heavily on their young daughters for daytime infant care. These caregivers are under orders to soothe their charges and keep them calm and quiet, and they do so, though not as well as the mother. The mother continues to monitor the baby for normal growth in size, and for attainment of motor skills such as standing and walking at the normal ages. Infants who are not doing well attract maternal attention (the "squeaky wheel" approach) and are the most likely candidates for special attention – including a trip to the clinic. Thus Gusii mothers are responsive to signs of disease and growth faltering; they try to maintain a strong minimum standard for health so that none of their children dies or falls far behind, and they are often successful.

But the relatively intense attention of the first months is not continued afterward if the mother perceives the child to be doing well in terms of general health and growth, and there is a decline in the child's overall interaction with caregivers, which becomes even more marked after the first year (Chapter 8). This can be interpreted as partly reflecting the mother's own energy-efficient style, saving her attention for a crisis or the next child, and the scarcity of assistance from child caregivers when they are no longer seen as absolutely required. Furthermore, mothers are anticipating the weaning of the child at around 17 months, and they tend to avoid visual and verbal interaction with the baby

partly in order to make the inevitable separation less troublesome. The physical growth of Gusii children drops below Western
standards after 6 months of age; performance of our sample children on cognitive tests dropped after a year (although not below
the United States average), except for those children who get
more care from their mothers (Chapter 6). There is an overall
downward curve to the child's interaction and developmental performance even during the first year, and certainly afterward, reflecting the mother's timetable for phasing out her own involvement as the infant becomes a toddler and is deemed ready to be
weaned and incorporated into the group of older siblings.

This incorporation does not occur until the child is 2 years old.
A few months before that, when he is 21 or 22 months old, the
mother gives birth again and spends more time at home; initially,
her interaction with the toddler increases, but by 24 months, the
child is interacting more with the other children. The second year
can be a difficult emotional transition period for the child, who is
no longer cared for as a baby, is sometimes yearning for the
mother (who does not want to arouse false hopes), and is often
not ready to become part of the children's group. Furthermore,
weaning in the middle of this year poses a nutritional problem,
because the replacement of breast milk with protein-rich foods
(cow's milk, meat, eggs) is by no means universal for Gusii children (Chapter 7). The care of Gusii children during the second
year represents a general decline in quantitative and qualitative
terms from the treatment of the infant during the first 6 months.

This does not mean that Gusii children suffer a trauma from
weaning or replacement by a new sibling; they are sometimes
upset, but we observed no breakdown in the ability of children
to adjust to new circumstances or move on to new relationships,
possibly because mothers had begun lowering expectations for
interaction during the first year. Furthermore, there were great
individual differences in diet, emotional relationships, and other
aspects of the toddler environments observed. It is clear, however, that the robust and reliable protective care of early infancy
gives way to a variety of contingent arrangements that put some
children at risk by 12 months of age if not before. Given the
improved state of disease control in Morongo by the 1970s (i.e.,
protection from epidemics of diseases that had formerly killed
young children), the second year posed less extreme threats to

survival than the postpartum period, but the risks include growth faltering, morbidity, and slower development of those behavioral capacities that are facilitated by social interaction – developmental risks that appear transient but may have long-term effects unrecognized by Gusii parents.

One way of formulating this problem is that the soothing strategy and its scripts are specifically addressed to the biological and behavioral needs of a child in the first few months after birth. Gusii mothers have no model of care specifically addressed to the changing needs of older infants, so their practices tend to be attenuated forms of the original: The children are breast-fed, carried, and slept with until at least 15 months, as the mother reduces her attention while monitoring growth and motor development. But an effective formula for care in early infancy is not necessarily adequate as the child matures during the first and second year. For example, Gusii mothers supplement breast milk with other foods from quite early on, but the quality of the supplementary food is variable, and in many cases, inadequate to maintain physical growth at the same rate after the first 6 months (Chapter 7). Similarly, although attention devoted to physical care promotes biobehavioral development in that early period, the infant after 6 months is ready for more interaction and exploration than Gusii infants are typically permitted. The mother's scripts for infant care, carried out by child caregivers as well as by herself, remain what they were for the newborn infant, but are administered with less intensity. Child care is in a holding pattern just when the child is ready to take off. Some infants thrive under this regime, eliciting enough care and stimulation for their health and behavioral development while residing in a stable and protective milieu, but others do not. This is not seen as problematic from the perspective of Gusii mothers, with their focus on survival, protection, and early physical growth, but it appears so from any perspective that focuses on goals of health and maturation specific to later periods of infancy that might require (or benefit from) developmentally sensitive facilitation.

This situation can be analyzed as the result of a parental investment strategy premised on scarce domestic resources (including maternal attention), in which the child's optimal health and behavioral development after early infancy are traded (i.e., put in jeopardy) for the survival of the maximum number of infants. The plausibility of such an analysis is supported by considering that the Gusii when we studied them had one of the highest fertility rates in the world, yet an increasing survival rate, with the average woman bearing about ten live children and losing about two. Reduced birth intervals meant that a woman might well have three children under 6 years of age to care for, and to grow food for, simultaneously, while the help that older children could give her had been diminished by increasing school attendance. Furthermore, mothers had virtually no access to help from other adults or to the money to hire caregivers. Operating on a regular reproductive schedule shaped by the necessity to bear children so long as they were able (Chapter 4), heavily burdened mothers had to allocate their time and energy strategically to give each child what was absolutely essential without raising the child's expectations for more. Hence the trading off of "quality" (enhanced or optimal care for each child) for "quantity" (number of surviving children), which resulted in diminished care for older children.[25]

This utilitarian analysis, though plausible in its own terms, leaves out two crucial factors, cultural and historical. First, Gusii mothers, however burdened by work and constrained by the birth succession in their reproductive lives, had enough leisure time to give their older infants more attention, including play and other forms of visual and verbal interaction than they did. For example, we have many times observed Gusii mothers breast-feeding babies for prolonged bouts without looking at them, though the mothers were relaxed and talking to others and could have looked down had they chosen to do so.[26] Furthermore, their reduction of attention during the second half of the infant's first year – at the very time when infants are forming a strong attachment to mother and tend to seek her attention – seemed to reflect a preference for interaction influenced by the Respect-Obedience model and observable in many other interactions with their children, as well as a strategy to conserve maternal energy and keep infant expectations low. In other words, the time-energy budget embedded in the parental investment strategy of the Gusii mother may only partly explain her declining interactive attention to the infant after 6 months; a culturally influenced perference involving moral feelings about *ogosika* (respect) and *ensoni* (a sense of sexually tinged shame between parents and children) is required for a fuller explanation.

Second, there is the historical factor of the contracting birth interval. At the time when the Gusii parental investment strategy developed historically, and as recently as 1940, Gusii birth intervals were longer, probably well over 30 months, with weaning after 2 years and much higher rates of infant and child mortality. The birth succession then was not such a rushed affair, with important consequences for the diet, health, and development of toddlers. Children of that time, in comparison with Morongo children of the 1970s who were weaned at 15 to 17 months and replaced by a sibling at 21 to 23 months, had a longer period of access to the protein supply in mother's milk (and cow's milk, because all families then had cows), and to the healthier eleusine grain used in gruel as well as being the mother's youngest until close to 3 years, an age at which they would be better able to negotiate their relationships in the sibling group. Thus there is reason to believe that their diet was healthier, that they had a later and more gradual transition from mother to the sibling group, and that the mothers did not feel so pressed to prevent the development of interactive expectations in the baby. If this is true, then it would not be accurate to assume that maternal attention was as scarce in the past as it was in the 1970s or that the health and interaction of children in the second year of life had to be sacrificed for the survival of newborns at the earlier time. The parental investment strategy as we have described, in other words, would be specific to the stresses and strains of the 1970s rather than representing a precolonial tradition inherited from the past.

This assessment has brought out weaknesses as well as strengths in the application of the Pediatric model to infant care by Gusii mothers in the 1970s. Following the model, they had done the best they could in the struggle to maximize the number of their surviving infants, and when new resources became available during the 1970s, they used them effectively toward that goal. Thus the mortality rate for children during the first 2 years born to mothers 20 to 24 years of age declined by almost 25% between 1969 and 1979 (Chapter 4). But measures of physical growth and behavioral development after the first 6 months suggest that, by the external standards of child development research, there were inadequate resources devoted to facilitating the maturation of the child when survival was not clearly at stake, particularly during the second year. This reflected the large number of children (most of whom survive) born to each mother, the lack of help for mothers with their multiple responsibilities, insufficiencies in family income and food supply, and a cultural model of care attuned primarily to the vital needs of newborn infants.

The costs of high fertility deserve special emphasis. Although the Gusii as parents were remarkably successful in achieving their historic goal of maximizing the number of surviving offspring, their reproductive success came at a high price to healthy child development in the 1970s. Mothers who had borne more children reported more reproductive difficulties such as miscarriage and gave birth to infants of lower birth weight who gained less weight in the first 10 days postpartum – children more vulnerable to disease in the future (Chapter 7). Extended childbearing jeopardizes the health of Gusii women and that of their children. More children on a limited landbase can also mean not enough high-quality food such as milk and meat to go around, creating scarcities affecting the health of young children, particularly in the period after weaning. Other family resources, from clothing to school fees, are subject to the same arithmetic – the more children, the less for each – yet by the 1970s, the contribution of children to the domestic economy was too slight to compensate for their increased costs. In a few generations, the advantages to high fertility were replaced by disadvantages, some of them insidious and invisible to Gusii parents but nonetheless damaging to health and development, and contrary to the goals of the Pediatric model. There are limits to the efficacy of the Pediatric model under conditions of high fertility, and Gusii parents in the 1970s seemed to have found them.

### Acquiring respect and obedience

At the level of cultural ideals, the benefits and costs of the Respect and Obedience model are obvious: Gusii parents expect to benefit from having children who are easy to manage as infants, participate in domestic production during childhood, and continue to help their parents as adults; they also expect the children to benefit from their acquisition of moral virtues prized in the Gusii community. The costs of applying the model are equally obvious from the American middle-class perspective, namely, failure to prepare the child for schooling through the early development of language skills, self-confidence, and assertiveness, and an excessive emphasis on compliance to authority instead of equality and independence – thus leaving the child without the skills and virtues thought to be needed in the modern world. There is a measure of cogency to this simple analysis, and by 1988 it was consistent with the views of a growing number of Gusii parents who saw educational advancement as the primary hope for their children's future. At the level of practice, however, a different understanding of the Respect and Obedience model emerges.

Respect and obedience are long-term goals of Gusii socialization, only partly attained during the preschool years and only partly in the context of the mother–child relationship. Lessons learned with the mother in early childhood are elaborated and redefined in the sibling group and the initiation ceremonies of later childhood and in relationships with older adults during adolescence and young adulthood, both before and during marriage. *The mother does not "inculcate" these virtues once and for all; she provides age-appropriate experience constituting preparation for the next setting in the child's life.* At the apex of the household hierarchy from a young child's point of view, the Gusii mother does not assume responsibility for teaching the desirable forms of competence and virtue but rather for managing a household organization of production and consumption from which its youngest members, her children, can learn skills and virtuous behavior through their participation. Thus, apart from some tutoring in obeying commands, the mother assumes the young child will learn what is necessary from its older siblings, to whom she has delegated tasks that need doing and general responsibility for the home in her absence. She intervenes in the young child's learning only when needed to support the hierarchy and enforce its rules of operation.

The Gusii mother is not able to supervise all of her children all of the time, nor does she control all the settings in their lives, particularly after they reach 5 or 6 years of age – ages beyond the focus of our 1970s study. In the 1950s, those children who spent much of their day herding cattle in pastures beyond maternal supervision, engaged in rough and tumble play and other activities that were not tolerated at home – at least until they were caught letting the cows into someone else's fields and were chastised by the mother.[27] By the 1970s, no one had herds of cattle, but children over 5 spent much time going to and from school, where they had opportunities for escaping the supervision of parents and adult siblings. Despite the ideological emphasis on respect and obedience, then, the practical system of control over children has always been loose, and it was expected by parents that their children would misbehave in the pastures and other places outside the home. The dialectic between parental control in the home and freedom among siblings and friends outside is an old and persistent theme in Gusii folklore, recognized in proverbs and initiation songs and fundamental to intergenerational avoidance as a model of moral order.[28]

Thus the Respect-Obedience model authorizes not a closed system of authoritarian repression for the child but guided participation in appropriate face-to-face relations with those above the child in a hierarchy.[29] The lessons are: Look down, don't initiate speech, don't talk back, do what you're told, and get away as soon as possible – though they are not formulated as such. This is not a guide to conduct in all situations but only in those defined by a hierarchical role relationship, which the child finds eventually to be escapable. Some children become particularly skilled at evading parental authority; all have experiences not covered, or authorized, by the model. Although Gusii mothers use commands with their infants and toddlers to a remarkable degree, the children, as they get older, participate in a freer social environment that is more varied linguistically. This means that in practice the Respect-Obedience model is neither as beneficial as Gusii parents might hope nor as costly as an outside observer might fear – though we can see grounds for both hopes and fears. Much of its impact on the training of children seems to depend on later development, that is, on the guided participation of the older child.

For Morongo children of the 1970s, the environment had already altered in ways not anticipated by the Respect-Obedience model, due to the expansion of primary schooling (declared universal by President Kenyatta in 1974) and the continuing contraction of family landholdings. Children were increasingly defined socially by their roles as pupils in school rather than as workers in domestic production. The relevance of the Gusii life course as an age-gender hierarchy to *their* lives, outlined in the stages shown in Tables 3.1 and 3.2, was fading in favor of the Western academic-occupational hierarchy introduced during the colonial period. But the children's early experience, guided by the Pediatric and Respect-Obedience models of child care, did not promote the package of academic skills (cognitive, language, and social) that enhances learning and performance in school. How would they be able to adapt to new conditions?

### The sample at 13 years of age

Most of the children we studied as infants attended school, and we gathered some information on them when they were about 13 years old. In August 1988, 12 years after the fieldwork of the Gusii infant study ended, and when the sample children were 12 to 14 years old, Sarah and Robert LeVine returned to Morongo for a brief 10-day visit.[30] Each available child in the sample was photographed, and the parents were asked about the child's formal education. One male child had died in 1977 at less than 2 years of age, and information was unobtainable on another, who had moved away with his parents. Of the other 26 children, 17 were currently going to school at the fifth grade level or higher, 3 were in fourth grade, and 6 were at the third grade level or lower (including 2 not in school).

The 17 in the first category included 5 in seventh grade, 3 in sixth grade, and 9 in fifth grade. Children in the second category (in fourth grade) seemed to have begun school at a later age than others, probably due to parental convenience or poverty. The third group was comprised of children who had been seriously ill or had parents who were in some way disorganized as well as poor. In this last group of 6, there was a girl who had never been sent to school (both parents were alcoholics); a boy, still in the first grade, reported to have had meningitis that affected his brain; a girl sent by her impoverished parents to care for the children of a family in Nairobi (the parents had lived on her pay, but she had returned and was "waiting" to get into third grade); a girl who had been seriously malnourished at the time of our study (third grade); and two rather mysterious cases, one of whom refused to attend school after second grade, though she seemed intelligent, and another currently in third grade, though it was not clear why.

Information on academic performance is largely lacking, although several children were said to rank high in their classes (the highest was a girl ranked 6th out of 56 in her sixth-grade class), and four were repeating grades (but one girl said to be repeating was in seventh grade at 13 years of age – the youngest at that level). The sample as a whole seemed average in their academic performance, with almost two-thirds at or near their proper grade level, whereas most of the others were affected by adverse health, economic, or behavioral conditions in their families, or by a late start in school because of parental postponement. These children who were off course in their educational advancement, and the one who died in infancy, were disproportionately from households we had noted for extreme poverty and/or heavy drinking in the 1970s, and by 1988 their parents clearly had not shared the majority condition of material improvement during the intervening years. This seemed to reflect the growth of a rural underclass – landless, unemployed, and afflicted by alcoholism – in which the parents cannot provide the support necessary for the health and schooling of their children even when those government services are offered at low cost.

Thus the majority of our sample children, despite their lack of tutoring or interaction that promoted academically relevant skills during infancy and early childhood, were able to perform adequately in the rural primary schools of 1980s Kenya, and most of those who did not had been hampered by health problems or home conditions that were exceptionally adverse in local terms. This does not mean that those who did well in Kisii schools were performing at the level of their urban middle-class counterparts in Nairobi, Europe, or North America, whose parents follow the Pedagogical model of early child care. A large body of educational and child development research suggests that they were *not* performing at the same level, and the average performance in rural primary schools of Kenya at that time may well have been low by international standards. But the fact that they were able to adapt to classroom instruction and progress to the end of primary school indicates that their early child care, under the guidance of the Pediatric and Respect-Obedience models, did not prevent them from being retrained after the age of 6. There is evidence of resilience here that warns against exaggerating the influence of the early years and emphasizes the importance of greater exactitude in our assumptions concerning what that influence is – and what it is not.[31]

## Conclusions from the assessment of benefits and costs

The Gusii case shows that there are economic and demographic contexts to child care practices, having to do with how many children the average woman bears, their chances for survival, and their contributions to domestic production. In agrarian populations at an early stage of demographic transition like the Gusii, cultural models of child care reflect conditions of high fertility and risks to infants, as well as the value of child labor, influencing the parents' agenda for their own young children. But parental practices that are adaptive or effective under one set of historical conditions may not be so when conditions change. The Gusii goal of maximizing the number of surviving children made more adaptive sense at the onset of the 20th century, when mortality was high, landholdings were large, and children were available to work under parental control, than 75 years later, when most children survived, land was scarce, and children's futures depended on school attendance and employment rather than working for their parents. In other words, Gusii reproductive and child care practices viewed as a parental investment strategy had lost much of their basis in economic utility by the 1970s. But given high fertility as a yet unchallenged goal among the Gusii, practices guided by the Pediatric and Respect-Obedience models remained advantageous for child survival, growth, and the development of indigenous moral virtues, while permitting children to attend school.

## ENCULTURATION AND EMOTIONS: THE CHILD'S PERSPECTIVE

Detecting, or divining, subjective experience during infancy and early childhood involves guesswork. We have no direct evidence on infants' internal working models of their interpersonal environment,[32] but it is possible to use behavioral data to narrow the range of speculations about the experience of young Gusii children. We have described their interpersonal environments over the first 30 months after birth and related our description to the goals and strategies of Gusii parents, finding their strengths and weaknesses as culturally organized practices of child care. We have compared the models and practices of Gusii parents with those of the American white middle class and found striking differences. Now we turn to the question of how the Gusii pattern of early care affects the early social and emotional experience of Gusii children.

The soothing of distress initiated in the neonatal period creates on average a quiescent baby who cries less, is more easily calmed (especially by mother), and – as found in the videotaped teaching task (Chapter 8) – can be prodded by mother without the negative reactions of American infants. By 1 year of age, then, Gusii babies are already more compliant than their American middle-class counterparts. The Gusii soothing strategy lays the groundwork during the first year of the child's future compliance to maternal wishes.

Even though infant-directed speech is relatively rare, we can find clues to the child's experience in how the mother responds and talks to the child.[33] In the mother's first and most consistent response to the infant's cry – physical soothing sometimes accompanied by verbal endearments – there are the implicit messages that maternal intervention brings comfort after the experience of distress, and that maternal speech is addressed to the baby only when it is in trouble. As the infant becomes a toddler, soothing is gradually replaced by the command script, particularly negative commands to stop doing something or get away from a place or object (Chapter 8). Once again, the child learns that its own action elicits maternal speech and that the mother intervenes only when something goes wrong, but in this case the mother's scolding words and impatient tone of voice arouse a measure of anxiety rather than comfort, indicating that it is the child's action that is wrong. Given the scarcity of mother-initiated speech or locutions of praise and approval, the mother's speaking to the child in itself becomes an index not only of prior wrongdoing that has attracted her attention but also more generally of the authority of her role as expressed in commands. The predominance of imperatives in maternal speech implies and teaches the hierarchical relationship between mother and child. The rarity of questions directed toward the child conveys the message that the mother has the knowledge rather than the child, further reinforcing her hierarchical position. (When questions are asked they are often rhetorical ones intended to scold the child.) Finally, when learning skills through participation in family work activities, the child receives only *corrective* feedback, some of it harsh, for mistakes made in imitating the mature performance of the mother or older siblings. The language environment of Gusii infancy and early childhood is quite consistent in making the mother's child-directed speech itself indexical of her higher status and superior knowledge vis à vis her child, thus preparing the infant and toddler for an initially subordinate position in the domestic age hierarchy.

In addition to the lessons in social status conveyed by this pattern of early communication, there are also implicit messages about emotional expression. Adults express disapproval and sometimes anger, but not approval or praise, in their words addressed to the young child. Older siblings acting as caregivers for infants do not act substantially different from mothers in this regard. Gusii adults nonetheless report that they knew as children that their mothers were attached and devoted to them, even though the mother never said so. Thus positive emotional attachment is not marked by words but is understood as an unspoken background phenomenon, whereas negative emotions, such as the mother's displeasure, are directly expressed in verbal communication, and the child's fear is sometimes deliberately elicited verbally for purposes of control.

As Gusii children grow up, they learn through everyday experience that prevailing norms put a damper on emotional expression in words or facial affect. Personal feelings and motives are usually hidden and must be divined, as in the Gusii proverb, "Two people may be seen together but their hearts don't know each other."[34] Finding out what people really feel or intend involves deciphering indirect reference in speech, detecting hesitations, decoding nonverbal leakages of affect in the eyes, watching people's movements and other actions over time, and listening to gossip from their neighbors. In this context, children learn that what is said publicly can often be discounted in favor of a diagnosis of motives from fragments of unarticulated evidence. But framing this rather elusive interpersonal environment is the public focus on people's kinship roles and the rules governing them, including the obligations of role relationships, and the prescriptions and proscriptions of routines and ritual. This is impersonal information, much of which is shared by all who have grown up in Gusiiland, and it constitutes the framework for their interactions. As children grow up, they learn the rules, acquire the skills of diagnosing private motives, and interact without intentionally disclosing their own motives, feelings, and even actions. A full account of enculturation among the Gusii would have to describe these acquisitions of later childhood and adolescence.

These facts present a challenge to the understanding of emotional development in the Gusii context. Without attempting a definitive interpretation, we point to the following aspects: (1) Gusii children do not receive, from their mothers or anyone else, the kind of enthusiastic support for their personal mastery and individual initiatives in the early years that is widely regarded as a prerequisite for normal self-esteem and cognitive development in Euroamerican populations. (2) The early emotional experience of Gusii children is shaped by highly consistent physical nurturance, involving co-sleeping, breast-feeding, and carrying, together with very little infant-directed visual and verbal interaction – a paradoxical combination by Western standards. (3) The constant presence of young children in family life while rarely being the focus of attention, children's integration into the sibling group at 2 years of age, and their participation in the productive and other activities of the household from an early age appear to provide emotional security without verbal expressiveness by mother and others. Gusii children do not have the kind of self-confident loquaciousness at the time they go to school that is common among American children, but they are definitely able to perform and advance in school, as shown by our sample children at 13 years old. Making sense of this will require changes in our notions of emotional and communicative development.

## LESSONS FOR CHILD
## DEVELOPMENT RESEARCH

Our case study of infant care in an African community has enough detail so that readers can draw their own conclusions from our data, and no doubt some readers will draw conclusions different from our own. Though our data were far from comprehensive, there is abundant food for thought in this book, indeed for rethinking many aspects of infant care and early child development. Here we focus on a few lessons for child development research.

The typical environment of Gusii infants contrasts sharply with that of American white middle-class infants in ways that have been theoretically related to schooling and mental health. From that perspective, Gusii infants and toddlers are deprived by a lack of support for their cognitive and language development and their healthy emotional and social development. Hcwever, we do not find that they suffer from glaring mental deficits or psychiatric abnormalities. This suggests that the social experience of Gusii children *after* 30 months facilitates the development of capacities that were not evidently acquired earlier. It raises fundamental problems for developmental theories that posit a single "average expectable environment" for the human infant, with universal prerequisites for normal development resembling the infant care practices of the contemporary American white middle class or other Euroamerican populations.

In generalizing from research on these Western populations, there has been a tendency to assume that factors shown to *optimize* children's performance in those cultural settings – guided by what we call the Pedagogical model – constitute *minimal* requirements for human development in general. Facilitating a young child's ability to answer questions may optimize the child's preparation for entry to a school where children are asked questions, for example, but this skill is not useful for all children – such as those in hierarchical societies without schools – and children growing up in the latter settings are not prevented by their lack of skill in answering questions from acquiring whatever language skills are locally valued. The Gusii study shows that the leap from factors that optimize school skills to universal prerequisites of cognitive, language, and emotional development is misguided, that children whose early environments lack these factors can develop normally in a different interpersonal environment, on a different schedule of experience, based on a divergent cultural model of child care. Knowledge of the minimal requirements for infant development will come from comparative evidence on numerous populations, as well as from laboratory and clinical studies, but when we look at a single population, Western or non-Western, we see their particular cultural priorities in action.

Peoples as different as the Gusii and the American white middle class vary in the maturational processes of the infant and child they facilitate from birth onward (e.g., physical growth vs. language development), in the types of stimulation they provide (e.g., tactile vs. vocal and visual), in the levels of activity and excitement parents regard as optimal (e.g., low vs. high), and in the relative concentration of maternal attention to the child in the first or second year of life. These divergent parental practices, together with the culturally mediated economic and interpersonal conditions in which they occur, create different pathways for early development that are evident through longitudinal research covering the period from early infancy to the third year of life. The long-term influence of these divergent patterns of infant care seems heavily dependent on the subsequent environment of the child.

The Gusii case teaches us that the absence, during the first 2 to 3 years, of specific parental practices that promote cognitive, emotional, and language skills in Western contexts, does not necessarily constitute failure to provide what every child needs. Like many other peoples in Africa and elsewhere, the Gusii had socially organized ways of cultivating skill, virtue, and personal fulfillment that were not dependent on mothers after weaning and were not concluded until long after the third year of life; they involved learning through participation in established, hierarchical, structures of interaction at home and in the larger community – a kind of apprenticeship learning, once widespread in the West, that we are only beginning to understand.[35] This does not mean that Gusii eventually became like Westerners, though on a slower schedule and through a less didactic social experience, but rather that they acquired different skills, virtues, and preferences, in accordance with their own goals for human development. If these findings seem surprising in the context of existing theories of child development, then that indicates how far we have to go in integrating evidence from other cultures into our conceptions of what is possible during childhood.

# Appendix A

## Fieldwork procedures: Initial phases and planning

The Gusii Infant Study brought together a team of social and medical researchers for field research into infancy and parenthood in Kisii District, Kenya, from 1974 to 1976. Planning for the study began in June 1973 at the Wenner-Gren Conference on Cultural and Social Influences in Infancy and Early Childhood, in Burg-Wartenstein, Austria, where the pediatrician T. Berry Brazelton and P. Herbert Leiderman, a psychiatrist and organizer of the conference, proposed to Robert A. LeVine, an anthropologist, the idea of a collaborative field project in Africa to examine the environments and development of children from birth through the transition to early childhood.

Brazelton and Leiderman had conducted previous infant studies in Africa (in Zambia and Kenya, respectively), but what they had in mind this time was an intensive and extended multidisciplinary project that would permit understanding of the social and cultural contexts in which infants developed over the first 2 to 3 years of life. LeVine, having worked since the 1950s on child care in Kenya and Nigeria, had come to believe that the investigation of how children acquire culture must begin in infancy; the proposed project offered not only collaborators experienced in infant research but also the possibility of a research relationship in which the parents being studied would gain medical service for their children. It was decided to locate the study among the Gusii people in southwestern Kenya, among whom LeVine had initially worked from 1955 to 1957 (with Barbara B. Lloyd) and whom he had revisited in four briefer trips from 1964 to 1969.

LeVine's work with the Gusii in the 1950s had been part of the Study of Socialization in Six Cultures, organized by John and Beatrice Whiting and their colleagues Irvin L. Child and William Lambert, which focused on child rearing from birth and child behavior from 3 to 11 years; a great deal of contextual material had been collected in a Gusii community that was directly relevant to infancy. In the new study, Robert LeVine and his wife Sarah LeVine (who had conducted research on mother–infant interaction in Nigeria), set up a field project in Kisii District, where they lived for 22 months and managed the data collection program, as the other research collaborators came for varying periods of time.

During August and September of 1974, the LeVines lived in Nairobi, where – based at the Bureau of Educational Research of the University of Nairobi – they applied for government permission to conduct the research, hired Gusii student assistants, and purchased the equipment needed for a research station in Kisii. They met G. M. Blankhart of the Royal Dutch Tropical Institute of Nutrition in Nairobi and learned of his methods for studying child nutrition and growth in Machakos District. At the end of September, they moved to Kisii Town to initiate the background work needed to plan the longitudinal study in detail.

The original plan had been to study infant care and development in three Gusii communities differing in social conditions that would affect the environments of early childhood, but the need to sustain an intensive study of parents and children over the long term narrowed the field of possible communities to those accessible to Kisii Town, where the investigators would be living in houses close to the Kisii General Hospital. To explore the problem, we conducted a nutrition and growth survey in the area surrounding "Nyansongo" (site of the 1950s study), called "Morongo" in this book, and in an area southwest of Kisii Town that was reputed to have a higher incidence of malnutrition. Blankhart sent a member of his staff to Kisii to train our Gusii university students in anthropometrics, identification of clinical signs of malnutrition, and dietary interviewing. The surveys of 150 children in each area revealed Morongo to be so heterogeneous in household economic resources and child nutrition that we could concentrate all data collection activities there without sacrificing the possibility of examining variations in child environments.

Detailed planning of the data collection program took place in Kisii during January of 1975, by Brazelton, Leiderman, and the LeVines, together with Constance Keefer, Gloria Leiderman, Edward Z. Tronick, and John O. Orora. There were visits to the field site for observation of mothers, babies, and their environments, as well as preliminary trials of neonatal assessment and other methods in the Gusii context. The planning group decided to select a sample of 36 children, consisting of three overlapping cohorts – newborn, 6 months old, and 12 months old, at the start – each with equal numbers of males and females and all to be studied for about 18 months, so that the data as a whole would cover the period from birth to 30 months of age. Each child would be studied with naturalistic observations at home and in a setting amenable to video recording as well as through anthropometrics and testing procedures ranging from the Brazelton Neonatal Behavioral Assessment Scale to repeated Bayley testing; the repertoire of instruments was expanded in the course of the fieldwork. Each mother, and insofar as possible, each father, was to be interviewed, and case materials were to be built up on each child's family. A community census and ethnographic studies would provide further context for the developmental investigation. The interpersonal environment of the child, the nature of caregiving, and interactions between the baby and others, were to be in the foreground of the research. Further, a pediatric clinic would be established to provide limited medical care to the community from which the sample was drawn.

We presented the project, the clinic, and ourselves to the administrative chief at Morongo and his elders at the weekly *baraza* (assembly), then in a series of ad hoc meetings in different neighborhoods of Morongo. Robert LeVine was remembered rather fondly by many people over 40 as *Getuka,* "The Investigator" (from the verb *ogotuka,* which means to follow a scent like a dog), from his residence at Morongo during the 1950s. His return with the offer of a free clinic at which their children could be treated by an American doctor was received with interest, but old people wanted to know why they would be excluded from the new medical care (there was no clinic at or near Morongo), and residents of Nyansongo itself wanted to know what other benefits they would receive. Thus to supplement the pediatric clinic, Robert LeVine ran an irregular ambulance service to the Kisii General Hospital for those of any age who needed emergency medical attention, even though buses were available.

When the weekly clinic for children under 5 opened in February 1975 in an old building provided by the local chief at the administrative headquarters of Morongo, so many mothers came from afar that we had to use our local census records of the research area (population 2,100) to define those who were eligible for service. The clinic was heavily used throughout the project period, and many children were treated there who would otherwise have had no medical attention at all. Its existence precipitated a *harrambee* (fund-raising effort) in 1976 by prominent men (who had grown up in Morongo) to raise funds for a permanent clinic, which was built with these private funds after our project had terminated and was eventually staffed by the government. Thus the clinic started by the Gusii Infant Study became a permanent and, in the course of the 1980s, large health care facility.

The clinic, located just across the road from the central marketplace in the area, was operated on Thursday afternoons from February 1975 to July 1976 by a succession of American physicians who were also collaborators in the infant study itself: Constance Keefer, T. Berry Brazelton, Suzanne Dixon, P. Herbert Leiderman, and David Feigal. They devoted themselves to field research the rest of the week, but also attended to medical emergencies among the sample children. Other emergency cases were taken to the Kisii General Hospital by Robert LeVine. (In addition, Michael Hennessy, an American orthopedic surgeon and husband of Suzanne Dixon, worked at the Kisii General Hospital performing corrective surgery on polio victims who would otherwise have gone untreated as well as many other patients from the district.)

The clinic building served as headquarters for the field research. Christopher Getoi, our senior field assistant, lived there with his wife Anna, a nurse in training who also worked at the clinic. Everyone else working on the project spent part of the day there, and people in the community knew they could reach us there. Thus there was a strong identification of the research project with the clinic and its medical service. After the initial community meetings announcing the project and requesting cooperation, no one explicitly mentioned to us the reciprocity involved or discussed the medical service as quid pro quo, but there was a high level of cooperation – reinforced by the local origins of many of our field assistants.

During the last months of 1974, Sarah LeVine had conducted a survey of pregnant women and mothers with young babies in the

Morongo area for a pool from which the longitudinal sample was to be drawn. This survey was continued in 1975 as a census of the area was completed, and samples of children for each of the three cohorts were chosen. In January and February 1975, Constance Keefer organized a schedule for spot observations and initiated the developmental monitoring of the sample children. The following month, Suzanne Dixon arrived to continue and add to the longitudinal study, particularly with video studies of mother–infant interaction, some of which had been used by Brazelton and Tronick at the Child Development Unit of Children's Hospital in Boston.

We drew a sample that was balanced by sex within each cohort and spread as widely across the neighborhoods of Morongo (to represent the spectrum of social conditions there) as was possible within the constraints set on age and sex of child. The sample was chosen from a roster of all infants in the area surveyed; substitutes of the same age, sex, and (if possible) area were substituted for those who moved away or were found to have congenital diseases. The longitudinal sample was reduced from 36 to 28 children once it became clear how much time was entailed in collecting data on each child, and in traveling from one sample family to another in the dispersed settlements of the Kisii hills during a period of unusually heavy rain that lasted during most of the field period. Even travel by car was difficult because of road building in the community, as we discovered one day when both of our vehicles became stuck in intractable mud and took most of the day to get out. Cohort I (the newborns) still had 12 children, but we reduced Cohorts II and III to 8 each, for a total of 28.

Once the clinic was established and the longitudinal study was initiated, project research activities as a whole fell into three categories: (1) Implementing the plan for monitoring the environment and development of the 28 children over the rest of the period of fieldwork, 17 months (February 1975 to July 1976); (2) supplementing the basic data collection on the longitudinal sample with studies at particular developmental moments; (3) collecting a wide variety of contextual data on the families and communities of Morongo.

1. The longitudinal data collection plan included monitoring the caregiving environment of the child (three methods of naturalistic observation), developmental assessment of the child using

standard instruments such as the Brazelton NBAS, the Bayley Infant Scales, anthropometrics; interviews with the mother and (when possible) the father. The three observational methods were the spot observations of Joseph Obongo, described in Chapter 6; the 1-hour narrative records of Sarah LeVine, described in Chapter 8 and illustrated in Chapter 9; and the precoded observations with vernacular transcriptions by Truphena Onyango and Mary Kepha Ayonga, described in the last section of Chapter 8.

2. Major supplements to the longitudinal data program included the pregnancy study of Keefer and Sarah LeVine reported in Chapter 5, which was based on 24 women, some of whom were in Cohort I; the mother–infant face-to-face interaction and teaching task studies reported in Chapter 8, both using video and carried out by Dixon; a video study of infant–caregiver attachment, carried out by P. H. Leiderman and David Feigal, used for the temperament assessment described in Appendix D and reported in Chapter 7; and the follow-up study of malnourished children by Dixon, also reported in Chapter 7.

3. The contextual data on the families and communities of Morongo included the census analysis of Chapter 4; Sarah LeVine's case studies of Gusii women (mostly sample mothers), in her monograph *Mothers and Wives: Gusii Women of East Africa;* studies of actual childbirths by Keefer, Dixon, and Sarah LeVine, reported in Chapter 5, and of birth and naming rituals by Robert LeVine, reported in Chapters 4 and 5. As in all ethnographic work in this study some of the best contextual understanding came from serendipities such as when Keefer told Robert LeVine of having visited a woman with her newborn twins, who were being confined in ritual seclusion. LeVine visited and learned about Gusii rituals of abnormal birth and eventually, how they are related to other rituals in the Gusii life course.

# Appendix B

## Coding categories for spot observations

Mother holds/Total holds
*Omoreri* holds/Total holds
Other sister holds/Total holds
Other brother holds/Total holds
Father holds/Total holds
Grandmother holds/Total holds
Other adult holds/Total holds
Other child holds/Total holds
Female under 5 within 5 ft./Total
Female over 5 within 5 ft./Total
Male under 5 within 5 ft./Total
Male over 5 within 5 ft./Total
Male child unspecified within 5 ft./Total
Female child unspecified within 5 ft./Total
Father within 5 ft./Total
Female adult within 5 ft./Total
Male adult within 5 ft./Total
Adult unspecified within 5 ft./Total
Child unspecified within 5 ft./Total
0 people within 5 ft./Total
1 person within 5 ft./Total
2 people within 5 ft./Total
3 people within 5 ft./Total
4 people within 5 ft./Total
5 people within 5 ft./Total
Min. 0 people within 5 ft./Total
Min. 1 person within 5 ft./Total
Min. 2 people within 5 ft./Total
Min. 3 people within 5 ft./Total
Min. 4 people within 5 ft./Total
Min. 5 people within 5 ft./Total

Mother within 5 ft./Nonmissing observations on mom
Mother 6–50 ft./Nonmissing observations on mother
Mother 50+ ft./Nonmissing observations on mother
Lying down/Nonmissing observations on position
Sitting/Nonmissing observations on position
Standing/Nonmissing observations on position
Being held/Nonmissing observations on position
Awake/Nonmissing observations on state
Inside/Nonmissing observations on location
Social/Social & nonsocial
Not play/Nonmissing observations on infant activity
Nonsocial play/Nonmissing observations on infant activity
Social play/Nonmissing observations on infant activity
Asleep/Nonmissing observations on new state
Unhappy/Nonmissing observations on new state
Neutral/Nonmissing observations on new state
Happy/Nonmissing observations on new state
Mother focus on baby/Total observations on focus
Mother focus on self/Total observations on focus
Mother focus on others/Total observations on focus
Mother focus elsewhere, missing/Total observations of focus
Mother hold/Total
Mother nurse/Total
Mother other care/Total
Mother not doing infant care/Total
*Omoreri* hold/Total
*Omoreri* physical or social care/Total
*Omoreri* not doing infant care/Total
*Omoreri* within 5 ft./Total
Baby focus on mother/Total
Baby focus on *omoreri*/Total
Baby focus on others/Total
Total observations on holding/Total observations
Child holds/Total hold
Adult other than mother holds/Total hold
Female child within 5 ft./Total
Male child within 5 ft./Total
Child within 5 ft./Total
1 or 2 people within 5 ft./Total
3 or 4 people within 5 ft./Total
Mother within 50 ft./Nonmissing observations on mother

# Appendix C

## Blankhart Nutrition Questionnaire

Child's name
* Mother's name
* Father's name
* Subarea of residence
* Informant birthdate: (Probably quite reliable because of the use of local time markers and ubiquity of calendars, newspapers, etc.)
* Age – months (to nearest half-month)
Weight in kg (reliably assessed to ± 0.5 kg). Spring balance with weighing points zeroed prior to weighing. Verified with standard weights weekly.
Length in cm (reliably assessed to ± 1 cm). Vinyl tape with child held supine and fully extended. Two or three examiners.
Head circumference in cm (reliably assessed to ± 0.5 cm), occipital-frontal using vinyl tape.
Who fed the child yesterday?
# Previous day's diet; meals and snacks, including breast-feeding
Presence of: hair changes (lightening, marked thinness)

| | |
|---|---|
| Edema (supra-tibial pitting) | Yes, |
| **Mosaic skin | No, |
| **Moon-face | Slight |

Note of any abnormal physical findings (e.g., skin infections, swollen belly, burns).

---

* Cross-verified with area census. **Field identification unreliable and data disregarded. # Quantification problematic because of variability of relative measures, e.g., "a bowl."

# Appendix D

## Temperament Assessment Method

Two assessments of temperament were made between 8 and 11 months of age to describe qualitative aspects of infant behavior during the second half of the first year. Ratings were made by staff pediatricians during videotaped sessions designed to investigate infant–caregiver attachment, using the following categories:

| | |
|---|---|
| Rapidity | Abruptness or tempo of state changes |
| Degree of change | Range of state changes during the observation, from little vacillation to extreme degree of change |
| Approach/withdrawal | Positive or negative initial response to novel object or person |
| Adaptability | After initial reaction, ease and speed of becoming involved with new object |
| Irritability/reactivity | Level of stimulation required to produce a reaction |
| Distractibility | Degree of turning attention to extraneous environmental stimuli |
| Persistence and attention span | Persistence in own activity, or if distracted, ease of returning to previous activity |
| Intensity of reaction | Level of response after initial reaction |
| Quality of mood | Overall mood, from negative to positive |

| Number of state changes | Not a rating, but the frequency of observed state changes over the course of the observation, such as from asleep to awake, alert or crying |
|---|---|

Table D.1. *Factor loadings on temperament summary factors*

| Variable | Factor 1 Irritability | Factor 2 Adaptability |
|---|---|---|
| *First assessment* | | |
| Number of state changes | .720 | .200 |
| Rapidity | .736 | .336 |
| Degree of change | .694 | .382 |
| Approach/withdrawal | − .068 | − .057 |
| Adaptability | .064 | .482 |
| Irritability/reactivity | .972 | − .199 |
| Distractibility | − .167 | .537 |
| Persistence/attention span | − .040 | .919 |
| Intensity of reaction | .899 | − .143 |
| Quality of mood | − .818 | .402 |

| Variable | Factor 1 Irritability | Factor 2 Distractibility |
|---|---|---|
| *Second assessment* | | |
| Number of state changes | .873 | .141 |
| Rapidity | .926 | .242 |
| Degree of change | .886 | .190 |
| Approach/withdrawal | .354 | .854 |
| Adaptability | − .234 | − .576 |
| Irritability/reactivity | .775 | .482 |
| Distractibility | − .055 | .712 |
| Persistence/attention span | − .192 | − .818 |
| Intensity of reaction | .851 | .187 |
| Quality of mood | − .921 | − .065 |

Factor analyses on each set of temperament ratings yielded two relatively well-defined factors. For the first assessment, the strongest factor to emerge, labeled *Irritability,* had high positive loadings on irritability and intensity of reaction, as number and degree of state changes and rapidity, and high negative loadings on quality of mood. This factor accounted for 54% of the variance in the set of ratings, and infants with high scores on this factor would be described as having many and sudden state changes, highly intense reactions, and negative mood. The second factor, accounting for 29% of the variance, labeled *Adaptability,* had positive loadings on adaptability, distractibility, persistence/attention span, and quality of mood (positive).

For the second temperament assessment, the first factor to emerge, accounting for 77% of the variance, had a factor structure virtually identical to the Irritability factor on the first assessment, with the same set of variables loading positively on it. Thus a consistent qualitative aspect of behavior emerges as the strongest factor for both sets of ratings. Further information appears in Caron (1985, pp. 22–26).

# Appendix E

## Coding categories for narrative observations

Table E.1. *Coding categories for narrative observations*

*Baby Behaviors*

| | |
|---|---|
| 01. Unspecified Behavior | 60. Look |
| 02. Unspecified actor | 61. |
| 03. Pause; stop; end | 62. |
| 04. Playful behavior | 63. |
| 05. | 64. |
| | |
| 10. Any sound | 70. Physical contact |
| 11. Cry | 71. Touch |
| 12. Fret | 72. Hug |
| 13. Misc. noise | 73. Kiss, nuzzle |
| 14. Laugh | 74. Cross bodily contact |
| 15. Vocalize | 75. Push away |
| 16. Imitate | 76. Greet |
| 17. Talk | 77. Root |
| 18. Sing | 78. Hit |
| 19. | 79. |
| 20. Facial expression | 80. Locomote re person |
| 21. Scowl; frown | 81. Approach person |
| 22. Smile | 82. Move away from person |
| 23. | 83. Jump, skip, dance |
| 24. | 84. Follow |
| | 85. |
| 30. Hand gesture | 86. |
| 31. | 87. |
| 38. Head gesture | |
| | 90. Noninteractive |
| 40. Object-mediated | 91. Passive |
| 41. Give object | 92. Gross motor behavior |
| 42. Take object | 93. Self-engaged |
| 43. Look at object | 94. Sleep |
| 44. Touch object | 95. Bodily functions |
| 45. Reach for object | 96. Get food; eat |
| 46. Reject object | 97. Locomote to object |
| 47. Point, display object | 98. |

Table E.1 *(cont.)*

---

*Interactor behaviors*

---

| | |
|---|---|
| 01. Unspecified behavior | 50. Phys. Caretaking |
| 02. Unspecified actor | 51. Wash, clean, bathe |
| 03. Pause; stop; end | 52. Groom |
| 04. Playful behavior | 53. Dress; undress |
| 05. | 54. Offer food, breast |
| | 55. Tie on, secure |
| 10. Any sound | 56. Take away food |
| 11. Talk | 57. |
| 12. Sing | 58. |
| 13. Imitate | 59. Restrain |
| 14. Misc. noise | |
| 15. Declarative | 60. Look |
| 16. Interrogation | 61. |
| 17. Imperative | 62. |
| 18. Laugh | |
| 19. | 70. Physical contact |
| | 71. Jostle, jiggle, bounce |
| 20. | 72. Pick up |
| 21. Praise | 73. Put down |
| 22. Reprimand | 74. Cuddle, hug |
| 23. Threaten | 75. Kiss, nuzzle |
| 24. | 76. Touch |
| | 77. Shift |
| 30. Facial expression | 78. Hit |
| 31. Scowl; frown | 79. Carry |
| 32. Smile | |
| 33. | 80. Other-directed |
| 38. Head gesture | 81. Other-directed comm. |
| | 82. Talk about Baby |
| 40. Object-mediated | 83. Talk not about Baby |
| 41. Give baby object | 84. Nonverbal other |
| 42. Take object from baby | 85. |
| 43. Display object | |
| 44. Reject object | 90. Noninteractive |
| 45. | 91. |

---

*Abbreviated code*

Col. 06 - Sex
1 = Male
2 = Female

Col. 19 - Setting
1 = Solitary    3 = Play         5 = Feeding
2 = Interactive 4 = Phys. Caretaking 6 = Nursing

# Appendix F

## Coding categories for face-to-face interaction

Table F.1. *Face-to-face interaction: Behaviors scored for adult and infant*

| Infant | Adult |
|---|---|
| 1. *Vocalization:*<br>  1. none<br>  2. isolated sound<br>  3. grunt<br>  4. coo<br>  5. cry<br>  6. fuss<br><br>  7. laugh<br>  8. repeated positive sounds | 1. *Vocalization:*<br>  1. abrupt shout<br>  2. stern, adult narrative<br>  3. rapid tense voice<br>  4. whispering<br>  5. little or no vocalizing<br>  6. rhythmic sounds with little modulation<br>  7. burst pause talking<br>  8. single bursts in rapid succession with wide pitch range<br>  9. burst of sound that peaks with much change of modulation and pitch |
| 2. *Direction of gaze:*<br>  1. toward mother's face<br>  2. away from mother's face<br>  3. follows mother<br><br>  4. looking at toy or hand mother is using as part of interaction | 2. *Direction of gaze:*<br>  1. toward infant's face<br>  2. toward infant's body<br>  3. away from infant but related to interaction<br>  4. away from infant and not related to interaction |
| 3. *Head orientation:*<br>  1. head toward, nose level<br>  2. head toward, nose level<br>  3. head toward, nose level<br>  4. head part side, nose level<br>  5. head part side, nose down<br>  6. head part side, nose up<br>  7. head complete side, nose level | 3. *Head orientation:*<br>  1. toward and down<br>  2. toward and up<br>  3. toward and level<br>  4. part side and down<br>  5. part side and up<br>  6. part side level<br>  7. head complete side, nose level |

Table F.1. *(cont.)*

| Infant | Adult |
|---|---|
| 8. head complete side, nose down | 8. head complete side, nose down |
| 9. head complete side, nose up | 9. head complete side, nose up |
| | 10. thrusting |
| | 11. nodding |
| | 12. nuzzling |
| | 13. cocked head |
| 4. *Facial expression:* | 4. *Facial expression:* |
| 1. cry face | 1. angry |
| 2. grimace | 2. frown |
| 3. pout | 3. serious, sad, sober |
| 4. wary/sober | 4. lidded |
| 5. lidding | 5. neutral flat |
| 6. yawn | 6. bright |
| 7. neutral | 7. animated |
| 8. sneeze | 8. simple smile |
| 9. softening | 9. imitative play face |
| 10. bright | 10. kisses |
| 11. simple smile | 11. exaggerated |
| 12. coo face | 12. broad full smile |
| 13. broad smile | 13. "ooo" face |
| 5. *Body position:* | 5. *Body position:* |
| 1. doubled over or complete away | 1. turns body full away |
| 2. arching | 2. sits back and still |
| 3. slumped | 3. slumping |
| 4. off to one side | 4. neutral slight forward |
| 5. neutral or being adjusted | 5. sideways shifts |
| 6. up into vertical | 6. slight rocking |
| 7. up and off backrest | 7. large sideways shifts into line of vision |
| 8. body vertical and extended | 8. medium close forward |
| 9. leaning forward with back straight | 9. going close and staying close |
| | 10. large shifts forward and back |
| | 6. *Specific handling of the infant:* |
| | 1. abrupt shift of baby's position |
| | 2. abrupt but no shift |
| | 3. jerky movement of limbs |
| | 4. no contact |
| | 5. gentle containing |
| | 6. small rhythmic patting |
| | 7. rhythmic movements of limbs |
| | 8. intensive movement, fast rhythm |

*Source:* Tronick, Als, and Brazelton (1980).

Table F.2a. *Infant monadic phases*

| | Gaze | Head orientation | Body orientation | Facial expression | Voice |
|---|---|---|---|---|---|
| Aoid | Away[a] (2) | Away (7, 8, 9) | Away (1–4) | Negative to neutral (1–7) | Cry and others (1, 3, 5, 6) |
| Avert | Away[a] (2) | Partially away (5, 6, 7) | Partially away (3, 4) | Negative to neutral (2–7) | Negative to neutral (1, 3, 6) |
| Monitor | Toward[a] (1) | Toward (1–6) | Toward (5–9) | Negative to bright(2–10) | Negative to neutral(1, 3, 6) |
| Set | Toward[a] (1) | Toward (1–6) | Toward (5–9) | Neutral to positive (7, 9, 10) | Neutral (1, 3) |
| Play | Toward (1) | Toward (1–6) | Toward (5–9) | Positive (11, 12, 13) | None, single laugh (1, 2, 7) |
| Talk | Toward (1) | Toward (1–6) | Toward (5–9) | Positive (11, 12, 13) | Repeated and coo (8, 4) |

[a]Necessary behavior for a monadic phase but not sufficient. Must be in combination with other behaviors.
*Source:* Tronick, Als, and Brazelton (1980).

Table F.2b. *Adult monadic phases*

| | Gaze | Head orientation | Body orientation | Facial expression | Voice | Specific handling |
|---|---|---|---|---|---|---|
| Avoid | Away[a] (4) | Away (7, 8, 9) | Away (1–4) | Negative to none (1–5) | Negative (1, 2, 3, 5) | None or negative (2, 3, 4) |
| Avert | Away[a] (4) | Partially away (4, 5, 6) | Away (1–4) | Negative to none (1–5) | Negative adult (1, 2, 3, 5) | Varied (2, 3, 4) |
| Monitor | Toward[a] (1) | Toward (1–6) | Toward (4, 8) | Negative to none (3–6) | Little infant-alization (4, 5, 6) | Varied (4, 5, 6) |
| Elicit | Toward[a] (1) | Toward/moving (1–6, 10, 11, 13) | Toward/moving (4–10) | Varied (2–9, 11, 12) | Rapid/none (3, 5) | Abrupt/touching (1, 2, 4, 8) |
| Set | Toward (1) | Toward (1–6) | Toward (4, 8) | Neutral to positive (5, 6, 7) | Infantalized (5, 6, 7) | Varied (4–7) |
| Play | Toward (1, 2) | Toward/moving (1–6, 10–13) | Toward (4, 6, 8, 9, 10) | Positive (8–13) | Infantalized (5, 6, 8, 9) | Varied (2, 4–7) |
| Talk | Toward (1) | Toward (1–6, 10, 11, 13) | Toward (4, 6, 8) | Positive (8–13) | Burst-pause (7) | Varied (2, 4–7) |

[a]Necessary behavior for a monadic phase but not sufficient. Must be in combination with other behaviors.
*Source:* Tronick, Als, and Brazelton (1980).

Table F.3. *Examples of criteria for monadic phase coding*

| Infant | Mother |
|---|---|
| **A. Aversion (2)** | |
| Neutral to negative affect, but not crying or fussing: | Neutral to negative affect; |
| Gaze away from mother; | Gaze away from infant; |
| Posture neutral to slumped; | Distance medium to far back; |
| Head position variable; | Head position variable, toward to part-side away; |
| a) fully to part-side away with or without focused attention elsewhere; | Vocalizations variable: a) none to infant; b) may or may not vocalize to another adult; |
| b) any position, totally involved in object or hand play. | Contact with infant variable, none to simple touch. |
| **B. Monitor (3)** | |
| Affect slightly negative; | Affect neutral to slightly negative; |
| Head and/or gaze predominantly toward the mother. | Gaze intermittant or lidded; |
| Posture slumped to neutral. | Body in neutral position; No contact of infant; Head may be partially turned away. |
| **C. Set (5)** | |
| Affect neutral to positive; | Affect neutral to positive; |
| Bright look to simple smile; | Face bright or with simple smile; |
| Head & gaze toward mother; | Vocalizations of all types except abrupt and/or negative; |
| Eyes open & alert; | Body and head orientation toward infant in medium to close position; |
| Body upright; | |
| Vocalizations positive or none. | Touches may include containment or none. |
| **D. Play (6)** | |
| Affect greater than neutral; | Affect greater than neutral; |
| Head and gaze totally oriented to mother; | Body, head and gaze fully oriented to infant; |
| Posture upright; | Vocalizations variable, from none to low burst-pause narrative, playful-stern or nonverbal sounds and laugh; |
| Face variable, from simple smile to coo face; | |
| Vocalizations variable, from none to positive vocalization to laugh; | Contact with infant variable, from none to simple touch or tapping. |
| Movement variable, from none to large limb movements. | |

*Source:* Dixon et al. (1981), Table 8.1, p. 156.

# Appendix G

## Coding categories for maternal teaching task

Table G.1. *Maternal teaching task coding system: Major categories*

| | |
|---|---|
| *Infant behavior* | |
| 10 (Attends) | Child looks at the toys or mother's activities |
| 20 (Attempts) | Child works at the task as directed |
| 30 (Success) | Child completes the task as directed |
| 40 (Other play) | Child manipulates the toys not as directed |
| 50 (Social behavior) | Child interacts positively or negatively with mother |
| 60 (No attention) | Child's attention is away from task and toys |
| 70 (Distress) | Child fusses, cries, or expresses negative affect |
| | |
| *Maternal manual/visual behaviors* | |
| 10 (Model the task) | Demonstrate the task to the child in whole or in part |
| 20 (Setup) | Replace and recover toys; get things ready to begin |
| 30 (Simplify) | Make task easier for the child; subcategories: reduction of objects or steps, holding toys in place (stabilize), or incorporating task into the child's ongoing activity (incidental assist) |

Table G.1. *(cont.)*

| | |
|---|---|
| 40 (Complicate) | Make task more difficult; subcategories: adding steps or number of objects, or moving toys further from child |
| 50 (Focus) | Maneuvers designed to draw and hold attention to toys or task |
| 60 (Moving the child) | Restraining, tugging, or moving the child; either toward or away from the task |
| 80 (Social behavior) | Social, non–task-related behavior |
| 90 (Attend) | Look at the toys and the child's activity |
| *Maternal verbal* | |
| 10 (Instruct) | Give directions |
| 20 (Focus) | Words and short phrases, singly or in repetition, used to draw attention to toys or task |
| 70 (Reinforce) | Respond to the child's ongoing activity in a positive (e.g., "that's right, come on") or neutral ("OK"; "it's finished") way; subcategories: scolding or praise, either personal or task |
| 80 (Reflect) | Neutral comment on the child's activity or mood (e.g., "you are happy, you are working") |
| 02 (Question) | Ask a question of the child |

*Source:* Dixon, LeVine, Richman, and Brazelton (1984).

# Appendix H

## Supplementary tables

Table H.1. *Performance of Gusii and American infants on NBAS items and clusters*

| | Early exam | | Middle exam | | Late exam | | ANOVA effects | | |
|---|---|---|---|---|---|---|---|---|---|
| | G | A | G | A | G | A | Group | Age | Age × Group |
| *Motor Performance items* | | | | | | | | | |
| Tonus[a] | 5.8 | 5.7 | 5.8 | 5.5 | 6.1 | 5.9 | N.S. | N.S. | N.S. |
| Maturity | 6.6 | 4.3 | 6.8 | 5.2 | 6.9 | 5.3 | .001 | .01 | N.S. |
| Pull to sit | 6.2 | 6.0 | 5.5 | 5.8 | 5.3 | 5.7 | N.S. | N.S. | N.S. |
| Defensive reaction | 5.8 | 6.4 | 6.8 | 7.2 | 6.6 | 6.5 | N.S. | .05 | N.S. |
| Activity level | 5.0 | 4.8 | 4.8 | 4.6 | 4.8 | 4.6 | N.S. | N.S. | N.S. |
| Motor cluster | 5.6 | 5.2 | 5.7 | 5.4 | 5.6 | 5.1 | N.S. | N.S. | N.S. |
| *Reflex cluster* | | | | | | | | | |
| Reflex cluster | 1.4 | 2.2 | 1.2 | 1.0 | 1.4 | 1.0 | N.S. | .07 | N.S. |
| *Orientation items* | | | | | | | | | |
| Inanimate visual (ball) | 5.9 | 5.3 | 6.0 | 6.1 | 6.7 | 6.8 | N.S. | .01 | N.S. |
| Inanimate auditory (rattle) | 5.7 | 5.5 | 6.5 | 5.8 | 6.3 | 6.0 | N.S. | N.S. | N.S. |
| Animate visual (face) | 5.7 | 6.5 | 5.9 | 6.6 | 6.0 | 7.2 | N.S. | N.S. | N.S. |
| Animate auditory (voice) | 6.0 | 5.6 | 6.1 | 5.7 | 6.5 | 6.1 | N.S. | N.S. | N.S. |
| Animate visual, & auditory (Face & voice) | 6.1 | 6.6 | 6.1 | 6.8 | 6.7 | 7.5 | N.S. | N.S. | N.S. |
| Alertness | 5.0 | 5.4 | 5.6 | 6.0 | 6.2 | 6.2 | N.S. | .06 | N.S. |
| Orientation cluster | 5.6 | 5.6 | 6.0 | 6.0 | 6.3 | 6.2 | | | |

Table H.1. *(cont.)*

| | Early exam | | Middle exam | | Late exam | | ANOVA effects | | |
|---|---|---|---|---|---|---|---|---|---|
| | G | A | G | A | G | A | Group | Age | Age × Group |
| *Habituation items* | | | | | | | | | |
| Repeated light flash | 5.7 | 6.6 | 6.2 | 8.3 | 6.5 | 7.3 | .06 | N.S. | N.S. |
| Repeated rattle | 6.8 | 5.6 | 7.3 | 8.3 | 6.7 | 6.6 | N.S. | .03 | N.S. |
| Repeated bell | 7.4 | 6.0 | 7.0 | 9.0 | 7.4 | 6.0 | N.S. | N.S. | N.S. |
| Repeated pin prick | 3.5 | 4.6 | 4.7 | 4.6 | 5.5 | 3.0 | N.S. | N.S. | N.S. |
| Habituation cluster | 6.0 | 6.1 | 6.4 | 6.5 | 6.5 | 6.0 | N.S. | N.S. | N.S. |
| *Regulation of state items* | | | | | | | | | |
| Cuddliness | 4.8 | 6.0 | 6.1 | 5.6 | 6.0 | 6.7 | N.S. | .01 | .02 |
| Consolability | 6.4 | 7.1 | 6.4 | 5.1 | 6.3 | 4.8 | N.S. | N.S. | N.S. |
| Self quieting | 5.4 | 6.1 | 4.9 | 4.9 | 5.6 | 4.4 | N.S. | N.S. | N.S. |
| Hand to mouth | 6.8 | 5.6 | 6.4 | 5.6 | 6.1 | 4.8 | .08 | N.S. | N.S. |
| Regulation | 5.8 | 6.1 | 5.9 | 5.4 | 6.0 | 5.3 | N.S. | N.S. | N.S. |
| *Range of state items* | | | | | | | | | |
| Peak of excitement | 5.9 | 5.8 | 5.8 | 5.6 | 5.9 | 5.5 | N.S. | N.S. | N.S. |
| Rapidity of build-up | 3.1 | 3.9 | 4.1 | 3.5 | 4.1 | 3.8 | N.S. | N.S. | N.S. |
| Irritability | 5.2 | 4.5 | 5.7 | 4.3 | 4.7 | 4.2 | .06 | N.S. | N.S. |
| Lability of state | 3.3 | 2.9 | 3.4 | 2.4 | 3.4 | 3.0 | .10 | N.S. | N.S. |
| Range cluster | 3.7 | 3.9 | 3.9 | 3.6 | 3.8 | 3.6 | N.S. | N.S. | N.S. |
| *Autonomic regulation items* | | | | | | | | | |
| Tremors | 3.1 | 5.1 | 3.4 | 3.7 | 2.7 | 3.7 | .09 | N.S. | N.S. |
| Startles | 3.0 | 4.7 | 3.5 | 3.7 | 3.0 | 3.2 | .10 | .10 | .04 |
| Lability of skin color[a] | | 4.2 | | 2.9 | | 4.1 | | | |
| Autonomic cluster[a] | | | | | | | | | |
| *Supplemental analysis* (n = 24) | | | | | | | | | |
| Habituation to light | | | 6.0 | 8.0 | 6.4 | 7.5 | .001 | N.S. | N.S. |
| Habituation to pin prick | | | 4.5 | 3.6 | 5.3 | 4.1 | .03 | N.S. | N.S. |
| Orientation to animate visual and auditory stimulus | | | 6.0 | 6.7 | 6.0 | 7.2 | .01 | N.S. | N.S. |
| Motor maturity | | | 6.9 | 5.0 | 6.7 | 5.3 | .001 | N.S. | N.S. |
| Cuddliness | | | 6.1 | 5.6 | 5.9 | 6.6 | N.S. | N.S. | .02 |

[a]Using scores as given in manual.

Table H.2. Correlations of infant physical characteristics and NBAS scores

| | Birth weight | Length | Head circumference | Gestational age | % Wt/G.A. | Ponderal index | Postnatal wt. gain |
|---|---|---|---|---|---|---|---|
| *State organization* | | | | | | | |
| Habituation: | | | | | | | |
| Light | -.46[3] | | | | -.45[3] | | -.68[3] |
| Rattle | | | | | | | -.66[1] |
| Bell | | | | | | | |
| Pinprick | | | * -.74[2] | | | | |
| Peak of excitement | | | | | | -.56[3] | -.63[1] |
| Rapidity of buildup | | | | | -.55[3] | | * -.74[1] |
| Irritability | | | | -.49[3] | | | |
| Lability of state | -.48[3] | | | | | -.59[3] | -.65[1] |
| Self-quieting | -.46[3] | | | | .55[3] | | .58[1] |
| | | | | | | | |
| *Interactional dimension* | | | -.42[3] | | | | |
| Orientation: | | | | | | | |
| Bell | | | | | | | |
| Rattle | | | | | | | |
| Face | | | | | | | |
| Voice | | | | | | | -.43[2] |
| Face & voice | | | | | | | |

| | | | | |
|---|---|---|---|---|
| Alertness | | | | |
| Cuddliness | | | | |
| Consolability | .43[2] | −.54[2] | | |
| *Motoric processes* | | | | |
| General tone | −.67[1] | | −.47[2] | |
| Motor maturity: | | | | |
| Pull-to-sit | | .61[1] | | |
| Defensive | | | | −.49[3] |
| Activity | | | | |
| Hand-to-mouth | −.48[3]   *.76[1] | −.62[1] | *−.58[3]   −.66[1] | *.76[1] |
| *Physiological stability* | | − | − | − |
| Tremulousness | | | | |
| Startles | | | | |
| Smiles | −.64[2] | | | |

| |
|---|
| −.55[3] |
| −.44[2] |
| −.49[2] |
| −.46[3] |
| +.95[1] |

*Significance:* Unmarked = $p < .05$
  \* = $p < .01$
  \*\* = $p < .001$

*Superscripts:* [1] = early exam
  [2] = middle exam
  [3] = late exam

*Source:* Dixon, Keefer, Tronik, and Brazelton (1982).

Table H.3. *Correlations of maternal factors and NBAS scores*

| | Age | Parity | No. living children | Height | Head circumference | Pregnancy wt. gain | P.B.I. |
|---|---|---|---|---|---|---|---|
| *State organization* | | | | | | | |
| Habituation: | | | | | | | |
| Light | | | | | | −.96[3] | |
| Rattle | .61[1] | | | | −.63[2] | | |
| Bell | | | | | | −.99[2] | |
| Pinprick | | | | .78[1] | −.63[2] | | |
| Peak of excitement | **.66[3] | *.59[3] | .50[3] | | | .55[2] | |
| Rapidity of buildup | | | | | | −.94[3] | |
| Irritability | .50[3] | .47[3] | | | | | |
| Lability of state | .52[3] | .47[3] | | | | .89[3] | |
| Self-quieting | | −.44[3] | | | −.63[3] | | |
| *Interactional dimension* | *.53[3] | .47[3] | *.50[3] | | | −.40[1] | |
| Orientation: | | | | | | | |
| Ball | | | | | | | |
| Rattle | *−.60[3] | −.50[3] | −.41[3] | | | | |
| Face | | | | | | | |
| Voice | −.41[3] | −.41[3] | −.42[3] | | | | |
| Face & voice | | | | | | | |

| | | | | |
|---|---|---|---|---|
| Alertness | −.48[3] | | | |
| Cuddliness | −.50[3] | −.49[2] | .71[1] | −.71[2] |
| Consolability | −.45[3] | −.49[2] | *.76[3] | −.71[2] |
| | | | | |
| *Motoric processes* | | | | |
| General tones | | .67[3] | −.56[2] | *.98[3] |
| Motor maturity | | *.68[3] | | |
| Pull-to-sit | | .82[1] | | .89[2] |
| Defensive | | *.82[1] | | |
| Activity | *.59[3] | | | |
| Hand-to-mouth | .49[3] | | | −.98[2] |
| | | | | |
| *Physiological stability* | | | | |
| Tremulousness | — | ** −.82[3] ⎡−.62[2]⎤ ⎣−.55[3]⎦ .73[2] | — | — |
| Startles | | | −.88[2] | |
| | | | | |
| Smiles | ⎡.69[3]⎤ ⎣.65[2]⎦ | | | |

*Significance:* Unmarked = $p < .05$
          * = $p < .01$
        ** = $p < .001$

*Superscripts:* [1] = early exam
         [2] = middle exam
         [3] = late exam

*Source:* Dixon, Keefer, Tronick, and Brazelton (1982).

Table H.4. *Mean anthropometric measures by age group and year in Morongo, absolute and relative to Harvard Growth Standards*

| Age group (months) | 1974 (n = 150) | % of Std. | 1975 (n = 147) | % of Std. | 1976 (n = 150) | % of Std. | All % of Std. | S.D. |
|---|---|---|---|---|---|---|---|---|
| **Weight (kg)** | | | | | | | | |
| 0–6 | 6.07 | 105.2 | 5.58 | 101.4 | 5.96 | 103.4 | 104.2 | 26.7 |
| 7–12 | 8.12 | 85.2 | 8.05 | 83.8 | 7.89 | 98.0 | 84.1 | 16.6 |
| 13–18 | 9.35 | 82.3 | 9.09 | 81.0 | 9.16 | 82.2 | 82.1 | 11.1 |
| 19–24 | 10.65 | 84.3 | 10.67 | 86.2 | 10.42 | 82.8 | 84.0 | 11.2 |
| 25–36 | 12.08 | 87.1 | 11.59 | 82.8 | 11.42 | 81.8 | 86.0 | 13.7 |
| **Length (cm)** | | | | | | | | |
| 0–6 | 56.99 | 94.8 | 55.57 | 92.9 | 55.18 | 96.3 | 95.1 | 6.9 |
| 7–12 | 68.44 | 95.3 | 65.31 | 90.4 | 65.54 | 91.3 | 92.3 | 6.9 |
| 13–18 | 73.8 | 93.9 | 71.26 | 90.8 | 73.33 | 94.0 | 92.9 | 5.3 |
| 19–24 | 79.13 | 93.5 | 76.54 | 91.0 | 78.09 | 92.1 | 92.3 | 4.3 |
| 25–36 | 87.11 | 95.6 | 80.99 | 88.4 | 83.45 | 90.9 | 93.3 | 6.0 |
| **Head circumference (cm)** | | | | | | | | |
| 0–6 | 41.03 | 103.1 | 40.83 | 103.5 | 40.13 | 101.4 | 103.2 | 6.6 |
| 7–12 | 45.69 | 101.1 | 45.41 | 100.0 | 46.00 | 102.1 | 101.0 | 3.8 |
| 13–18 | 46.65 | 98.2 | 46.58 | 98.3 | 46.99 | 99.3 | 98.3 | 3.5 |
| 19–24 | 47.80 | 98.4 | 48.07 | 99.0 | 48.62 | 100.0 | 99.3 | 2.7 |
| 25–36 | 48.35 | 98.1 | 48.14 | 97.7 | 48.65 | 98.6 | 98.2 | 3.1 |

Table H.5. *Proportion of children having certain foods, and frequency of serving, in a one-day dietary history*

| | Maize | Meat | Eggs | Green veg. | Beans | Cow's milk |
|---|---|---|---|---|---|---|
| *Age group* | | | | | | |
| 0–6 mos. | .53 | 0 | .01 | .07 | 0 | .18 |
| 7–12 mos. | .84 | .08 | .02 | .22 | .02 | .36 |
| 13–18 mos. | .95 | .13 | .02 | .45 | .25 | .49 |
| 19–24 mos. | .98 | .17 | .06 | .53 | .23 | .73 |
| 25–36 mos. | .99 | .15 | .04 | .66 | .25 | .69 |
| All | .86 | .11 | .04 | .41 | .16 | .52 |
| Number of servings/ | 2.39±1.28 | .13±.43 | .05±.25 | .61±.85 | .21±.53 | 1.16±1.38 |

Table H.6. *Growth parameters (percentage of standard) by area and milk consumption for children aged 7–12 and 13–18 months*

| | | Area X | | Area Y | | Area Z | | ANOVAS | | | |
|---|---|---|---|---|---|---|---|---|---|---|---|
| | | Milk | No milk | Milk | No milk | Milk | No milk | Area | Milk | Area & milk | |
| *PEXPWt* | | | | | | | | | | | |
| | 7–12 | 69.9±4.3 | 83.8±2.9 | 89.5±5.1 | 79.2±4.1 | 117.6±4.1 | 72.3±8.1 | $F = 5.63$, df = 2, $p < .008$ | N.S. | $F = 14.95$, df = 2, $p < .0001$ | $F = 9.90$, df = 5/36, $p < .001$ |
| | 13–18 | 83.1±5.2 | 15.2±2.4 | 94.9±6.4 | 80.4±9.1 | 81.0±5.9 | 82.4±6.4 | $F = 3.46$, df = 2, $p < .05$ | $F = 3.43$, df = 1, $p < .03$ | N.S. | $F = 2.73$, df = 5/28, $p < .02$ |
| *PEXPHt* | | | | | | | | | | | |
| | 7–12 | 87.1±2.2 | 93.7±1.5 | 90.5±1.9 | 89.8±1.9 | 103.6±2.9 | 95.2±2.9 | $F = 8.03$, df = 2, $p < .001$ | N.S. | $F = 5.00$, df = 2, $p < .01$ | $F = 4.99$, df = 5/45, $p < .001$ |
| | 13–18 | 96.9±2.3 | 92.9±2.8 | 93.4±3.3 | 95.7±4.9 | 94.1±1.9 | 96.9±3.4 | N.S. | N.S. | N.S. | N.S. |
| *PEXPHC* | | | | | | | | | | | |
| | 7–12 | 100.4±1.2 | 98.9±0.8 | 100.1±1.0 | 102.9±1.0 | 106.7±1.6 | 102.7±1.6 | $F = 6.81$, df = 2, $p < .003$ | N.S. | $F = 3.86$, df = 2, $p < .03$ | $F = 4.83$, df = 5/45, $p < .001$ |
| | 13–18 | 98.1±1.8 | 93.9±2.0 | 99.7±2.4 | 98.5±3.4 | 98.7±1.3 | 97.4±2.4 | N.S. | N.S. | N.S. | N.S. |
| *Wt/Ht* | | | | | | | | | | | |
| | 7–12 | .107±.006 | .117±.004 | .129±.005 | .119±.005 | .155±.009 | .111±.005 | $F = 5.14$, df = 2, $p < .01$ | $F = 7.37$, df = 2, $p < .01$ | $F = 6.93$, df = 2, $p < .002$ | $F = 5.07$, df = 5/45, $p < .001$ |
| | 13–18 | .122±.005 | .121±.008 | .128±.008 | .114±.013 | .129±.005 | .122±.009 | N.S. | N.S. | N.S. | N.S. |

Table H.7a. *Gusii and American infant behaviors:*
*Proportion of time in monadic phases and the mean*
*duration of the phases*

|  | Proportion of time, % | | Mean duration in sec. | |
|---|---|---|---|---|
|  | Gusii | American | Gusii | American |
| Protest | 5.1 | 3.4 | 7.0 | 1.6 |
| Avert | 20.8 | 36.0 | 6.4 | 4.9 |
| Monitor | 19.0 | 20.4 | 8.2 | 2.7 |
| Set | 21.1 | 20.2 | 5.2 | 3.1 |
| Play | 19.5 | 16.6 | 3.0 | 3.2 |
| Talk | 13.3 | 3.4 | 1.7 | 1.11 |

Table H.7b. *Gusii and American maternal behaviors:*
*Proportion of time in monadic phases and the mean*
*duration of the phases*

|  | Proportion of time, % | | Mean duration in sec. | |
|---|---|---|---|---|
|  | Gusii | American | Gusii | American |
| Avoid | 4.9 | 0 | 1.1 | 0 |
| Avert | 3.8 | 1.8 | 3.0 | 1.2 |
| Monitor | 13.6 | 20.0 | 2.5 | 3.3 |
| Elicit | 11.1 | 17.4 | 1.7 | 4.4 |
| Set | 34.0 | 27.8 | 2.1 | 2.6 |
| Play | 20.5 | 15.2 | 1.4 | 3.6 |
| Talk | 11.7 | 17.2 | 1.2 | 3.4 |

# Notes

### 1. THE COMPARATIVE STUDY OF CHILD CARE

1. See LeVine (1970) for a critical review of "natural experiments" in child rearing.
2. See Ritchie's (1943) *The African as Suckling and Adult* for a particularly outrageous example of this kind of interpretation.
3. Goldschmidt (1975).
4. Hartmann (1958).
5. See Bowlby (1988), Papousek (1987), Stern (1977, 1985), Trevarthen (1988).
6. See Bateson and Mead (1942), Schieffelin and Ochs (1986), LeVine (1990), Richman, Miller, and LeVine (1992).
7. See Wilson (1975, pp. 548–549).
8. LeVine and Campbell (1972, pp. 104–109).
9. Adaptive organization at the population level in humans tends to be unstable when viewed from the perspective of an evolutionary timescale, but insofar as its changes are responsive to environmental pressures and opportunities, it provides a flexibility that fosters survival under varied conditions.
10. See Wilson (1975).
11. Nowadays, as indicated in Chapter 3, parents are also concerned with school performance.
12. See Chapter 4 of this volume and LeVine and LeVine (1966).
13. See Whiteley (1960, p. 13).
14. In the examination of both parent and child behavior, we are mindful of Blurton-Jones's (1971) advice to distinguish causal influences on behavior by Tinbergen's (1951) four questions concerning (1) the conditions that elicit and control the behavior, (2) the conditions under which it was learned or developed, (3) its utility or survival value, and (4) its evolutionary origins. We shall focus on the first three.
15. The parental perspective provides the social and cultural context as it affects those responsible for organizing child care; the infant's

perspective, however difficult to reconstruct, provides an indispensable basis for assessing the impact of caregiving and social exposure on behavioral development; and the comparative perspective, in which the ideals and practices of a community are seen as variants of a human predicament, makes possible a level of analysis that no particular population of parents can attain.

16. Bronfenbrenner (1979).

17. The quotation marks are used to suggest that the analogy is a metaphorical heuristic and not to be taken too seriously. Computer software as a metaphor for culture has its origins, so far as we know, in a 1966 article by Clifford Geertz, reprinted in his 1973 book *The Interpretation of Cultures:* "Culture is best seen . . . as a set of control mechanisms – plans, recipes, rules, instructions (what computer engineers call 'programs') – for the governing of behavior" (1973, p. 44). Sheila Ryan Johansson (1988, 1990) has developed the concept of cultural software in discussions of demography and health.

18. Additional features assumed here include small litter size, i.e., the fact that humans usually give birth to offspring one at a time; sexual dimorphism in anatomy and behavioral patterns; the monthly female cycle and its onset at menarche and termination at menopause, etc. For a review of the universals of infant behavioral development in the light of cross-cultural evidence, see Werner (1988); for an examination of gender differentiation in behavioral development based on cross-cultural analysis, see Whiting and Edwards (1988).

19. As evidence becomes available demonstrating that these features change in historical time, such an assumption becomes untenable unless heavily qualified. See Ellison (1990) and Worthman (1987, 1992) for evidence on population-specific historical changes in reproductive physiology.

20. For example, infant mortality rates remained high (probably over 200 deaths per thousand live births) through human prehistory and history until the late 19th century, when they began to decline in Western Europe; the decline accelerated in the industrial countries during the 20th century until they reached values under 10 per thousand live births in recent years. This precipitous drop in less than a century was due to technological and economic improvements limiting the spread of infectious diseases. A similar but less extreme change took place in fertility rates. Economic parameters affecting resource allocations available to children also show a similar pattern, in that they can be stable for centuries until technological and social change permits a major alteration in family income.

21. The ecological firmware adds a series of constraints and opportunities at the population level, constituting a theoretically optimal parental investment strategy, but this too is neither fully specified nor compelling as a guide to behavior. The optimal strategy, as constructed by an outside observer, may favor bearing many children rather than few and devoting resources to their survival rather than their education, but such general goals can be interpreted and attained in a variety of ways in different institutional contexts. Furthermore, a society can, at least in the short run, ignore incentives in its environment and organize parental resources in a nonoptimal way, thus leading to decline in the size, health, or economic welfare of its population. There is little doubt that this has happened many times in human history (Edgerton, 1992).

    Cultural software adds the impact of ideational models and scripts, which provide a parental agenda for child care and development, selecting which hardware-firmware potentials are to be realized and which left unused, according to a set of symbols – prototypes, norms, and plans offered as guides to behavior. Culturally diverse "programs" act as the *mediators* between hardware and firmware capacities on the one hand and parental behavior on the other. Through the labeling, interpretation, and organization of their cultural software, parents' experience of sexuality, reproduction, child development, and their socioeconomic environment is automatically assimilated to the normative categories of their active cultural traditions.

22. In addition to cultural mediation, there is another, slower-acting process not shown on Figure 1.1, but which could be indicated by an arrow *to* the cultural software box *from* parental behavior, suggesting that cultural models reflect as well as influence central tendencies in the parental behavior of a population. In other words, the actual practices of a population alter culturally formulated preferences over time, as our examination of Gusii child care in historical perspective will illustrate.

## 2. INFANT CARE IN SUB-SAHARAN AFRICA

1. The review in this chapter is limited to the argicultural and pastoral peoples of the sub-Saharan region, leaving out the foraging peoples, even though important studies of infant care and development have been conducted by Konner (1972, 1976, 1977; Barr, Konner, Bakeman, & Adamson, 1991) among the !Kung San of Botswana, Tronick and his collaborators (Tronick, Morelli, & Winn, 1987; Tronick, Morelli, & Ivey, 1992) among the Efe pyg-

mies of eastern Zaire, and Hewlett (1991) among the Aka pygmies of the Central African Republic. This exclusion is based on the judgment that the hunting and gathering peoples of Africa form a set of cultural environments for infant care quite distinct from the food-producing majority around them. Because the Gusii were agropastoralists, it is the literature on other food producers that provides the regional context for understanding their patterns.

2.  Bryant (1949), Junod (1962), Smith and Dale (1920).
3.  Junod (1962, p. 59).
4.  Krige (1937).
5.  Krige (1937, p. 95).
6.  There is no direct quantitative basis for estimating infant and child mortality rates in most of sub-Saharan Africa before 1945, but a wide range of indirect evidence strongly suggests that infant mortality throughout the region was at least 200 per thousand live births (during the first year) and might have been considerably higher, particularly where malaria was endemic and during epidemics of smallpox, measles, and typhoid. These diseases, as well as other diarrheal and acute respiratory infections, particularly when combined with malnutrition during periodic famines, caused high rates of postinfancy mortality too, providing a basis for extending maternal protection, including breast-feeding and intensive monitoring, as a preventive measure for children older than 12 months.
7.  Brazelton, Koslowski, and Tronick (1976).
8.  J. Whiting (1964).
9.  Page and Lesthaeghe (1981).
10. Saucier (1972).
11. Lesthaeghe et al. (1981, p. 7). For further information on the contraceptive effect of breast-feeding, see McNeilly (1988).
12. Varkevisser (1973, p. 94).
13. Varkevisser (1973, p. 135).
14. Varkevisser (1973, p. 100).
15. Southwold (1973). In other African societies, the birth interval is protected by warnings of poor behavioral development. Thus Bryant (1949, p. 637) reports of the Zulu: "A wife bearing children at too short intervals, that is, becoming pregnant again while the preceding child is still at the breast, is said to *nyemfuza,* that is, to bear lifeless, indolent, good-for-nothing children."
16. Lesthaeghe et al. (1981, p. 7).
17. Schoenmakers et al. (1981).
18. For example, LeVine and LeVine (1966, p. 131), Sangree (1981), Smith (1954), Varkevisser (1973, pp. 163–164). In Gusii, the word for lastborn is *omokogooti;* see Chapter 6 for more information.
19. Evans-Pritchard (1953).

20. See Sangree (1987).
21. See Bledsoe and Isiugo-Abanihe (1989) on the Mende of Sierra Leone, Goody (1982, p. 44) on the Gonja of Ghana, Riesman (1992, p. 96) on the Fulani of Burkina Faso.
22. Deng (1972).
23. Deng (1972, p.9).
24. Deng (1972, p. 94).
25. LeVine (1973, pp. 131–133).
26. Bledsoe and Isiugo-Abanihe (1989, pp. 447–449).
27. Gluckman (1950).
28. Hakansson (1989).
29. See Weisner and Gallimore (1977) and Weisner (1982, 1987, 1989a, 1989b).
30. See Bledsoe and Isiugo-Abanihe (1989) for description of foster care by grandmothers.
31. Wenger (1989).
32. Riesman (1992).
33. This research was supported by a grant from the Carnegie Corporation of New York to Ahmadu Bello University and by the Early Education Research Center of the University of Chicago. See LeVine, LeVine, Iwanaga, and Marvin (1970) and Marvin, VanDevender, Iwanaga, LeVine, and LeVine (1977).
34. As it happens, however, the peoples with a high social density in the domestic group permitting the infant access to a greater range of caregivers, viz, the Yoruba, Hausa, Giryama, and Fulani (of Burkina Faso) were also characterized by low fertility and high child mortality at the time of observation. Thus in comparison with low-density populations in the East African highlands, the demographic and organizational factors supporting a more varied cast of caregivers were confounded with each other and appeared to be mutually reinforcing.
35. Munroe and Munroe (1971, 1980).
36. Borgerhoff Mulder (1985).
37. In Kenya, universal primary schooling and, more recently, the advent of rural nursery schools have altered the indigenous pattern without eliminating the phenomenon of children caring for infants.
38. Weisner (1987), Whiting and Whiting (1975).
39. Konner (1976).
40. Leiderman et al. (1973), Leiderman and Leiderman (1974a, 1974b, 1977).
41. Munroe and Munroe (1971); see Chapter 6 of this volume for a description of their method.
42. Sigman, Neumann, Carter, Cattle, D'Souza, and Bwibo (1988).
43. Sigman et al. (1988, p. 1259).

44. A similar point could be made about foster care during the early years. See Bledsoe and Isiugo-Abanihe (1989).
45. LeVine (1980); LeVine, Klein, and Owen (1967); Lloyd (1966, 1967, 1970).
46. Lloyd (1970, pp. 76–77).
47. Lloyd (1970, pp. 79–90). Daytime care was provided by hired young adolescent girls from rural areas who did not attend or, in some cases by the mother's mother or another older woman from her family.
48. LeVine (1980).
49. Goldberg (1977).
50. Albino and Thompson (1956).
51. Ainsworth (1967, 1977). The study was conducted in 1954–1955.
52. Ritchie (1943).
53. The Hausa of Nigeria also practice abrupt weaning, but many other African peoples do not; the practice varies greatly across the sub-Saharan region.
54. See J. Whiting, Child, and Lambert (1966).
55. LeVine and LeVine (1966).
56. LeVine (1963).
57. See Fadipe (1970).
58. Whiting and Whiting (1975).
59. Whiting and Whiting (1975).
60. Super (1976), Wober (1975).
61. Super and Harkness (1982, p. 14).
62. Kilbride and Kilbride (1974, 1975, 1983, 1990).
63. Harkness and Super (1977).
64. Super and Harkness (1986).
65. Trevarthen (1988).
66. Trevarthen (1988, p. 57).
67. Trevarthen (1988, pp. 80–81).
68. Ainsworth (1967, 1977).
69. Bowlby (1969, 1988).
70. R. LeVine, S. LeVine, Iwanaga, and Marvin (1970); Marvin, VanDevender, Iwanaga, S. LeVine, and R. LeVine (1977).
71. Leiderman and Leiderman (1974a).
72. Ainsworth et al. (1978).

## 3. GUSII CULTURE

1. See LeVine and LeVine (1991).
2. See I. Mayer (1965).
3. See R. LeVine (1982).

4. P. Mayer (1949).
5. I. Mayer (1965).
6. R. LeVine (1962).
7. R. LeVine (1963, 1980).
8. Soja (1968).
9. R. LeVine (1964).
10. R. LeVine and B. LeVine (1966).
11. R. LeVine (1980), S. LeVine and G. Pfeifer (1982).
12. See Chapter 2, Gluckman (1950), Hakansson (1989).
13. See Lave and Wenger (1991) for the theoretical statement, Fortes (1938) for the original African description.

## 4. GUSII FERTILITY, MARRIAGE, AND FAMILY

1. Dow and Werner (1983).
2. Moseley (1983); we have used his measure of child mortality, viz, the proportion of children born alive who died during the first 24 months to mothers 20–24 years of age.
3. Nag (1980).
4. Bongaarts (1978); Bongaarts, Frank, and Lesthaeghe (1984).
5. LeVine (1982).
6. Frank (1983).
7. Frank (1938, p. 138).
8. Frank (1983, p. 140).
9. Central Bureau of Statistics (1981).
10. See Raikes (1990) for 1985–86 and Hammerslough (1992) for the DHS of 1989.
11. Central Bureau of Statistics (1981).
12. R. LeVine (1959).
13. Central Bureau of Statistics (1981) and Moseley, Werner, and Becker (1982).
14. Our longitudinal sample of 28 mothers in 1975–1976 had an average age of 29.2 years, with a standard deviation of 6.4 and a range of 20 to 40; the KNFS sample included women up to 44 years of age.
15. LeVine and LeVine (1966, pp. 130–131).
16. See Sangree (1987).
17. See the desciption of the rituals for anomalous births in Chapter 5.
18. Caldwell and Caldwell (1987).
19. The KNFS found that only 12% of Gusii ever-married women had a first marriage that was dissolved (Central Bureau of Statistics, 1979).
20. Central Bureau of Statistics (1979, p. 19, Table 12).

21. Pebley and Mbugua (1989).
22. Knodel (1983).
23. Page and Lesthaeghe (1981), Bongaarts, Frank, and Lesthaeghe (1984).
24. LeVine and LeVine (1966, pp. 46–47).
25. Levine and LeVine (1966, p. 51).


## 5. PREGNANCY AND BIRTH

1. Some of these women were enrolled in Cohort I of our longitudinal study.
2. This was found in the 1950s, too; see LeVine and LeVine (1966, p. 116).
3. LeVine and LeVine (1966, pp. 165–176).
4. P. Mayer (1950).
5. LeVine and LeVine (1966, p. 114).
6. LeVine and LeVine (1966, pp. 116–117).
7. See Barkow (1989, pp. 305–309) for a cross-cultural study of customs concerning the feeding of colostrum to newborns; he argues that this is one area in which a substantial proportion of human populations have maladaptive customs.
8. There are other Gusii names that do not fit neatly into these categories, including those referring to personal qualities of the parents or to omens seen near the time of birth, after which the diviner (*omoragori*) may tell the parents to name the child.
9. There are other variants of these names and this ritual, e.g., *Bisieri* (from *ebisieri,* which means "doors"), when a female child in born after a mother has lost several children, and the mother takes the newborn to the doorways of people in the community for token presents instead of sitting by the side of the road. There is also the name *Ntabo* (from *entabo,* "the only one"), usually for a male child whose mother has lost several children and is so old she might be unable to have more; the same ritual is performed. For children named Bisieri or Ntabo, the earlobe is punctured (left lobe for girls, right for boys) and a bead inserted until the child's circumcision.
10. At the funeral of a female elder, her adult grandchildren will sing laments recalling how she called them by their praise-names, as they weep and dance slowly on her grave.


## 6. INFANT CARE

1. LeVine and LeVine (1966, pp. 119–137).
2. Geertz (1973, 1983).

3. See Chapter 9 for a more complete analysis of cultural models of infant and child care.
4. *Omwana obande mamiria makendu.*
5. We heard of one case in the 1950s in which the mother-in-law of a young woman who died in childbirth breast-fed the surviving new-born along with her own nursing child, but it was recognized as contrary to prevailing norms.
6. *Tuga ntakana ngombe totuga ntakana monto.*
7. One woman who insisted on the validity of the proverb gave herself as an example of an ungrateful orphan.
8. LeVine and LeVine (1966, p. 128).
9. An exception is described in LeVine and LeVine (1966, pp. 132–133), but the child whose mother ignored her crying was 22 months old and trying to get at her mother's breasts when the mother was desperately attempting to wean the child before the father's return on a particular date, so she could conceive another child. Furthermore, this woman had a reputation for being somewhat irresponsible, then and in the 1970s, so this instance should not be interpreted as typical of Gusii mothers.
10. LeVine and LeVine (1966, p. 121).
11. Munroe and Munroe (1971); for subsequent uses of their technique in child development research, see Rogoff (1978).
12. Intercoder reliabilities ranged from .79 to .93, with an average of .86. For purposes of analysis, summary scores for each coding category across 3-month intervals were generated for each of the 28 infants. These summary scores were generated by calculating, for each infant, the proportion of observations over a 3-month interval in which a particular event occurred. For example, if the mother were observed to hold the infant for 5 of 20 observations, the variable "mother holding" would have a value of 25% for that infant. Mean values of these proportions were then calculated for each 3-month interval.

## 7. SURVIVAL AND HEALTH

1. See Table 4.2
2. Moseley (1983).
3. Brazelton (1973).
4. Specific modifications of the BNBAS to the Gusii situation are described in Keefer, Tronick, Dixon, and Brazelton (1982) and Keefer, Dixon, Tronick, and Brazelton (1991).
5. Brazelton et al. (1977).
6. Als et al. (1976).

7. Lester (1979).
8. Blankhart (1971).
9. See Appendix A.
10. Werner (1979).
11. See Appendix B for tables.
12. See Caron (1985).
13. See Appendix B.
14. See Appendix A for methods and categories.

## 8. COMMUNICATION AND SOCIAL LEARNING DURING INFANCY

1. Gottman and Bakeman (1978).
2. Barr (1990), Barr and Elias (1988), Bell and Ainsworth (1972), Hunziker and Barr (1986).
3. Richman et al. (1988).
4. See Richman, Miller, and LeVine (1992, p. 617, Table 3).
5. Leiderman and Leiderman (1974a); the nonmaternal caregivers in that study were older on average than those in the Gusii study.
6. Tronick, Als, and Brazelton (1977, 1980).
7. Tronick, Als, and Brazelton (1977).
8. Dixon, Tronick, Keefer, and Brazelton (1981).
9. Dixon, LeVine, Richman, and Brazelton (1984).
10. For example, Kaye (1976).
11. Lave and Wenger (1991).
12. A full account of the method and findings appears in Yaman (1993).
13. See LeVine and LeVine (1966, pp. 125–126) for a description of this phenomenon in the 1950s.
14. Harkness and Super (1977).

## 10. EARLY CHILD DEVELOPMENT IN AN AFRICAN CONTEXT

1. Winnicott (1957, 1965).
2. We do not mean to imply that the child care practices of London as Winnicott knew them between 1920 and 1970 were similar to those of our suburban Boston comparison groups (although they were derived from a broadly common Anglo-American cultural tradition) but only that Gusii practices are different from both.
3. See Geertz (1983, pp. 73–93) for a discussion of "common sense as a cultural system." For the concept of cultural model, see Quinn and Holland (1983) and D'Andrade and Strauss (1992).

4. See Chapter 2 of this volume and LeVine (1974, 1977, 1988).

5. The American model described here is drawn from our home observations of and interviews with suburban Boston mothers, conducted to provide comparison with the Gusii data (Richman, Miller, and Solomon, 1988), the videotaped laboratory observations conducted at the Child Development Unit, Children's Hospital Medical Center, Boston (Dixon et al., 1981, 1984), and the research literature on white middle-class child care in the United States.

6. Gusii infant mortality in 1974 was probably about 80 births per thousand live births (during the first 12 months), whereas the United States white middle class had a rate that was undoubtedly under 15 at that time.

7. Barr (1990) refers to these as the !Kung San package of caregiver behaviors, because they are found among the Kalahari huntergatherers in Botswana, as documented by Konner (1972, 1977). LeVine (1974, 1977) has suggested that they are common to many peoples living in tropical areas around the world.

8. Tronick, Als, and Brazelton (1977).

9. For the concept of scaffolding, see Wood, Bruner, and Ross (1976), Wood (1988), Bruner (1990); for the analysis of baby talk, see Snow and Ferguson (1977); for a discussion of the use of recasting and expanding in the linguistic socialization of American middle-class infants, see Ochs and Schieffelin (1984) and Schieffelin and Ochs (1986).

10. Heath (1986, p. 99).

11. See LeVine and LeVine (1966, pp. 128–129).

12. See LeVine and LeVine (1966, pp. 124–125).

13. This is paraphrased from a Gusii mother in the Nyansongo study of the 1950s; only 2 out of the 24 mothers interviewed then said they praised their children for good behavior (LeVine & LeVine, 1966, p. 147). For another African case in which parents repudiate the praising of children, see Riesman on the Fulani of Burkina Faso (1992, pp. 174–178); he also discusses the emotional effects on the child of not being directly praised for good behavior.

14. See Harkness and Super (1977).

15. Lave and Wenger (1991).

16. The optimal method for eliciting this kind of cultural reaction is to show videotapes from one people to those of another culture, as in the study of nursery schools in Japan, China, and the United States by Tobin, Wu, and Davidson (1989).

17. See Richman (1983, p. 41).

18. Scafidi et al. (1990), Field et al. (1986), Schanberg and Field (1987).

19. DeCarvalho et al. (1983), Barr and Elias (1988).
20. See Barr (1990) for a review of the studies supporting this statement.
21. Koner and Super (1987).
22. See Barr (1990).
23. See Lamb and Malkin (1986).
24. Anisfeld et al. (1990). See also Leiderman and Reed (1981, 1983).
25. The quality of children in purely physical terms, and hence their chances of survival are also adversely affected by high fertility among the Gusii. As shown in Chapter 7, infants born to mothers who had already had five or more children tended to be smaller and more vulnerable than those earlier in the birth order.
26. See the case of Justin in the previous chapter.
27. See Whiting and Whiting (1975).
28. For example, the girls' initiation songs quoted in LeVine and LeVine (1966, pp. 171–172).
29. See Rogoff (1989).
30. Sarah LeVine had been back for 3 weeks in October 1979 (3 years after the original study), when she interviewed each of the mothers concerning their own lives (see S. LeVine and Pfeifer, 1982) and learned that one of the 29 children had died. In 1988, working with Agnes Nyabeta, she found the rest of the children and mothers and collected the data reported here.
31. For further discussion of resilience in child development, see Kagan (1984).
32. For discussion of the "internal working model" of the infant, see Bretherton (1987).
33. This analysis is based on the theoretical discussion and framework of Ochs (1990).
34. *Banto mbamaiso nemioyo etamanyaini.*
35. See Lave and Wenger (1991).

# References

Ainsworth, M. D. S. 1967. *Infancy in Uganda*. Baltimore: Johns Hopkins University Press.

Ainsworth, M. D. S. 1977. Infant Development and Mother–Infant Interaction among Ganda and American Families. In P. H. Leiderman, S. R. Tulkin, & A. Rosenfeld, eds., *Culture and Infancy*. New York: Academic Press.

Ainsworth, M. D. S., Blehar, M. C., Water, E., & Wall, S. 1978. *Patterns of Attachment: A Psychological Study of the Strange Situation*. Hillsdale, N.J.: Erlbaum.

Albino, R. C. & Thompson, V. J. 1956. The Effects of Sudden Weaning on Zulu Children. *British Journal of Medical Psychology 29:* 177–210.

Als, H., Tronick, E., Adamson, L., & Brazelton, T. B. 1976. The Behavior of the Full-term yet Underweight Newborn Infant. *Developmental Medicine and Child Neurology 18:* 590–602.

Anisfield, E., Casper, V., Nozyce, M., & Cunningham, N. 1990. Does Infant Carrying Promote Attachment? An Experimental Study of the Effects of Increased Physical Contact on the Development of Attachment. *Child Development 61:* 1617–1627.

Barkow, J. H. 1989. *Darwin, Sex and Status: Biological Approaches to Mind and Culture*. Toronto: University of Toronto Press.

Barr, R. G. 1990. The Early Crying Paradox: A Modest Proposal. *Human Nature 1:* 355–389.

Barr, R. G. & Elias, M. F. 1988. Nursing Interval and Maternal Responsivity: Effect on Early Infant Crying. *Pediatrics 81:* 529–536.

Barr, R. G., Konner, M., Bakeman, R., & Adamson, L. 1991. Crying in !Kung San Infants: A Test of the Cultural Specificity Hypothesis. *Developmental Medicine and Child Neurology 33:* 601–610.

Bateson, G. & Mead, M. 1942. *Balinese Character: A Photographic Analysis*. New York: New York Academy of Sciences.

Bell, S. M. & Ainsworth, M. D. S. 1972. Infant Crying and Maternal Responsiveness. *Child Development 43:* 1171–1190.

Blankhart, G. M. 1971. Outline for a Survey of the Feeding and Nutritional Status of Children under Three Years and their Mothers. *Journal of Tropical Pediatrics and Environmental Child Health 17:* 175–185.

Bledsoe, C. & Isiugo-Abanihe, U. 1989. Strategies of Child-Fosterage among Mende Grannies in Sierra Leone. In R. J. Lesthaeghe, ed., *Reproduction and Social Organization in Sub-Saharan Africa.* Berkeley: University of California Press.

Blurton-Jones, N. 1971. Characteristics of Ethological Studies of Human Behavior. In N. Blurton-Jones, ed., *Ethological Studies of Child Behaviour.* Cambridge: Cambridge University Press.

Bongaarts, J. 1978. A Framework for Analyzing the Proximate Determinants of Fertility. *Population and Devlopment Review 4:* 105–132.

Bongaarts, J., Frank, O., & Lesthaeghe, R. 1984. The Proximate Determinants of Fertility in Sub-Saharan Africa. *Population and Development Review 10:* 511–537.

Borgerhoff Mulder, M. 1985. Factors Affecting Infant Care in the Kipsigis. *Journal of Anthropological Research 41:* 231–261.

Bowlby, J. 1969. *Attachment.* New York: Basic Books.

Bowlby, J. 1988. *A Secure Base.* New York: Basic Books.

Brazelton, T. B. 1973. *Neonatal Behavioral Assessment Scale.* London: Heinemann; Philadelphia: J.P. Lippincott.

Brazelton, T. B., Koslowski, B., & Tronick, E. 1976. Neonatal Behavior among Urban Zambians and Americans. *Journal of American Academy of Child Psychiatry 1:* 97–107.

Brazelton, T. B., Tronick, E., Lechtig, A., Lasky, R. E., & Klein, E. R. 1977. The Behavior of Nutritionally Deprived Guatemalans. *Developmental Medicine and Child Neurology 19:* 364–372.

Bretherton, I. 1987. New Perspectives on Attachment Relations: Security, Communication and Internal Working Models. In J. Osofsky, ed., *Handbook of Infant Development,* 2nd edition. New York: Wiley.

Bronfenbrenner. U. 1979. *The Ecology of Human Development.* Cambridge, Mass.: Harvard University Press.

Bruner, J. 1990. *Acts of Meaning.* Cambridge, Mass.: Harvard University Press.

Bryant, A. T. 1949. *The Zulu People.* Pietermaritzburg, South Africa: Shuter and Shooter.

Caldwell, J. C. & Caldwell, P. 1987. The Cultural Context of High Fertility in Sub-Saharan Africa. *Population and Development Review 13:* 409–437.

Caron, J. W. 1985. Infant Effects on Caretaker Responsiveness: Influences of Infant Characteristics on the Infant Care Environment among the Gusii of Kenya. Unpublished Ed.D. thesis, Harvard University Graduate School of Education.

Central Bureau of Statistics, Ministry of Economic Planning and Development, Kenya. 1979. Major Highlights of the Kenya Fertility Survey. *Social Perspectives 4,* No. 2, pp. 1–20.

Central Bureau of Statistics, Ministry of Economic Planning and Development, Kenya. 1981. Modernization, Birth Spacing and Marital Fertility in Kenya. *Social Perspectives 6,* No. 5, pp. 1–12.

D'Andrade, R. G. & Strauss, C., eds. 1992. *Human Motives and Cultural Models.* Cambridge: Cambridge University Press.

De Carvalho, M., Robertson, S., Friedman, A. 1983. Effect of Frequent Breast-feeding on Early Milk Production and Infant Weight Gain. *Pediatrics 72:* 307–316.

Deng, F. M. 1972. *The Dinka of the Southern Sudan.* New York: Holt, Rinehart and Winston.

Dixon, S., Keefer, C., Tronick, E., & Brazelton, T. B. 1982. Perinatal Circumstances and Newborn Outcome among the Gusii of Kenya: Assessment of Risk. *Infant Behavior and Development 5:* 11–32.

Dixon, S., LeVine, R. A., & Brazelton, T. B. 1982. Malnutrition: A Closer Look at the Problem in an East African Village. *Developmental Medicine and Child Neurology 24:* 670–685.

Dixon, S., LeVine, R. A., Richman, A., & Brazelton, T. B. 1984. Mother–Child Interaction around a Teaching Task: An African-American Comparison. *Child Development 55:* 1252–1264.

Dixon, S., Tronick, E., Keefer, C., & Brazelton, T. B. 1981. Mother–Infant interaction among the Gusii of Kenya. In T. M. Field, A. M. Sostek, P. Vietze, & P. H. Leiderman, eds., *Culture and Early Interactions.* Hillsdale, N.J.: Erlbaum.

Dow, T. E. & Werner, L. H. 1983. Prospects for Fertility Decline in Rural Kenya. *Population and Development Review 9:* 77–97.

Dubowitz, L. M. S., Dubowitz, V., & Goldberg, C. 1970. Clinical Assessment of Gestational Age in the Newborn Infant. *Journal of Pediatrics 77,* 1–10.

Edgerton, R. 1992. *Sick Societies.* New York: The Free Press.

Ellison, P. T. 1990. Human Ovarian Function and Reproductive Ecology: New Hypotheses. *American Anthropologist 92,* 933–952.

Evans-Pritchard, E. E. 1953. *Kinship and Marriage among the Nuer.* London: Oxford University Press.

Fadipe, N. A. 1970. *The Sociology of the Yoruba.* Ibadan, Nigeria: Ibadan University Press.

Field, T. M., Schanberg, S. M., Scafidi, F., Bauer, C., Vega-Lahr, N., Garcia, R., Nystrom, J., & Kuhn, C. 1986. Tactile/Kinesthetic Stimulation Effects on Preterm Neonates. *Pediatrics 77:* 654–658.

Fortes, M. 1938. *Social and Psychological Aspects of Education in Taleland.* International African Institute Memorandum No. 17. London: Oxford University Press.

Frank, O. 1983. Infertility in Sub-Saharan Africa: Estimates and Implications. *Population and Development Review 9:* 137–144.

Geertz, C. 1973. *The Interpretation of Cultures.* New York: Basic Books.

Geertz, C. 1983. *Local Knowledge.* New York: Basic Books.

Gluckman, M. 1950. Kinship and Marriage among Lozi of Northern Rhodesia and the Zulu of Natal. In A. R. Radcliffe-Brown and D. Forde, eds., *African Systems of Kinship and Marriage.* London: Oxford University Press.

Goldberg. S. 1977. Infant Development and Mother–Infant Interaction in Urban Zambia. In P. H. Leiderman. S. Tulkin, & A. Rosenfeld, eds., *Culture and Infancy.* New York: Academic Press.

Goldschmidt, W. 1975. Absent Eyes and Idle Hands: Socialization for Low Affect among the Sebei. *Ethos 3:* 157–164.

Goody, E. 1982. *Parenthood and Social Reproduction.* Cambridge; Cambridge University Press.

Gottman, J. & Bakeman, R. 1978. The Sequential Analysis of Observational Data. In M. Lamb, S. Suomi, & G. Stephenson, eds., *Methodological Problems in the Study of Social Interaction.* Madison: University of Wisconsin Press.

Hakansson, N. T. 1985. Why Do Gusii Women Get Married? A Study of Cultural Constraints and Women's Strategies in a Rural Community in Kenya. *Folk 27:* 89–114.

Hakansson, N. T. 1988. *Bridewealth, Women and Land: Social Change among the Gusii of Kenya.* Uppsala, Sweden: Uppsala Studies in Cultural Anthropology, No. 10.

Hakansson, N. T. 1989. Family Structure, Bridewealth, and Environment in Eastern Africa: A Comparative Study of House Property Systems. *Ethnology 28*(2): 117–134.

Hammerslough, C. R. 1992. The Mystery of Machakos: Contraceptive Method Choice in Rural Kenya. Paper presented to the Department of Population and International Health, Harvard School of Public Health, June 11, 1992.

Harkness, S. & Super, C. 1977. Why African Children Are So Hard to Test. In L. L. Adler, ed., Issues on Cross-Cultural Research. *Annals of the New York Academy of Sciences 285:* 326–331.

Hartmann, H. 1958. *The Ego and the Problem of Adaptation.* New York: International Universities Press.

Heath, S. B. 1986. What No Bedtime Story Means: Narrative Skills at Home and School. In B. Schieffelin and E. Ochs, eds., *Language*

*Socialization Across Cultures.* Cambridge: Cambridge University Press.

Hennessy, M. J., Dixon, S. D., & Simon, S. R. 1984. The Development of Gait: A Study in African Children Ages One to Five. *Child Development 55*, 844–853.

Hewlett, B. 1991. *Intimate Fathers: The Nature and Context of Aka Pygmy Paternal Infant Care.* Ann Arbor: University of Michigan Press.

Hunziker, U. & Barr, R. 1986. Increased Carrying Reduces Infant Crying: A Randomized Controlled Trial. *Pediatrics 77:* 641–648.

Johansson, S. R. 1988. The Computer Paradigm and the Role of Cultural Information in Social Systems. *Historical Methods 21,* 172–188.

Johansson, S. R. 1990. Cultural Software, Institution Hardware, and Health Information Processing in Social Systems. In John C. Caldwell, ed., *What We Know About Health Transition: The Cultural, Social and Behavioral Determinants of Health.* Australian National University: Canberra.

Junod, H. 1962. *The Life of a South African Tribe,* Volumes I and II. (reprinted from second edition, 1926). New Hyde Park, N.Y.: University Books.

Kagan, J. *The Nature of the Child.* 1984. New York: Basic Books.

Kaye, K. 1976. Infants' Effects Upon their Mothers' Teaching Strategies. In J. C. Glidewell, ed., *The Social Context of Learning and Development.* New York: Gardner.

Keefer, C. H., Dixon, S., Tronick, E. Z., & Brazelton, T. B. 1991. Cultural Mediation between Newborn Behavior and Later Development: Implications for Methodology in Cross-Cultural Research. In J. K. Nugent, B. M. Lester, & T. B. Brazelton, eds., *The Cultural Context of Infancy,* Vol. 2. Norwood, N.J.: Ablex.

Keefer, C. H., Tronick, E. Z., Dixon, S., & Brazelton, T. B. 1982. Specific Differences in Motor Performance between Gusii and American Newborns and a Modification of the Neonatal Behavioral Assessment Scale. *Child Development 53:* 754–759.

Kilbride, J. E. & Kilbride, P. L. 1975. Sitting and Smiling Behavior of Baganda Infants. *Journal of Cross-Cultural Psychology 6:* 88–107.

Kilbride, P. L. & Kilbride, J. E. 1974. Sociocultural Factors and the Early Manifestation of Socioability Behavior among Baganda Infants. *Ethos 2:* 296–314.

Kilbride, P. L. & Kilbride, J. E. 1983. Socialization for High Positive Affect between Mother and Infant among the Baganda of Uganda. *Ethos 11:* 232–245.

324    *References*

Kilbride, P. L. & Kilbride, J. E. 1990. Changing Family Life in East Africa: Women and Children at Risk. University Park, Pa: Pennsylvania State University Press.

Knodel, J. 1983. Natural Fertility: Age Patterns, Levels and Trends. In R. Bulatao & R. Lee, eds., *Determinants of Fertility in Developing Countries.* Volume I. New York: Academic Press.

Konner, M. J. 1972. Aspects of the Developmental Ethology of a Foraging People. In N. Blurton-Jones, ed., *Ethological Studies of Child Behavior.* Cambridge: Cambridge University Press.

Konner, M. J. 1976. Maternal Care, Infant Behavior and Development among the !Kung. In R. B. Lee & I. DeVore, eds., *Kalahari Hunter-Gatherers.* Cambridge, Mass.: Harvard University Press.

Konner, M. J. 1977. Infancy among the Kalahari Desert San. In P. H. Leiderman, S. Tulkin, & A. Rosenfeld, eds., *Culture and Infancy.* New York: Academic Press.

Konner, M. J. & Super, C. 1987. Sudden Infant Death Syndrome: An Anthropological Hypothesis. In C. Super, ed., *The Role of Culture in Developmental Disorder.* New York: Academic Press.

Krige, E. J. 1937. Individual Development. In I. Schapera, ed., *The Bantu-Speaking Tribes of South Africa.* London: Routledge & Sons.

Lamb, M. & Malkin, C. 1986. The Development of Social Expectations in Distress-Relief Sequences: A Longitudinal Study. *International Journal of Behavioral Development 9:* 235–249.

Lave, J. & Wenger, E. 1991. *Situated Learning: Legitimate Peripheral Participation.* Cambridge: Cambridge University Press.

Leiderman, P. H., Babu, B., Kagia, J. Craemer, H. C., & Leiderman, G. F. 1973. African Infant Precocity and Some Social Influences during the First Year. *Nature 242:* 247–249.

Leiderman, P. H. & Leiderman, G. F. 1974a. Affective and Cognitive Consequences of Polymatric Infant Care in the East African Highlands. In A. D. Pick, ed., *Minnesota Symposia on Child Psychology,* Volume 8. Minneapolis: University of Minnesota Press.

Leiderman, P. H. & Leiderman, G. F. 1974a. Familial Influences on Infant Development in an East African Agricultural Community. In E. J. Anthony & C. Koupernik, eds., *The Child in his Family – Children at Psychiatric Risk.* Volume 3. New York: Wiley.

Leiderman, P. H. & Leiderman, G. F. 1977. Economic Changes and Infant Care in an East African Agricultural Community. In P. H. Leiderman, S. Tulkin, & A. Rosenfeld, eds., *Culture and Infancy.* New York: Academic Press.

Lesthaeghe, R., Ohadike, P. O., Kocher, J., & Page, H. J. 1981. Child-Spacing and Fertility in Sub-Saharan Africa: An Overview of Issues. In H. J. Page and R. Lesthaeghe, eds., *Child-Spacing in Tropical Africa.* New York: Academic Press.

Lester, B. 1979. A Synergistic Approach to the Study of Parental Malnutrition. *International Journal of Behavioral Development 2:* 377–393.

LeVine, R. A. 1959. Gusii Sex Offenses: A Study in Social Control. *American Anthropologist 61,* 965–990.

LeVine, R. 1962. Witchcraft and Co-Wife Proximity in Southwestern Kenya. *Ethnology, 1:* 39–45.

LeVine, R. 1963. Witchcraft and Sorcery in a Gusii Community. In J. Middleton & E. Winter, eds., *Witchcraft and Sorcery in East Africa.* London: Routledge and Kegan Paul.

LeVine, R. A. 1964. The Gusii Family. In R. F. Gray & P. H. Gulliver, eds., *The Family Estate in Africa.* London: Routledge Kegan Paul.

LeVine R. 1970. Cross-Cultural Study in Child Psychology. In P. Mussen, ed., *Carmichael's Manual of Child Psychology,* third edition. New York: Wiley.

LeVine, R. A. 1973. Patterns of Personality in Africa. *Ethos, 1,* 123–152.

LeVine, R. 1974. Parental Goals: A Cross-Cultural View. *Teachers College Record 76:* 226–239.

LeVine, R. 1977. Child Rearing as Adaptation. In P. H. Leiderman, S. Tulkin, & A. Rosenfeld, eds., *Culture and Infancy.* New York: Academic Press.

LeVine, R. 1980. Adulthood among the Gusii of Kenya. In N. Smelser & E. Erikson, eds., *Themes of Work and Love in Adulthood.* Cambridge, Mass.: Harvard University Press.

LeVine, R. 1982. Gusii Funerals: Meanings of Life and Death in an African Community. *Ethos 10:* 26–65.

LeVine, R. A. 1988. Human Parental Care: Universal Goals, Cultural Strategies, Individual Behavior. In R. A. LeVine, P. M. Miller & M. M. West, eds., *Parental Behavior in Diverse Societies.* New Directions for Child Development No. 40. San Francisco: Jossey-Bass.

LeVine, R. 1990. Infant Environments in Psychoanalysis. In J. Stigler, R. Schweder, & G. Herdt, eds., *Cultural Psychology.* New York: Cambridge University Press.

LeVine, R. & Campbell, D. T. 1972. *Ethnocentrism: Theories of Conflict, Ethnic Attitudes and Group Behavior.* New York: Wiley.

LeVine, R. & Dixon, S. 1990. Child Survival in a Kenyan Community: Changing Risks Over Thirty Years. In J. Caldwell et al., eds., *What We Know About Health Transition.* Canberra, Australia: Australian National Printing Service.

LeVine, R., Klein, N., & Owen, C. R. 1967. Father–Child Relationships and Changing Life-Styles in Ibadan, Nigeria. In H. Miner, ed., *The City in Modern Africa*. New York: Praeger.

LeVine, R. & LeVine, B. B. 1966. *Nyansongo: A Gusii Community in Kenya*. New York: Wiley.

LeVine, R. & LeVine, S. 1988. Parental Strategies among the Gusii of Kenya. In R. LeVine, P. Miller, & M. West, eds., *Parental Behavior in Diverse Societies*. San Francisco, Calif.: Jossey-Bass Inc., Publishers.

LeVine, R. & LeVine, S. 1991. House Design and the Self in an African Culture. In L. B. Boyer and S. Grolnick, eds., *Psychoanalytic Study of Society*. Hillsdale, N.J.: Analytic Press.

LeVine, R., LeVine, S., Iwanaga, M., & Marvin, R. 1970. Child Care and Social Attachment in a Nigerian Community: A Preliminary Report. Paper presented at panel on "Grandparents, Parents and Grandchildren – Interdisciplinary Perspectives on Three Generations," at the Annual Meeting of the American Psychological Association.

LeVine, S. 1979. *Mothers and Wives: Gusii Women of East Africa*. Chicago: University of Chicago Press.

LeVine, S. & Pfeifer, G. 1982. Separation and Individuation in an African Society: The Developmental Tasks of the Gusii Married Woman. *Psychiatry 45:* 61–75.

Lloyd, B. 1967. Indigenous Ibadan. In P. Lloyd, A. Mabogunje, & B. Awe, eds., *The City of Ibadan*. Cambridge: Cambridge University Press.

Lloyd, B. 1970. Socialization among the Yoruba of Ibadan. In P. Mayer, ed., *Socialization: The Approach from Social Anthropology*. London: Tavistock.

Lubchenco, L. Hansman, C., Dressler, M., & Boyd, E. 1963. Intrauterine Growth As Estimated from Liveborn Birth Weight Data at 24 and 42 Weeks of Gestation. *Pediatrics 32,* 193.

McNeilly, A. S. 1988. Suckling and the Control of Gonadotropin Secretion. In E. Knobil & J. Neill, eds., *The Physiology of Reproduction*. New York: Raven Press.

Marvin, R., VanDevender, T., Iwanaga, M., LeVine, S., & LeVine, R. 1977. Infant-Caregiver Attachment among the Hausa of Nigeria. In H. McGurk, ed., *Ecological Factors in Human Development*. Amsterdam: North-Holland.

Mayer, I. 1965. *The Nature of Kinship Relations: The Significance of the Use of Kinship Terms among the Gusii*. The Rhodes-Livingstone Papers No. 37. Manchester: Manchester University Press.

Mayer, P. 1949. *The Lineage Principle in Gusii Society*. International African Institute No. 24. London: Oxford University Press.

Mayer, P. 1950. *Gusii Bridewealth Law and Custom.* Rhodes-Livingstone Papers No. 18. London: Oxford University Press.

Mead, M. 1930. *Growing Up in New Guinea.* New York: William Morrow.

Moseley, W. H. 1983. Will Primary Health Care Reduce Infant and Child Mortality? A Critique of Some Current Strategies, with Special Reference to Africa and Asia. In the Seminar on Social Policy, Health Policy and Mortality Prospects for the International Union for the Scientific Study of Population.

Moseley, W. H., Werner, L. H., & Becker, S. 1982. The Dynamics of Birth Spacing and Marital Fertility in Kenya. The Hague: International Statistical Institute, World Fertility Survey Scientific Reports No. 30.

Munroe, R. H. & Munroe, R. L. 1971. Household Density and Infant Care in an East African Society. *Journal of Social Psychology 83:* 9–13.

Munroe, R. H. and Munroe, R. L. 1980. Infant Experience and Childhood Affect among the Logoli: A Longitudinal Study. *Ethos 8:* 295–315.

Nag, M. 1980. How Modernization Can also Increase Fertility. *Current Anthropology 21:* 571–587.

Ochs, E. Indexicality and Socialization. 1990. In J. Stigler, R. Shweder, & G. Herdt, eds., *Cultural Psychology.* New York: Cambridge University Press.

Ochs, E. & Schieffelin, B. 1984. Language Acquisition and Socialization: Three Developmental Stories. In R. Shweder and R. LeVine, eds., *Culture Theory.* New York: Cambridge University Press.

Page, H. T. & Lesthaeghe, R., eds., 1981. *Child-Spacing in Tropical Africa.* New York: Academic Press.

Papousek, H. & Papousek, M. 1987. Intuitive Parenting: A Dialectic Counterpart to the Infant's Integrative Competence. In J. D. Osofsky, ed., *Handbook of Infant Development,* second edition. New York: Wiley.

Pebley, A. & Mbugua, W. 1989. Polygyny and Fertility in Sub-Saharan Africa. In R. Lesthaeghe, ed., *Reproduction and Social Organization in Sub-Saharan Africa.* Berkeley: University of California Press.

Quinn, N. & Holland, D. 1987. Cognition and Culture. In D. Holland and N. Quinn, eds., *Cultural Models in Language and Thought.* Cambridge: Cambridge University Press.

Raikes, A. 1990. *Pregnancy, Birthing and Family Planning in Kenya: Changing Patterns of Behavior.* Copenhagen: Centre for Development Research.

328     *References*

Reed, G. & Leiderman, P. H. 1981. Age-Related Changes in Attach-
ment Behavior in Polymatrically Rearing Infants: The Kenyan
Gusii. In T. Field, P. H. Leiderman, P. Vietze, & S. Sostek, eds.
*Culture and Early Interactions.* Hillsdale, N.J.: Erlbaum.

Reed, G. & Leiderman, P. H. 1983. Is Imprinting an Appropriate Model
for Human Infant Attachment? *International Journal of Behavioral
Development 6:* 51–69.

Richman, A. 1983. Learning about Communication: Cultural Influences
on Caretaker-Infant Interaction. Unpublished Ed.D. thesis, Harvard University Graduate School of Education.

Richman, A., Miller, P., LeVine, R. 1992. Cultural and Educational
Variations in Maternal Responsiveness. *Developmental Psychology
28:* 614–621.

Richman, A., Miller, P., & Solomon, M. 1988. The Socialization of
Infants in Suburban Boston. In R. LeVine, P. Miller, & M. M.
West, eds., *Parental Behavior in Diverse Societies.* New Directions
for Child Development No. 40. San Francisco: Jossey-Bass.

Richman, A., LeVine, R., New, R. S., Howrigan, G., Welles-Nystrom,
B., & LeVine, S. 1988. Maternal Behavior to Infants in Five Societies. In R. LeVine, P. Miller, & M. M. West, eds., *Parental Behavior in Diverse Societies.* New Directions for Child Development No.
40. San Francisco: Jossey-Bass.

Riesman, P. 1992. *First Find Your Child a Good Mother: The Construction of Self in Two African Communities.* New Brunswick, N.J.:
Rutgers University Press.

Ritchie, J. F. 1943. The African as Suckling and as Adult (a Psychological
Study). Livingstone, Northern Rhodesia: *The Rhodes-Livingstone
Papers* No. 9.

Rogoff, B. 1978. Spot Observation: An Introduction and Examination.
*Quarterly Newsletter of the Institute for Comparative Human Devel-
opment 2:* 21–26.

Rogoff, B. 1989. *Apprenticeship in Thinking: Cognitive Development in
Social Context.* New York: Oxford University Press.

Sangree, W. H. 1981. The "Last Born" (*Muxogosi*) and Complementary
Filiation in Tiriki, Kenya. *Ethos 9:* 188–200.

Sangree, W. H. 1987. The Childless Elderly in Tiriki, Kenya and Irigwe,
Nigeria: A Comparative Analysis of the Relationship between Beliefs about Childlessness and the Social Status of the Childless Elderly. *Journal of Cross-Cultural Gerontology 2:* 201–223.

Saucier, J. F. 1972. Correlates of the Long Postpartum Taboo: A Cross-
Cultural Study. *Current Anthropology 13:* 238–249.

Scafidi, F., Field, T., Schanberg, S., Bauer, C., Tucci, K., Roberts, J.,
Morrow, C., & Kuhn, C. 1990. Massage Stimulates Growth in

Preterm Infants: A Replication. *Infant Behavior and Development 13:* 167–188.

Schanberg, S. M. & Field, T. M. 1987. Sensory Deprivation Stress and Supplemental Stimulation in the Rat Pup and Preterm Human Neonate. *Child Development 58:* 1431–1447.

Schieffelin, B. & Ochs, E. 1986. Language Socialization. *Annual Review of Anthropology 15:* 163–191.

Schoenmakers, R., Shah, I. H., Lesthaeghe, R., & Tambashe, O. 1981. The Child-Spacing Tradition and the Postpartum Taboo in Tropical Africa: Anthropological Evidence. In H. J. Page & R. Lesthaeghe, eds., *Child-Spacing in Tropical Africa.* New York: Academic Press.

Sigman, M., Neumann, C., Carter, E., Cattle, D., D'Souza, & N. Bwibo, 1988. Home Interactions and the Development of Embu Toddlers in Kenya. *Child Development 59:* 1251–1261.

Smith, M. F. 1954. *Baba of Karo: The Autobiography of a Hausa Woman.* London: Faber and Faber.

Smith, E. W. & Dale, A. M. 1920. *The Ila-Speaking Peoples of Northern Rhodesia.* Volumes I and II.

Snow, C. & Ferguson, C. 1977. *Talking to Children.* Cambridge: Cambridge University Press.

Soja, E. W. 1968. *The Geography of Modernization in Kenya.* Syracuse, N.Y.: Syracuse University Press.

Southwold, M. 1973. The Baganda of Central Uganda. In A. Molnos, ed., *Cultural Source Materials for Population Planning in East Africa.* Volume III, Beliefs and Practices. Nairobi: East African Publishing House.

Stern, D. N. 1977. *The First Relationship: Infant and Mother.* Cambridge, MA: Harvard University Press.

Stern, D. N. 1985. *The Interpersonal World of the Infant.* New York: Basic Books.

Super, C. 1976. Environmental Influences on Motor Development: The Case of "African Infant Precocity." *Developmental Medicine and Child Neurology 18:* 561–567.

Super, C. 1981. Cross-Cultural Research on Infancy. In H. C. Triandis and A. Heron, eds., *Handbook of Cross-Cultural Psychology, Vol. 4, Developmental Psychology.* Boston: Allyn & Bacon.

Super, C. & Harkness, S. 1982. The Development of Affect in Infancy and Early Childhood. In D. Wagner and H. W. Stevenson, eds., *Cultural Perspective on Child Development.* San Francisco: W. H. Freeman.

Super, C. & Harkness, S. 1986. The Developmental Niche: A Conceptualization at the Interface of Child and Culture. *International Journal of Behavioral Development 9:* 1–25.

Tinbergen, N. 1951. *The Study of Instinct*. London: Oxford University Press.

Tobin, J., Wu, D., & Davidson, D. 1989. *Preschool in Three Cultures*. New Haven, Conn.: Yale University Press.

Trevarthen, C. 1988. Universal Cooperative Motives: How Infants Begin to Know the Language and Culture of their Parents. In G. Jahoda and I. M. Lewis, eds., *Acquiring Culture*. London: Croom Helm.

Tronick, E., Als, H., & Brazelton, T. B. 1977. Mutuality in Mother-Infant Interaction. *Journal of Communication 27:* 74–79.

Tronick, E., Als, H., & Brazelton, T. B. 1980. Monadic Phases: A Structural Description Analysis of Infant–Mother Face-to-Face Interaction. *Merrill-Palmer Quarterly 26:* 3–24.

Tronick, E., Morelli, G., & Ivey, P. 1992. The Efe Forager Infant and Toddler's Pattern of Social Relationships: Multiple and Simultaneous. *Developmental Psychology 28:* 568–577.

Tronick, E., Morelli, G., & Winn, S. 1987. Multiple Caretaking of Efe (Pygmy) Infants. *American Anthropologist 89:* 96–106.

Varkevisser, C. M. 1973. *Socialization in a Changing Society: Sukuma Childhood in Rural and Urban Mwanza, Tanzania*. The Hague: Centre for the Study of Education in Developing Societies.

Weisner, T. S. 1982. Sibling Interdependence and Sibling Caretaking: A Cross-Cultural View. In M. Lamb and B. Sutton-Smith, eds., *Sibling Relationships: Their Nature and Significance across the Lifespan*. Hillsdale, N.J.: Erlbaum.

Weisner, T. S. 1987. Socialization for parenthood in sibling caretaking societies. In J. Lancaster, A. Rossi, & J. Altmann, eds., *Parenting Across the Lifespan*. New York: Aldine.

Weisner, T. S. 1989a. Cultural and Universal Aspects of Social Support for Children: Evidence from the Abaluyia of Kenya. In D. Belle, ed., *Children's Social Networks and Social Supports*. New York: Wiley.

Weisner, T. S. 1989b. Comparing Sibling Relationships Across Cultures. In P. Zukow, ed., *Sibling Interaction Across Cultures*. New York: Springer-Verlag.

Weisner, T. S. & Gallimore, R. 1977. My Brother's Keeper: Child and Sibling Caretaking. *Current Anthropology 18:* 169–180.

Wenger, M. 1989. Work, Play and Social Relationships Among Children in a Giriama Community. In D. Belle, ed., *Children's Social Networks and Social Supports*. New York: Wiley.

Werner, E. E. 1979. *Cross-Cultural Child Development*. Belmont, Calif.: Wadsworth.

Werner, E. E. 1988. A Cross-Cultural Perspective on Infancy. *Journal of Cross-Cultural Psychology 19:* 96–113.

Whitely, W. H. 1960. *The Tense System of Gusii*. East African Lingusitic Studies No. 4. Kampala, Uganda: East African Institute of Social Research.

Whiting, B. B., ed., 1963. *Six Cultures: Studies of Child Rearing*. New York: Wiley.

Whiting, B. B. 1974. Folk Wisdom and Child Rearing. *Merrill-Palmer Quarterly 20:* 9–19.

Whiting, B. B. & Edwards, C. P. 1988. *Children of Different Worlds*. Cambridge, Mass.: Harvard University Press.

Whiting, B. B. & J. W. M. Whiting. 1975. *Children of Six Cultures*. Cambridge, Mass.: Harvard University Press.

Whiting, J. W. M. 1964. Effects of Climate on Certain Cultural Practices. In W. Goodenough, ed., *Explorations in Cultural Anthropology*. New York: McGraw-Hill.

Whiting, J. W. M., Child, I. L., & Lambert, W. W. 1966. *Field Guide for the Study of Socialization*. New York: Wiley.

Wilson, E. O. 1975. *Sociobiology: The Modern Synthesis*. Cambridge, Mass.: Harvard University Press.

Winnicott, D. W. 1957. *The Child and the Family: First Relationships*. London: Tavistock.

Winnicott, D. W. 1965. *The Maturational Processes and the Facilitating Environment: Studies in the Theory of Emotional Development*. New York: International Universities Press.

Wober, M. 1975. *Psychology in Africa*. London: International African Institute.

Wood, D. 1988. *Children's Learning*. Oxford: Blackwell.

Wood, D., Bruner, J. S., & Ross, G. 1976. The role of tutoring in problem-solving. *Journal of Child Psychology and Psychiatry 66:* 181–191.

Worthman, C. M. 1987. Interactions of Physical Maturation and Cultural Practice in Ontogeny: Kikuyu Adolescents. *Cultural Anthropology 2,* 29–38.

Worthman, C. M. 1992. Cupid and Psyche: Investigative Syncretism in Biological and Psychosocial Anthropology. In T. Schwartz, G. White, and C. Lutz, eds., *New Directions in Psychological Anthropology*. Cambridge: Cambridge University Press.

Yaman, Josephine. 1993. Patterns of Caretaker Utterances to Children Aged 3 to 31 Months among the Gusii of Southwestern Kenya. Unpublished qualifying paper. Harvard Graduate School of Education.

# Index

Abagusii (people), 59
abnormal births: confinement with placenta, 135–6; rituals for, 134–5; *see also* birth anomalies
academic performance, 8, 267–8, 272
academic skills, 267, 273
active engagement: goal of American child care, 250–1, 252
adaptation, 11, 12–13, 15; cultural, 97; infant care as, 169, 194–5
adulthood: stages of maturity for, 81–3
advance organizers, 215
affective display (infant), 211, 212, 213, 215, 222
age: and child caregiving, 40–1; and division of labor, 60; and domestic hierarchy, 33
age-appropriate experience, 265
age-appropriate goals: and caregiver responsiveness, 188–92
age at marriage, 30, 70, 96, 102; decline in, 97–8
age-gender hierarchy, 65, 266, 271; progress in, 104
age-seniority, 243
agriculture, 31, 57, 59, 71, 73, 83
agropastoralists, 13
Ainsworth, Mary, 37, 45–6, 50–1, 52
albinism, 105
Albino, R. C., 45, 46
alcoholism, 186; *see also* drinking
Als, H., 210
amenorrhea, lactational, 101–3
amenorrhea, postpartum, 26
American white middle class: infant care, compared with Gusii, 1, 2, 247–56

ancestor cult, 64
ancestor spirits, 104–5
anthropological literature: infant care in, 22–4
anthropometric measurements, 177
antibiotics, 170
apprenticeship learning, 274
arousal states, 201
attachment, 45–6, 50–2, 88, 207–8, 221, 243, 258, 262; to caregivers, 208, 209–10; interference in, 187; nonmaternal care and, 40–1; as unspoken phenomenon, 271
attention, expectations for, 152
authority structure, age-based, 221
average expectable environment, 2, 10, 273
avoidance, intergenerational, 266; as moral order (model), 60, 66–8, 222–3; norms/rules of, 37, 38, 65, 70; system of: parent–child, 65; taboos (*chinsoni*), 63

baby bottles, 147, 170, 195
"baby talk," 251
Baganda (people), 26
Bantu-speaking peoples, 22, 57, 67
Bayley Scales of Infant Development, 40, 143, 214; Bayley Mental Development Index (MDI), 40, 41, 42, 167t, 168
beer-drinking, 77, 80
behavioral characteristics, neonatal, 171–7
behavioral development, 50, 196, 250, 261–2, 263
behavioral recovery, 176–7
biopsychological models, 18–19, 21